The Veil of Signs

SHELDON BRIVIC

The Veil of Signs

JOYCE, LACAN, AND PERCEPTION

UNIVERSITY OF ILLINOIS PRESS
Urbana and Chicago

Library of Congress Cataloging-in-Publication Data

Brivic, Sheldon, 1943–
    The veil of signs : Joyce, Lacan, and perception /
Sheldon Brivic.
      p. cm.
    Includes bibliographical references and index.
    ISBN 0-252-01765-X (cl : alk. paper). — ISBN 0-252-06159-4 (pb :
alk paper)
    1. Joyce, James, 1882–1941—Criticism and interpretation.
2. Lacan, Jacques, 1901– —Contributions in criticism.
3. Psychoanalysis and literature. 4. Desire in literature.
I. Title.
PR6019.09Z526318 1991
823'.912—dc20

                                0990-41246
                                      CIP

For Barbara
u.s.w.

Contents

Acknowledgments

The Veil of Signs was the most difficult to write of my three books on Joyce because of the uncertainties involved in Lacan's system as I see it, which stimulated my awareness of uncertainties in Joyce. With Lacan, as with Joyce, I feel that to put his ideas into definite form is to violate them, yet I must try to make my argument cohere. Fortunately Lacan, like Joyce, provides such a profusion of new ways of understanding thought, writing, and experience that I feel that the parts I apprehend are bountiful.

A remarkable concentration of sharp Lacanian studies of Joyce reflects the affinity between the two thinkers. Books on Joyce that are substantially influenced by Lacan include those of Christine van Boheemen, Colin MacCabe, Patrick McGee, Margot Norris, and Beryl Schlossman that are listed in my Works Cited, and more will soon follow. My book focuses on Lacan's and Joyce's theories of perception, but perception leads to other areas; and while my primary aim has been to use Lacan to explain Joyce, I hope that my delineation of the field of signification/desire in Joyce will suggest new perspectives on the verbal media of experience elsewhere.

I organized panels on Joyce and Lacan at the Copenhagen Joyce Symposium of 1986, the Milwaukee Joyce Conference of 1987, the Venice Joyce Symposium of 1988, and the Philadelphia Joyce Conference of 1989. Participants in these groups included Rosemarie Battaglia, Marilyn Brownstein, Kim Devlin, Daniel Ferrer, Patrick Colm Hogan, Garry Leonard, Catherine Millot, Ellie Ragland-Sullivan, Claudine Raynaud, and Beryl Schlossman. I am grateful to all of them for contributing to my ideas, especially insofar as they disagreed with me. Jacques Aubert and Ellie Ragland-Sullivan were kind enough to read parts of the manuscript. My mistakes are not their faults. Others who have helped include Elliott Gose, Patrick McGee, Dan O'Hara, and the members of the Philadelphia Ideal Insomniacs, my *Finnegans Wake* reading group: Dick Beckman (first cause), David Borodin, Martha Davis, Mort Levitt, Tim Martin, Mike O'Shea, and Steve Steinhoff.

I owe thanks to the following people for providing suggestions on translating Lacan: Daniel Ferrer, Marthe Lavallee-Williams, Catherine Millot,

Al Omans, Bob Storey, and Bill Van Wert. My greatest help in translation came from the generosity and acumen of Kevin Moore.

Portions of this book have appeared in different form in *ELH,* in *Joyce's "Ulysses": The Larger Perspective,* edited by Robert D. Newman and Weldon Thornton, and in *Coping with Joyce: Essays from the Copenhagen Symposium,* edited by Morris Beja and Shari Benstock.

I am grateful to Temple University for a study leave that helped me to complete the book.

The amazing David Bloom has often studied Joyce and Lacan with me over the last decade, but my friendship with him—and indeed most of the knowledge I have that is of value—proceeds from my love for my wife Barbara.

Abbreviations

The following abbreviations are used to refer to the corresponding works of Joyce and to Ellmann's revised biography. Bibliographical data on these books is given in my Works Cited.

CW	*Critical Writings*
D	*Dubliners*
E	*Exiles*
FW	*Finnegans Wake. References to the Wake* will give the page number, a period, and the line number.
JJ	Richard Ellmann, *James Joyce.*
Letters 1	*Letters of James Joyce,* Vol. 1
P	The Viking Critical Edition of *A Portrait of the Artist.* The pagination of the novel in this edition never differs by more than a few lines from the Penguin edition of 1976.
SH	*Stephen Hero*
U	References to *Ulysses* will start with the page number of the 1961 edition, followed by a slash, followed by episode number, period, and line number of the *Corrected Text* of Hans Walter Gabler. The text quoted is Gabler's unless otherwise indicated.

Introduction:
The Other End of Thought

Seeing through Language

The search for perception in which Joyce engages his characters and readers advances by finding the source of appearance in the movement of language. For perception in Joyce's novels operates as a circulation of signifiers between the self and its field, and it usually derives its insight from recognizing this circuit. What the characters of the novels perceive is always made up of language in motion, whether they focus on external objects or on internal feelings. Joyce can see no more; nor can we in our lives. He validates the verbal lives of his figures by developing the idea that the world is made up of words in progress, as they are. And as they wander through their urban labyrinths seeking understanding, many of their sharpest insights are impressions of discourse as a substance that moves.

As Stephen Dedalus walks to the University in the last chapter of *A Portrait of the Artist,* his annoyance at the corruption of language around him leads him to see the truth about how language constitutes his life:

> His own consciousness of language was ebbing from his brain and trickling into the very words themselves which set to band and disband themselves in wayward rhythms:
>
> *The ivy whines upon the wall*
>
> . . . . .
>
> Did anyone ever hear such drivel? Lord Almighty! Who ever heard of ivy whining on a wall? (*P* 179)

When Stephen sees his consciousness as a linguistic liquid ebbing and trickling in a cycle that alternates form and disintegration ("band and disband"), he is seeing the actuality of both mind and matter in Joyce's novels. The word variations and associations that spring up here—eventually shifting from "ivy" to "ivory"—exasperate Stephen as "drivel." But it is because he cannot tell where they come from that exasperation yields revelation about how language operates. A distinguishing feature of stream of consciousness is that in following unpredictable associations rather than logic, it comes from outside consciousness; so Stephen is diving deep into the stream here. He also notices here that the word *ivory* shines "in his brain, clearer and brighter than any ivory sawn from . . . elephants" (179), that the word is more vivid than the thing. In his impression that life is made up of language that comes from an unknown source and keeps changing, he grasps the actuality not only of his life, but of all life in Joyce, and these uneasy reflections lead ultimately to the wordshifts of *Finnegans Wake*.

In *Ulysses*, Stephen remembers meeting an intense writer, Synge, and realizing where he found himself: "In words of words for words, palabras" (*U* 200/9.577). A similar perspective is presented by Jacques Lacan, who hears a voice saying, "Everything is language: language when my heart beats faster . . . "[1] An increase in speed has to be felt as language because it can only appear within a scale of discriminations of movement, so movement itself must be verbal to be perceived. The place the increase of speed occupies on this scale functions as a word or signifier—but in fact it does not stay in any one place, for words are always moving from one place to another when they are used. Every word, then, combines a stable component that can be seen clearly with a dynamic one that cannot, but we are trained to disregard the dynamic aspect. Convention makes us "see" words as static, logocentric structures, but this is not what we see at all. Even if I stop reading to focus on a single word, I can never see the word sitting on the page. What I see is the word coming into my eyes, received at a certain angle in a given light by a particular mind in a specific, unstable state. This word will probably never look the same again. Therefore the reality of words is seen when they are seen changing. They alternate between the clearness we grasp and the unclearness we slip into so that their "band and disband" revolves into and out of consciousness.

The Rotary Process Us

Such a circulation of language constitutes the minds of Joyce's characters, and I intend to trace a few of the shapes these circuits take. My primary figure is the loop, and I will revolve around several kinds of circular movement. While the obvious model for such loops is dialogue, I am less concerned with spoken words than with unspoken ones. The actual conversations, which have been much examined, are only part of the spectrum of dialogic circulation in Joyce's texts. Most of the looping of signification involving Joyce's characters connects them to other characters to whom they are not speaking, to inanimate objects, to ideas, and to something outside their known, conscious worlds—the unknown source from which Stephen feels his words coming. The term I use for this source is one Lacan uses to emphasize the alterity of the unconscious, the Other. The recognition of the Other as a narrative agency will allow me to describe the narrative framework of interior monologue, which narratologists have missed.

I was enabled to see these circuits by the work of Lacan, and I have followed Lacan's ideas as my main source, but there are places where my view of Joyce leads me to depart from Lacan, and places where I draw ideas from other thinkers. There are also places where I present ideas that are in Lacan, but have not been recognized, and this is especially true when I draw on Lacan's writings on Joyce.

Lacan's work is based on Freud's, which sees libido, the energy of desire, as continually being sent toward its object and then drawn back.[2] Lacan develops a linguistic version of this looping movement of desire as the basis for what can be perceived of both the object and the subject. The Lacanian subject, a complex personal construction involving external connections, is the unconscious basis of the self. Lacan argues that the subject can only be known through the stages of the movement of desire outward and back that constitutes personality. In another theory, Lacan describes visual perception as a loop in which the eye sends out vision that the object returns (*Four* 67–77). Neither existence nor perception can take place for Lacan except as a looping involvement of words, and so I see his field of desire as essentially equivalent to that of perception. In the *Wake*, Butt arranges his sleeve "so as to loop more life the jauntlyman" (343.14), looking or appearing vital and attractive as he loops.

For Lacan, the linguistic construction of personality (the signifier) is first formed by reflection from parents, who convey the social structure of language. As a result, a subject is constituted by the interchange of speech with another, so that identity is a process of return, just as a word has meaning only by relation to other words. The subject is constantly changed by its circulation, and words in Joyce gravitate toward the dynamic status they have in the *Wake*, where, with certain functional exceptions, each word takes a new form (spelling) each time it appears.

The fundamental source of the process of identity, the invisible otherness behind any particular other who represents it by responding, is the Other: "The Other is, therefore, the locus in which is constituted the I who speaks to him who hears, that which is said by the one being already the reply . . . " (*Selection* 141). The subject exists only by relation to an unknown external agency. Other definitions of the elusive concept of the Other will follow. Its basic otherness dictates that it can never be known, yet only it can make its perceiver known.

Some of Joyce's most explicit development of the idea of identity as a process between figures appears in his portrayal of Shem and Shaun in the *Wake*. Neither brother can exist without the other, and Joyce refers to the way they define each other as *"the rotary processus and its reestablishment of reciprocities"* (304.29–31, Joyce's italics). Lacan criticizes Descartes's *Cogito, ergo sum* because it overlooks the dependence of the individual's thought on someone else (*Four* 140–41), and Joyce seems to agree, for in the passage cited one brother asks the other to sing to him so that they can be added together: "...cog [wheedle] it out, here goes a sum" (304.31), implying that the Latin 'I am' must be attached to "sumwon" else.

In "The Freudian thing," Lacan demonstrates how much more important the circulation of speech is than the conscious mind by engaging in a conversation with the nearest thing, his desk. He labels the desk's speeches as "the discourse of the other" (*Selection* 135), and the desk brings out new areas of Lacan's mind by leading him to speak from a new point of view. Lacan may not have been consistent about capitalizing *Other* in 1955, but he was to use "the discourse of the Other" to refer to the voice of desire or the unconscious that speaks for the subject through the object. It should be remembered that words themselves are objects. The Other is the real motivator of speech and so it is the giver of voice.

This pattern corresponds to one of Joyce's early conceptions of writing, the epiphany, in which the object expresses to the artist "a sudden spiritual manifestation, whether in the vulgarity of speech or of gesture or in a memorable phase of the mind itself" (*SH* 211). While most epiphanies are scenes of people, the main definition of epiphany, in *Stephen Hero,* says that when the "spiritual eye" adjusts its "vision to an exact focus," an epiphany can be received from "the clock of the Ballast Office" (211). Whether the object is alive or inanimate, it is perceived as a sign. To give a thing voice or make it known, to narrate it (the Latin *narrare* is from *gnarus*, 'knowing'), involves, for Stephen Daedalus (the *SH* spelling), invoking the spirit of art through a series of stages that issue from the artist's mind and return to it.[3] What finally has to be sensed through sight or hearing is the otherness of the object, but the voice of this otherness speaks for the artist—speaks not only for what he has been, but for what he will be after this vision, so that epiphany reveals the artist to come. For Stephen the artist's goal is to express himself, yet this self can only appear as an interaction with objects.

"The Freudian thing" says, "The trade route of truth...now seems to pass through things" (*Selection* 122). This chimes with Joyce's devotion to facts, but if truth must be heard through objects, it does not reside in them. It is a vagabond that must pass through because it can only be truth by expressing the human subject. For Lacan, there is no "objective" truth without the subject and its Other (*Selection* 305), without the looping of narration. A person is made of words grounded in the Other, so that everyone has an author, or an authoress.

In the "Scylla and Charybdis" episode of *Ulysses*, Stephen says that the physical solidity of his existence consists of a looping or weaving process analogous to artistic signification: "As we, or mother Dana, weave and unweave our bodies . . . from day to day, their molecules shuttled to and fro, so does the artist weave and unweave his image" (194/9.376–78). A corresponding passage of Leopold Bloom's appears in "Sirens" when he focuses on a cat's cradle and ponders what may be on the other side of soundsigns: "Words? Music? No: it's what's behind./ Bloom looped, unlooped, noded, disnoded" (274/11.703–4).

The looping or weaving of signification that makes physical reality in Joyce always suggests an invisible force behind it; and this force, which I describe by the Other, is sometimes linked to a mother goddess such as the Celtic Dana in recognition of woman's power over the movement of language. What is woven is a tissue of signs into which perception loops, a curtain of appearances. This veil of semisolidified language conceals and suggests the Other that can never be seen. The arrangement of this veil and its operation in *Ulysses* are my main concerns, and I will examine a series of forms the veil takes in all of Joyce's novels; but at present I want to say more about the revolving movement that leads to and from it, and also to explain where Joyce got the idea of this movement.

Linking Sources: Hegel

Joyce was helped toward anticipating Lacan's ideas of being and sensing as loops of language by a number of thinkers with related conceptions. Freud's revelations of the symbolic field were important, and Daniel Ferrer has augmented our awareness that Joyce read many books by Freud;[4] but other sources were particularly useful to Joyce for these patterns. Berkeley, in arguing that the appearance of the world is shaped by our thought, proved that everything we see is made of language, and I will describe the influence of Berkeley's thinking on *Ulysses*.

Giordano Bruno was a favorite thinker of Joyce's from 1901 ("The Day of the Rabblement," *CW* 69–72) to 1939 (the *Wake*). Bruno's theory of the coincidence of contraries described experience and sensation as a constant circular movement. For Bruno such opposites as cold and hot are indivisible aspects of a single element, in this case, temperature. J. Lewis McIntyre's 1903 book on Bruno, reviewed favorably by Joyce, says, "One contrary is the 'principle' or starting point of the other, and therefore transmutations are circular" (177). Cold has to interact with hot to become itself, and as nothing stays the same, every quality is incessantly involved in a "circular" intercourse with its opposite or other.

Such circular movement is seen as basic to all language by Umberto Eco in *A Theory of Semiotics*. He says that a "cultural unit," such as a word, "'exists' and is recognized insofar as there exists another one which is opposed to it" (73). Because a sign has to oppose another one to exist, "continual circularity is the normal condition of signification . . ." (71).

Joyce's favorite expression of the coincidence of contraries is a footnote from Coleridge's *The Friend* (1818), which Joyce paraphrases in the Bruno review (*CW* 134) and again in the *Wake* (92.7–10). In this note (I 94) Coleridge refers to "Thesis . . . Antithesis" and "Synthesis," implying a parallel between Bruno's thinking and Hegel's *Phenomenology of Spirit* (1807). The technologically sophisticated version of dialectic that exfoliates in Hegel was a major influence on Lacan, but it is not clear what Joyce read of Hegel. Although Leopold Bloom is referred to as a "phenomenologist" in the "Cyclops" episode (*U* 343/12.1822), clear references to Hegel do not appear in Joyce until the *Wake*, and then they do not flatter. In the midst of some heavy weather, for example, "hegelstomes" appear (*FW* 416.33). Nevertheless, there are indications that Hegel influenced Joyce's thought.[5]

Jacques Aubert shows that Joyce's early esthetics theories, many of which went into *Portrait*, make extensive use of Hegelian ideas taken primarily from works by the English Hegelian Bernard Bosanquet (*Introduction* 22, 48–49). Jacques Derrida, whose own ideas (including his critique of Hegel) I will often cite, calls Joyce "perhaps the most Hegelian of modern novelists" (*Writing* 153). F. C. McGrath points out (237–48) that Joyce seems to have used Hegel in organizing *Portrait* and to have derived from him a sense that the ongoing process of dialectic is more important than any particular goal. This dialectic in both Hegel and Joyce is a continual, revolving cycle of joining with and separating oneself from otherness. An explicit statement of Joyce's indebtedness to Hegel appears in Joyce's letter to Harriet Shaw Weaver of 9 October 1923, which describes the theory of history of the four annalists in the *Wake* as "after Hegel and Giambattista Vico" (*Letters* 1:205).

I count on Joyce knowing enough of Hegel's theories to stimulate him to develop ideas that anticipate Lacan, despite the contrast between the integrative dialectic of Hegel and the disintegrative one of Lacan. Some points of Hegel that I cite, however, are used descriptively rather than as sources. I also make descriptive use of M. M. Bakhtin's dialogical principle, which applies dialectic to levels of language in the novel. R. B. Kershner points out in *Joyce, Bakhtin, and Popular Literature* that "Bakhtin's special interest is in the area of interpenetration of authorial voice and character's voice . . ." (19). Thus Bakhtin delineates an ongoing dialogical relationship between an author and his character, a process in which their distinct languages or idioms converse, blend, debate, and counterpoint each other on every page.

Having shown concern with Lacan's versions of dialectic and phenomenology, I should add that Lacan's field of the Other differs from earlier phenomenologies because of its linguistic dynamism, because the subject involved is not identifiable with consciousness, and because the Other is a process of perpetual displacement. The constant vanishing of the Other causes the shifting of the language and identity that depend on it. In his second book of seminars, *The Ego in Freud's Theory* . . . , Lacan defines the goal of analysis as communication with "a genuine Other, . . . the Other who gives the answer one doesn't expect" (246). The Other is identifiable as whatever slips beyond formulation. As the manifestation of the unconscious, it is for Lacan the source of truth.

Interceptions

If the circuits of language I am most concerned with connect Joyce's characters to people who are not in touch, to inanimate objects, and to something outside their awareness, these circuits share the situation of not being attached to actual listeners, a characteristic of thought. Words of thought either aim at someone who is not there or, if they aim at oneself, they come from someone not there.

In interior monologue, the distinction between words that aim at an unknown other and those that come from such another is often a distinction between the use of first and second person. When Bloom thinks, "I pass" in "Calypso" (*U* 57/4.98), he probably has no idea whom he is addressing. This is the most common person for interior monologue, and first person is usually implied when no pronoun appears. When Stephen, in "Proteus," thinks, "Whom were you trying to walk like?" (*U* 41/3.184), he is using an undefined external authority to judge himself. In his self-consciousness, he uses the second person more frequently than Bloom does. Stephen is more aware of the action of otherness than Bloom is because Bloom has enclosed the Other (and it has enclosed him) in conventions. The false Other is not seen as other, and Lacan values contact with the real Other because recognizing the unconscious is a step toward freeing oneself.

There are many exceptions to the rule that interior monologue in the first person is addressed to another, while such monologue in the second comes from another. When Bloom thinks, "Wonder what I look like to her [the cat]" (*U* 55/4.28), the first person expresses the Other's point of view; and when he thinks, "Makes you feel young" (57/4.83), it is he who speaks to the Other even though the person is second. In any case, it is impossible for speech to aim at itself, to avoid differing from itself, without reducing itself to nonsense (which brings its own intervention external to consciousness). So thought always aims at an absent party.

I reject Dorrit Cohn's statement that "interior monologue is, by definition, a discourse addressed to no one, a gratuitous verbal agitation without communicative aim" (225). While this is the appearance of such monologue, it would be unreal if it were not addressed to anyone: discourse cannot exist without an aim. Moreover, writing generally aims at someone (like yourself) who is not there.

If thinking and writing usually aim at someone absent, then when we actually speak to someone present, our discourse continues to follow internalized patterns. What the loop reaches outward to corresponds to otherness within, for although the Other includes whatever surprises us, it is also repressed. Ellie Ragland-Sullivan indicates this in *Jacques Lacan and the Philosophy of Psychoanalysis* (hereafter *R–S*) when she defines the Other comprehensively as "the discourse of the mother, father, culture, and of language itself, which has been repressed and is subsequently displaced into concrete language and relationships and onto other substitute objects" (191). The otherness we find in external objects expresses images from our backgrounds that have been stored out of sight because they could not be accepted. Our dependence on parents and other social signifiers through which we derived self-images is so deep that we must repress it to consolidate a sense of independent identity; but we continue to require the effect of a prior, unknown agent.

When I speak to a person, in this perspective, I speak to the Other through him. Whatever we say that is rational has a tendency to cover up communication on an outside level. He has his strongest effects on me when codes break down and we have trouble understanding each other. Such a view fits Joyce's works, in which external dialogue and what is clear are usually less important than the unclear flow of language within. This tendency grows stronger through Joyce's career, ending with the *Wake,* which takes place within the mind of a dreamer.

With regard to logical communication, rarely does anyone change anyone else's mind by speaking intentionally in Joyce. When it does happen, it tends to be seen negatively as brutal imposition, as when the Mooney family changes Bob Doran's mind in "The Boarding House," or as in the Sermons on Hell in *Portrait.* Most of the time, when characters speak to each other, the emphasis is on how little is understood. The most active lines of communication are intrapersonal and extrapersonal. The idea that unspoken discourse is more important than what is said is widely prevalent in Modernism, where it connects with emphasis on the unconscious. Lawrence, for example, concentrates in *The Rainbow* on what the body expresses; and the inadequacy of words is a prominent theme in both Woolf and Forster.

Insofar as one receives an answer from someone not in touch, it must express part of one's mind but that part need not be contained by the self. The field of the Other in which Lacan's loop of desire operates can be constituted without another person present, yet there is always an imagined consciousness implied by it. Desire and other effects of the unconscious come from outside the self in the field of the Other, which assembles the foundation of the self. On the visual level, no matter what the eye looks at, it has to receive an answering gaze, which must be imagined combining with the initial eyesight in a loop to constitute what is seen (*Four* 72). No point of sensation or existence can be felt without the sense of its being shared.

If Joyce followed this model, then every perception that appears in his work is an interception. Whatever is sensed is sensed with, by, and for someone else. Such interceptions appear in many forms. The teller may augment the thoughts of characters, for example, so that they say or think something of Joycean brilliance; or characters in *Ulysses* may be inseminated with Homeric parallels without being aware that they are acting out a version of the *Odyssey*. A character's interior monologue may be directed toward other persons, who may thereby be involved in it whether or not they are present. Stephen's thoughts, for example, may soften when he thinks of his mother or harden when he thinks of his father. In fact, figures in *Ulysses* tend to share thoughts without communicating them. As a minor example, in the first half of *Ulysses* before they meet, both Stephen and Bloom think of a woman's "seaweed hair" (243, 281/10.876, 11.942), a Homeric image. We have noticed a correspondence between Stephen's "weave and unweave" and Bloom's "looped, unlooped."

Perception in Joyce is always shared, and the input that contributes to the visions of the characters tends to pass through the mind of the author. In arguing that Joyce's mind is the central construction making connections in the works, I will consider current objections to the idea of the author as main source.[6] Patrick McGee, in his excellent *Paperspace,* sees that Joyce is a presence often referred to in *Ulysses,* but McGee argues that this presence cannot be an "integrative unity" (47) because the book uses so many different styles, and places such emphasis on role-playing and the falseness of authority. I agree that Joyce's authority has to appear in divided form, but for Lacan (whom McGee uses), the subject is always divided. That is, even the most determinate person standing directly before me can only appear to me as an interplay of opposed forces. In developing the complexity of the subject, Joyce aimed to be what Stephen calls Shakespeare, "All in all" (*U* 212/9.1020), and thereby he built on his division the comprehensiveness of the Other.

The Other may seem too impersonal to be matched with the author, but

Lacan often speaks of the Other as if it were a person. In "The direction of the treatment," for example, he says that the Other "has its own ideas" (*Selection* 263) and "arrange[s]" the circus of human relations "from the box reserved for the boredom of the Other" (265). This last image sounds like Stephen's idea of the indifferent artist who pares his fingernails.

McGee feels that the nature of the author cannot be known in *Ulysses*, but the truth about society can be. Yet Joyce's view of society, no matter how insightful, is personal. *Dubliners*, to use a relatively simple example, presents a city in which virtually everyone is trapped. The social criticism is powerful, but the Dublin of the period may well have had more range. Lacan describes Joyce as having "carefully testified to the symptom of Dublin, which takes its soul only from his own."[7]

The belief that Joyce could represent the society of Dublin with complete accuracy, while it may be justified, is an act of faith. Historical and cultural material could only enter his work by passing through his mind, and it was transformed in that passage. The Shakespeare who enters *Ulysses* is not necessarily the historical Shakespeare, nor is the social context in Joyce free from subjectivity. While the Other is strongly represented by the otherness of society, there is always in the Other something personal and irrational that has no objective equivalent. In his Seminar of 16 December 1975, Lacan says that "the imagination of the novelist . . . reigns in *Ulysses*" (*Ornicar?* 7:15).

The multitude of social codes in Joyce's novels are handled ironically and artistically so that the purposes they serve here are different from those they served in their social contexts. Joyce's novels are strong examples of dialogic fiction, works in which independent voices interact. Bakhtin says in *Problems of Dostoevsky's Poetics* (90–100) that any ideology that appears in a dialogic novel is changed into part of a system. Whether the author supports it or not, it is equal to any other idea in the artistic whole, and its meaning depends on its relation to the other voices.

For Lacan, social codes cannot exist objectively as determinate facts because they always depend on an Other whose workings are outside consciousness. In "The subversion of the subject and the dialectic of desire . . . ," he writes, "one can speak of code only if it is already the code of the Other, . . . since it is from this code that the subject is constituted, which means that it is from the Other that the subject receives even the message that he emits" (*Selection* 305). The paradoxical nature of the Other prevents any voice from being reduced to a definable message. There can be no objective word in Lacan because the signifier always speaks for the subject, though the subject is unknowable, and may be divided into a myriad of voices. Joyce's *Wake* seems to be about a single subject who speaks for all humanity. For the average person who does not confront the Other, its functions are fulfilled by society. In Joyce's works, where the Other is confronted by being re-presented in the uncertainty of language, the major center that generates these functions and controls values is not social, but authorial. This is the "genuine Other" that provides words that surprise.

Another objection to Joyce's authority involves the role of the reader, whose interpretations may supplement the visions of both character and author. Joyce, however, apprehends and includes his readers to a unique extent by designing ambiguities that anticipate a wide range of responses. Margot Norris lists a series of reader types and attitudes that Joyce manipulated as early as the 1905 story "Clay" ("Narration" 208–9). Derrida says that when he reads the *Wake,* he feels as if he inhabits Joyce's memory and is inscribed in advance in the book: " . . . everything we can say after it looks . . . like a minute self-commentary with which the work accompanies itself. It is already comprehended by it" ("Two Words" 149). Derrida does add that nevertheless new interpretations can enlarge the text in new directions, but if I misunderstand him correctly, these new views will be anticipated by Joyce, though not yet discovered.

Wolfgang Iser (21, 61) sees the reader as a cognitive performer who completes the text. Such a reader becomes an author, or part of the author, and is therefore included in the statement that Joyce's characters share their perceptions with the author. While Joyce had no monopoly over the author-ity of his work, his effort was to expand the range of his written implications so that as many as possible would be processed by his personality. Daniel R. Schwarz says that to make sense of *Ulysses,* each reader has to construct his own image of Joyce the artist (19), and some of these images are made of anti-matter.

When the thoughts of Joyce's speakers form themselves by looping around someone who is not there, the place of the implied interlocutor who adds to their thought is filled by a projection of the author. The image of the artist as one end of a circuit, receiving and giving back life from a wide variety of sources, appears in Joyce's definition of the poet in the 1902 essay "James Clarence Mangan." Here the intense life of the poet is seen "taking into its centre the life that surrounds it and flinging it abroad again amid planetary music" (*CW* 82). This construction is not specifically attached to narrative, but it presents the writer's material as circling through him and then going back to its subject. To indicate the persistence of this idea in Joyce's thought, a similar image appears in a late addition to Book IV of the *Wake* that describes a "millwheeling vicociclometer" (614.25–615.10). This mechanism receives the products of the world, digests them, and returns them recombined; and it stands not only for the body of the dreamer, but for both the *Wake* and its author.

The Other End of Thought

The narrative agencies of Joyce's fiction are always contrary on an active level to what they narrate. Bernard and Shari Benstock, in "The Benstock Principle," hold that the method of Joyce's narration, which changes frequently within each work, is always influenced by its subject matter; and that as the narrator grows stronger later in *Ulysses,* the content of the text and its style are increasingly divided against each other (18). I believe that many of the most vital effects of the narration are based on functions in opposition to the material presented. Because what is told interacts with what is telling, in what John Paul Riquelme refers to as oscillation, they distinguish themselves as opposed. This fits in with Bruno's idea that something can be perceived only through its opposite.

A few main outlines of this pattern in Joyce's novels can be sketched out quickly. John Gordon has suggested a principle of opposition for *Dubliners:* that each of these stories constitutes a dialogue between the central character and a narrator who sees beyond her or him (13ff.). Admittedly, these Dubliners rarely have access to the circulation of vision because they are so trapped by convention that the Other rarely has vitality for them. There are, however, a few stories in which vision is active, and these illustrate the patterns of Joycean linguistic looping.

In the epiphanies at the ends of "Araby" and "The Dead," the protagonists see the Other by seeing themselves from the viewpoints of others. As they do so, they gain access to language that expresses them beyond their own linguistic abilities, as in the boy's epiphany in "Araby": "Gazing up into the darkness I saw myself as a creature driven and derided by vanity . . ." (*D* 35).[8] The ordinary state of his mind could no more say this than Gabriel Conroy could compose the snowy coda of "The Dead." Both figures are lost in a gazing state that drifts into a transcendent perspective from which they see themselves. As the world becomes unreal for both, there is a veil before them, for the boy in "Araby" is standing in front of a curtain, while Gabriel looks through a window into the snow that fills space with translucent movement.

The circulation of language is more complex in the novels, and I only suggest here the most basic oppositions between the main figures and what tells them. In *A Portrait of the Artist,* as Riquelme points out in *Teller and Tale in Joyce's Fiction* (60–66), the narrator is a future version of the protagonist. So Stephen contrasts with the narrator by being an artist who is not mature. Whenever Stephen has a significant insight, he moves toward artistry by interacting with the author who is portraying him, and he gains access to Joyce's art by being inspired. In fact, as Stephen begins to understand his nature, he starts to sketch the first outlines of the artist he will become, so that the vision of art he gives out is the germ of the vision from which he receives. Stephen interloops with Joyce as they develop themselves by seeing the movement of language. On the crucial issue of the work—artistic development—the two young men are opposites.

In *Ulysses*, Stephen gains new depth because as he spins off his theories and ironies, we sense the desperation of his attitudes, the human lack behind him. The compassion that enriches Stephen represents Bloom, so that Stephen tends to be seen from Bloom's point of view. On the other hand, as Bloom weaves his materialistic daydreams, we find him funny and touching because Stephen's irony allows us to see through his self-delusions. Neither character would be the same without the other to counterpoint him.

In the *Wake*, one main opposition seems to be between the artist Shem and his conformist brother Shaun. Clive Hart points out that Shem tends to dominate the first half of the *Wake*, while Shaun clearly dominates the second (131–32). Shem, however, is usually viewed with disapproval by narrators who tend to resemble Shaun, while Shaun is presented with mockery from points of view that are often Shem-like. Here again, what is seen is opposed to what is showing it.

These are only one each of the largest contrasts working in the narration of Joyce's novels. Many other oppositions function on various levels, often several at once. I can illustrate readily by contrasting the different experimental styles developed in episodes of *Ulysses* with what is supposed to be happening in the scenes they describe. Consider the inflated stylistic parodies of "Cyclops" or the survey of English prose styles in "Oxen of the Sun," the phantasmagoria of "Circe" or the elaboration of minutiae in "Ithaca." By introducing dialects that contrast with the surface thoughts of the characters, Joyce here expresses their minds more accurately and fully than they could themselves, bringing out the social and psychological otherness behind those minds.

When Bloom's thoughts are expressed in medieval style in "Oxen" (14.71–276), or when the abstraction of the style makes him, as Joyce put it, a heavenly body "like the stars" in "Ithaca,"[9] he is systematically inserted into Joycean cultural contexts at variance with his own. The styles that attack realism in order to expand it throughout *Ulysses* are alien to the Dublin of 1904: they come from the experimentation of Zürich and Paris from 1915 to 1922. My point is that Bloom does not live in a historical context: he lives in a Joycean context that includes Joyce's idea of history.[10]

If we contrast these alien styles with the "actuality" of Bloom, we come up against the fact that the actuality of Bloom is a convention (at best a symposium). Assuming we could confront Bloom in his bloom and ask him to express his thoughts, what he would say (which would depend on how he was asked) would express only a small margin of his feelings. For conscious thought is only the surface crust of what is on one's mind. Joyce gives Bloom much more depth than conscious thought could express by inserting him dialogically into "other" discourses—not only those of his own culture, but those of Homer, psychoanalysis, anarchism, metaphysics, sociology, and various literary and linguistic movements, including those Joyce used to anticipate poststructuralism. This illustrates Lacan's idea that depth comes from otherness.

The truth of Bloom's experience is a dialogue between the convention of actuality that tries to enclose him and connections that come from beyond him to exceed "actuality." No one resides in Bloomsday Dublin who could be responsible for such styles as the music of "Sirens" or the unpunctuated flow of Molly's stream. The barfly narrator of "Cyclops," for example, could suggest but not execute the gigantic parodies of that episode. Moreover, the hundreds of psychic connections between the thoughts of the characters, which Joyce allowed Stuart Gilbert to emphasize, tend to be mediated by the author.[11]

The coincidences and the styles come from what David Hayman calls "the arranger," who selects technical frameworks for the narrative. Hayman's reference to the arranger as "the artist-God as cosmic joker" (93) implies that as artist he is personal to Joyce, as God he is divine, and as joker he is both funny and contrary. Schwarz notices this projection of Joyce: "By showing his power to make whatever metaphoric and metonymic substitutions he wishes, Joyce shows that he is, as Stephen puts it in 'Oxen of the Sun,' the 'lord and giver' of language, the God of his imagined world" (15). These substitutions constantly attach Joyce's characters to something outside their world (Schwarz 17), something that can never be known; yet every interpretation predicates some form of it, and the firmest identities it can be given pertain to Joyce.

Massive indication of this Joycean source of language is found in the interior monologues that dominate the first half of *Ulysses*. In these passages no narrator is apparent, but the characters are being fed technical devices that are outside their historical situation. Actually, if we turn from the novel to biography, we may be able to justify Stephen's stream of consciousness, for Joyce bought Edouard Dujardin's *Les Lauriers sont coupés* in 1903 and was impressed by its interior monologue (*JJ* 126). Therefore, it is conceivable that Stephen (if he follows Joyce) would have this technique running through his mind in 1904; but this cannot explain the streams of Bloom and Molly without recourse to Joyce's intervention.

According to Bakhtin, the artistic image of language must involve two linguistic consciousnesses, "the one being represented and the one doing the representing. . . . Indeed, if there is not a second representing consciousness . . . , then what results is not an image . . . of language but merely a sample . . . " (*Dialogic* 359). So the source of language for Joyce's figures must be what Bakhtin here calls an "individual" consciousness capable of dialogue, and not an abstraction. In Bakhtin's Dosteovsky study (58–73), the dialogic figure is engaged in an ongoing interchange with the author, and this is what keeps the character's ideas alive. Because he converses with another consciousness, he can never be finalized or reduced to a type or formula. So Bakhtin sees an author figure active in all vital interior discourse.

The source of language in Joyce, then, has to be personal, yet it seems to have endless linguistic resources and it strives constantly to extend the limits of omniscience. Such features match the image of the artist-God that Stephen describes. In *Joyce the Creator* I showed Joyce playing in his works the role of God as a group of voices that changed and multiplied. I emphasized that this divinity could never be seen, and I now regard it as a function of the Other. Jacqueline Rose points out that "the place of the Other is also the the place of God."[12] The need for God springs from the otherness of of the human situation of lack, the fact that reality is unattainable. René Girard, in *Deceit, Desire, and the Novel,* describes desire as an attempt to be the Other who seems to possess reality.[13] Lacan recognizes the creative role of the Other in generating thought insofar as it surprises. The Joycean artist provides his characters and readers with a series of oppositions against which they form their senses and feelings. Rather than pretending the need for God does not exist, Joyce co-opts it blasphemously by synthesizing God's functions. The role Joyce plays in the mental process of his figures corresponds to "the other end . . . of . . . thought."

Linguistic Mysticism

Surprisingly, both Lacan and Derrida, who have contributed to the critique of authorial presence, have been impressed by Joyce's authority in his work. If Joyce can only appear in his texts as a series of effects in language, these effects must be quite powerful. Lacan generally speaks of Joyce's writing as an expression of Joyce's own subject, while Derrida, with less irony than one might expect, speaks of Joyce as a divinity. Joyce wins their appreciation by disseminating language and by withdrawing his own image behind the text, and I will show that he could not engage in these dynamic activities so effectively without playing the role of God.

As a linguistic phenomenon, God has two opposing functions: he is not only the principle of phallocentric unity, but also that of multiplying meanings or dissemination. The "Oxen of the Sun" episode of *Ulysses* refers to God as a "Beneficent Disseminator" (405/14.766), and there is an extensive line of mysticism that sees God as a principle of creative differentiation.

This line includes Bruno and Blake,[14] and Gerard Manley Hopkins, who taught at University College, Dublin, until a decade before Joyce entered it. In "Pied Beauty," Hopkins typically finds the glory of God in "all things counter, original, spare, strange"—whatever is extra or outside of definition, other.

In *Writing Joyce: A Semiotics of the Joyce System,* Lorraine Weir describes Joyce's system for the production of language as having a theological basis, though she converts the theology of this system into logology, a science (derived by Kenneth Burke from Saint Augustine) in which words play the role of God (5–6). Weir says that Joyce's fundamental method for multiplying words was "the Ignatian [Loyola according to Roland Barthes] version of the *Lectio divina* or meditation on the (divine) name, the working of a series of variations upon all the signifieds of a single noun in order to arrive at an apprehension of the whole. Wresting from the form of the noun the whole gamut of its meanings. . . . 'exhausting the "pertinences" of a subject' [quote from Barthes]" (Weir 16).

Weir recognizes that Ignatius's system was "a mystical sequence to a higher order," but she precludes the possibility that such a level could exist in Joyce, though she does see him as progressing to a higher order (20). Weir insists that the "god term," which she sees as the origin of linguistic production, has no relation to Joyce or anything else outside language, so that for her, technique fills the place of motivation. Her semiotics fits Joyce because it is based on scholasticism, but she insists that "belief is never in question" in logology (36). With regard to Joyce, this apparently means that no one ever thought there was any truth to be found in his work, and yet Weir seems to find value in her conception of Joyce's intention.

I agree with Weir that the god term that operates as point of origin in Joyce's work should be seen as a linguistic function; but I think that by excluding the effects of the subject and of authority, she limits her apprehension of that function to the surface. Lacan, by seeing the dynamics of motivation as language in motion, provides linguistic models for understanding the activity and structuration of origin.

I said in *Creator* that the effect of Joyce's deity, like that of his prior competitor, can be seen primarily in gaps and incomprehensible moments in the text, miracles that indicate a voice speaking from outside established discourse (58, 84). Surprising turns of phrase indicate the limits of linguistic possibility, and the major linguistic definition of the Other, as Anika Lemaire points out (157), is that it is the totality of language out of which the individual emerges by contrast. This matches Eco's idea of unlimited semiosis. Because every sign has to be identified in relation to another one, all identity leads to an endless chain, and Eco says that unlimited semiosis is the foundation of all meaning (68).

While Lacan insists that no one can fill the role of the Other in its absolute otherness and linguistic totality, he indicates that it is common for someone to represent the Other for someone else, as parents and authorities often do.[15] Joyce was far from possessing totality in his life, but he realized that he would have to play this role to give his work a dynamic supplement. Nothing is more characteristic of his writing than the sense of projecting the totality of language. Yet there are unanswered questions and loose ends that point to a prevalent Joycean strategy of projecting himself as a source of transcendent knowledge that shifts and turns out to be a step beyond comprehension. By this use of his authority, Joyce lures his reader to confront the limitations of the reader's insight. Joyce's maneuver of projecting himself in and beyond his work as a linguistic movement (with a personal rhythm) succeeds in generating enormous authority without violating Lacan's strictures.

In fact Lacan, like Joyce, makes psychological use of theological ideas. In "The function and field of speech and language in psychoanalysis," the so-called "Rome Discourse" of 1953, he refers to the spirit of the unconscious as seen in jokes by Freud as "the spirit that lives as an exile in the creation whose invisible support it is" (*Selections* 60). This fits Joyce's role in his work. In *Seminar XX, Encore,* given in 1972–73, two years before his seminars on Joyce, Lacan cites a few mystics and then places himself squarely in their tradition: "These mystical ejaculations are neither idle gossip nor mere verbiage, in fact they are the best thing you can read—note right at the bottom of the page, *Add the* Ecrits *of Jacques Lacan,* which is of the same order. Given which, naturally you are all going to be convinced that I believe in God. I believe in the *jouissance* of the woman insofar as it is something more."[16]

What Lacan puts in the place of God here is *la jouissance,* a feminine effect of going beyond any particular form. The word means orgasm, joy, playfulness, and free usage, but Lacan uses it here to refer to a sliding of language from one meaning to the next that he sees as typically feminine. Rose says, "The concept of *jouissance* (what escapes in sexuality) and the concept of *significance* (what shifts within language) are inseparable" (*FS* 52). Lacan believes that joy consists of such flowing of signification, and he considers this the essence of mysticism, for he says of someone who senses "a *jouissance* which goes beyond. That is what we call a mystic" (*FS* 147). Finally, Lacan was to use *jouissance* to refer to the joy-sense of Joyce.

The Untranslatable

As early as 9 January 1973, Lacan observed that the *Wake* was *"plus"* close to analysis because it presented the slip that could be read in an infinite number of ways (*Encore* 37). In 1975, with the encouragement of his friend Aubert, he embarked on a year of discussion of Joyce. On June 16 he gave an address on "Joyce *le symptôme*" to the Fifth International Joyce Symposium (including myself) at the Sorbonne. He then wrote a brilliant essay with the same title for a volume of papers from the symposium. From November 1975 to May 1976 he gave a series of weekly seminars on Joyce under the general title *"Le sinthome,"* his term for Joyce's particular symptom. The address ("Joyce *le symptôme* I"), the essay ("Joyce *le symptôme* II"), and two of the seminars have now been gathered by Aubert in *Joyce avec Lacan.* Eight other *"sinthome"* seminars have appeared in the Lacanian periodical *Ornicar?*[17]

Ragland-Sullivan, in her chapter on the symptom, calls it a principle of repetition that constitutes identity (*R–S* 259). The repetition of the symptom relates to Lacan's idea of the real. This is a difficult term to define, and I will use it only glancingly as part of a first suggestion of what the *sinthome* is. The most economical way to hint at the nature of the real is to cite Rose's definition: "Lacan termed the order of language the symbolic, that of the ego and its identifications the imaginary. . . . The real was then his term for the moment of impossibility onto which both are grafted, the point of that moment's endless return" (*FS* 31).

In her review of *Joyce avec Lacan* ("More French Connections"), Ragland-Sullivan interprets the *sinthome:* "Joyce the *sinthome* becomes James Joyce's proper name, proper names having to do, ultimately, with God insofar as God approximates the Real where the something unsymbolizable joins the ineffable part of Woman. The impossible Real produces fissures and explosions in identity consistency and language" (116–17).

All of this is relevant, but what I will use from it immediately is its indication that the *sinthome* is both Joyce's identity and intensely involved in division. Ultimately, I hope to equate the *sinthome* with the overflow of the word into multiplicity and in this sense with *jouissance,* the linguistic shift that may be "the ineffable part of Woman."

In the essay *"Symptôme* II," Lacan praises the exuberance of Joyce's language, writing in a style like that of the *Wake,* complete with invented words like *eaubscene, faunetique,* and *hihanappat* (31). While Lacan is skeptical of the positive potential of the unconscious, he recognizes here that in breaking out of the verbal containers of conventional consciousness, one can gain access to the possibilities in the chain of signifiers, the totality of language.

Lacan finds the unconscious in the ambiguity of words, an uncertainty that can yield multiplicity and plenitude He sees in Joyce a fulfillment of release that comes from abandoning fixed meanings: "It is having and not being that characterizes it. There is a havingness in what have you?"[18] This indicates the fruitfulness that Joyce derives from giving the widest range of meanings to his words. What this essay celebrates and imitates in Joyce's language is *"Jouissance opaque d'exclure le sens"* (36), and the opaque joyance of excluding sense is a term that Lacan put in the place of God a few years earlier. Moreover, the attitude of having that Lacan identifies with Joyce seems to come from a quest for self-knowledge, for in the seminar of 16 March 1976, Lacan says, "There where one recognizes oneself, it's only in this that one has" (*Ornicar?* 9:36).

In the seminar of 10 February 1976, Lacan emphasizes that Joyce was intent on making his name a common noun and on being an artist who occupied all the world (*Ornicar?* 8:13). In fact, there are entries for "joycean" as adjective and noun in Webster's Third. Lacan also plays with *jouissance* so as to equate it with Joyce. In the address, for example, he says, *"cette jouasse, cette jouissance est la seule chose que de son texte nous puissions attraper. Là est le symptôme"* ('This *jouasse,* this *jouissance* is the only thing that we may entrap from his text. That is the symptom') (*J avec L* 27). According to a letter from Catherine Millot, *jouasse* is a slang (argot) word for pleasure, usually used as an adjective, so that *"il est jouasse"* means 'he enjoys himself.' Ferrer tells me that *jouasse* sounds like a common French mispronunciation of Joyce. So this is what Joyce sounds like in the language in which Lacan writes, and even in English his name varies with dialects. *Jouasse* also sounds like the vulgarity of *jouir,* a verb for 'enjoy' that is often used to mean 'come.' It may even suggest the potential for play in Joyce as the imperfect subjunctive of *jouer,* so that in the place of a noun, it might be translated 'this would-have-played.' A fourth level may be 'joyass,' for English puns are frequent in *Joyce avec Lacan.*[19]

The statement presents a light attitude in that nothing can be caught but joy. Yet the privileged position that Lacan had earlier given to *jouissance* implies a framework. If joy is the symptom, Lacan goes on in the four paragraphs that follow the quote to say that this symptom conditions Joyce's language and supports the structure of his work, and that Joyce's version of the symptom, the *sinthome,* is what identifies him as an individual. Ragland-Sullivan equates the Lacanian symptom with "identity itself" (259). So Joyce's identity, the *sinthome,* is at the heart of his work in the form of an indefinable feminine shifting, *jouissance,* something that cannot really be entrapped. And since Lacan has substituted *jouissance* for divinity, it is like the invisible spirit of humor that Lacan described in his *Rome Discourse.*

In the sentence after the quoted pair, Lacan says that through Joyce's language the symptom "supports this web, these strings, this weaving of earth and of air with which he opens *Chamber Music,* his first published book" (27). This refers to the opening line of Joyce's poem: "Strings in the earth and air. . . . " Lacan recognizes here that the world Joyce created was, from the start and ever after, a weaving of sensory appearances in loops of language, a veil of signs projected in many directions by Joyce's desire as *jouissance.*

The flow of *jouissance,* however, can only express itself in connection with discipline, though that discipline be concealed. Lacan says at the bottom of the page quoted from that the symptom "depends, in the last term, on a structure wherein the Name-of-the Father is an unconditional element." This suggests that Joyce cannot assert the feminine side of his personality without involving the masculine. If Lacan praises the overflow of linguistic excess in Joyce, he also recognizes the need for discretion and control to sustain this onrush. In "*Symptôme* II" he evidently sees Joyce as orchestrating the possibilities of his language by taking up an opposing position to every word because that is where the focus of creativity lies:

> Having is power to make something with. Always to be suspended among others, among others we were considering to be spoken as possible of "power." The only definition of the possible being that it can *not* "take place": what one takes for the other end, regarded as the general inversion of what one calls thought.[20]

The artist is seen here as suspended in otherness, suspended among alternatives. Only one of these others can differentiate itself into enunciation, but the others have to be felt to define it. Thought is always the contrary end (*"le bout contraire"*) of something—the Other, I think. And the writer gains power to create images by locating his receptivity at the other end of the circuit of thought. This would seem to involve self-awareness. He must hold himself back as he is surrounded by alternatives that suggest themselves for perception. Rather than fixing on a form, he stays open to the flow of possibilities. If he exerts this skill, the "having" power of language will appear from outside consciousness. By being in opposition to his own thoughts and in contact with the Other, he makes release possible.

The combination of the release of multiplicity and the control that allows that release is succinctly expressed in the *Wake* by ALP, the mother, speaking of a progress she makes with her husband: " . . . we go out in all directions on Wanterlond Road with my cubarola glide?" (618.21–22). As they proceed on the wandering path of want and wonderland, they disseminate themselves in every direction at once, but they also follow a definite pattern of movement. This pattern, the "cubarola glide," may be a Cuban guide and certainly is a Latin-American dance, but it also represents the Wakean structure that informs their movements. Referring to two opposing structural principles, Joyce described the *Wake* in a postcard as an engine with a square wheel.[21] The bumpy, rolling rhythm of such a wheel has to structure the outward spread in order to allow the image of movement or continuity. This rhythm (like most locutions in Joyce) is a unique Joycean contrivance, so however innate to ALP it may be, it is also partly imposed from outside her knowledge by the Other, the outhor.

The God of Laughter

Extensive refutation of the idea of the author-god appears in Frances Restuccia's *Joyce and the Law of the Father*. Restuccia focuses on typology, a pattern in which the echoing of one passage by another in the narrative shows the arranging power of the author as God. But she shows that as *Ulysses* proceeds, these symbolic echoes get repeated excessively, and as they multiply, they grow increasingly incoherent and debased. So that while bread may seem to represent the Eucharist of Joyce early in *Ulysses* (Restuccia 76), it proliferates later in the book in such silly forms as "tell me where is fancy bread . . . " (*U* 614/16.59, with apologies to Portia) and crumbs in bed (731/17.2124). The theological implications lose their authority as they abound ridiculously, and the anagogy of authorial intention becomes ludicrous.

Yet the argument that Joyce undoes his authority by excessive reference to it is equivocal. Restuccia traces a strong pattern of mockery, but this need not exclude other possibilities. Bakhtin (*Dialogic* 72–75) shows that indecent parody was very active during the middle ages, and suggests that mockery loses force when there is no belief to oppose it. According to Bruno, who was burned for heresy in 1600, God multiplies himself into every particle of matter and the most debased forms are the most exalted.[22]

Restuccia says that *Ulysses* loses referentiality in its second half to become a pure fabric of wordplay (a Barthesian text). But the narrative never stops, and most readers gain emotional involvement in the second half. People are moved to tears by such scenes as the apparition of the lost son Rudy at the end of "Circe," the alienation of the characters in "Ithaca," and Molly's reverie: and Joyce's sentimental tastes suggest that this was one of his intentions. The tissue of stylistic games is also a screen behind which emotions are generated. Late in *Ulysses* the reader tends to be overwhelmed by Joyce's power over both feelings and ideas. Restuccia's view that Joyce's authority disappears can refer only to a surface level, and is parallel to her odd claim that Joyce and his protagonists can escape the law of the Father by masochism. This argument, based on Gilles Deleuze, is valid and important as a fantasy Joyce was subject to, but in taking it for effectual (138–39, 174), Restuccia leaves both Freud and reality behind.[23] If the topic did not arouse repression, it would be obvious that no one is more severely subject to the law of the Father than someone who needs to be beaten. (The exception, someone who needs to be killed, does not tend to be around long.)

Joyce emphasizes that the woman by whom the male masochist needs to be beaten is really a paternal figure in "Circe," when he turns Bella Cohen into the mustachioed, cigar-smoking Bello. And Joyce's works end with resonant reaffirmation of the tortuous power of the Father. In 1932 he ended the poem "Ecce Puer" with "O, father forsaken/ Forgive your son!" And the last page of the *Wake* features "I go back to you . . . my cold mad father, my cold mad feary father. . . . "

Restuccia shows how strongly Joyce disintegrates reality by withdrawing his godhead, but she makes it clear that he could not get this effect unless he began *Ulysses* with a massive assumption of theological self-reference: " . . . Joyce needed to set up the illusion of full presence before he could do, or seem to do, away with it" (Restuccia 61). Her analysis of typology and Eucharistic imagery (20–53, 103–12) reveals more references to Joyce's divinity on each page of his work than I had suspected. I believe that what her observations reflect is a withdrawal of the effect of divinity behind a veil of language, a ruse in which Joyce acts as euchre-ist. The chief example of such withdrawal in the Bible is the destruction of the Tower of Babel, and this is the event that Derrida uses to describe Joyce's role in his work.

If Lacan sees a personal agency beyond consciousness in Joyce, Derrida virtually deifies him, and, while Derrida's views should not be imposed on Lacan, it may not be a coincidence that both thinkers are impressed by Joyce's method of increasing his authority by seeming to abandon it. I agree with Barbara Johnson that Derrida's work is an extension of Lacan's,[24] but I will be treating their differences as well as insights they share. In "Two Words for Joyce," Derrida describes Joyce's tendency in the *Wake* to overwhelm the reader with the multiplicity of his knowledge, and reads two words from the *Wake*, "he war" (258.12), as "God's signature" (157). Derrida is not sure if he likes Joyce's claim to absoluteness, but he justifies it as partly demonic and revolutionary. These lines are from the final paragraph of his essay: "At the beginning I spoke of resentment. Always possible with respect to Joyce's signature. But it was a way of considering, on a small scale, Joyce's revenge with respect to the God of Babel. . . . And God lets himself be prayed to, he condescends, he leans over. . . . This is art, Joyce's art, the space given for his signature made into the work. *He war,* it's a countersignature, it confirms and contradicts. . . . Countersigned God . . . God who signeth thyself in us, let us laugh, amen" (158).

The recognition of "he war" as a personal signature is solidly based on the self-referential aspect of Joyce's work. Derrida emphasizes the rebellion in Joyce's divinity partly because playing the role of God is the central sin of Satan.[25] But then elsewhere in this paragraph Derrida says that by confounding Babel, God himself expressed "revenge, resentment, reprisal," like Satan or Joyce. Joyce is more than a usurper here: he creates words, wins prayer, and signs himself in us. The athesis of the essay is that Joyce plays the role of God powerfully in the language of the *Wake*.

That Derrida sees the form of prayer appropriate to Joyce as laughter accords with Lacan's idea, derived from Freud, that laughter speaks for the unconscious. It may seem that the spirit of laughter that Lacan and Derrida see as essential to Joyce is an element that leaves authority behind, but Freud indicates otherwise. In his 1927 essay "Humour," he says that it involves a humorist in the role of a father who reduces his objects to the positions of children (*SE* 21:163). Freud's recognition that there is always an authority behind laughter suggests that the dissemination or analysis of language cannot be sustained without insemination or synthesis to oppose it. But the creative principle of Joyce's authority is dissemination or otherness, which means that it is always moving away from what we can see or express.

God appears in the work of Joyce as a series of gaps in understanding that indicate the unconscious. Lacan, referring to *Totem and Taboo,* says, "the true formula of atheism is not *God is dead* —even by basing the origin of the function of the father on his murder, Freud protects the father—the true formula of atheism is *God is unconscious*" (*Four* 59). Lacan warns here that attempts to eliminate the father end up consolidating his power through the unconscious. In a sense, every attempt to eliminate the father is masochistic. Think of Stephen in Nighttown breaking the lamp and then getting himself knocked down even though Bloom tries to stop him. Father William Noon observes that Joyce puts the unconscious in the place of God (135), and this corresponds to Rose's observation that for Lacan, the place of the Other is the place of God. There is even a parallel with Derrida in the sense that Joyce, Lacan, and Derrida all attach transcendent value to whatever moves beyond formulation.

Joyce finds effective images of the movement beyond form in woman as a figure of displacement, a verbal flow that cannot be contained. This is reflected in the way his main narrative units usually (or always, as I will show) end focused on the free fluency of a woman's mind. When Lacan asserts his belief in *jouissance,* he adds that some men have these mystical feelings of going beyond, but they are exceptions. Joyce cultivated such feelings in himself by developing his major female characters. While he presents an incisive critique of the entrapment of women, he also cele-brates their powers, especially the hegemony of women over the creation of language that Julia Kristeva describes, a power related to *jouissance.* [26] Joyce's attempts to see from the points of view of women at the ends of his works are another way in which he puts himself in the position of the Other.

Movement beyond corresponds to the place of the Other in creative discourse, which is continually shifting beyond sight to draw perception forward. This is one of the three main functions of the figure of divinity Joyce projects. It not only represents Joyce's authority and mocks religion, but it serves as what Lacan calls a lure: as the image of the subject-who-knows, it draws the reader onward with its promise of ultimate intelligence.

Because the locus of the Other is always somewhere else than you think it is, it can be a heuristic tool. In "The direction of the treatment and the principles of its power," Lacan says that the analyst has to project an image of authority to draw the patient's speech, but "frustration must prevail over gratification" (*Selection* 271). That is, the patient has to keep finding that he cannot grasp the analyst's authority even though he has to keep trying. In this way the patient is weaned from dependence on the analyst's truth and led to seek his own. By the same token, Joyce's readers must find that their attempts to capture his intention will be frustrated to promote their development. Lacan ends "Joyce *le symptôme* II" in amazement that Joyce could achieve the effect of analysis without having been trained (*J avec L* 36).

Joyce maintains the place of the Other as a constant displacement by endlessly changing the rules of language with each new stylistic experiment so that the principles underlying style recede into complexity. Such an uncapturable authority is stronger than any definable intention because it cannot be reduced and so it remains creative. It requires a knowledge greater than consciousness, which can only grasp one intention at a time. Joyce is always beyond any definition we try to enclose him in.

Dialogue as Veil

Having justified the idea of Joyce as a transcendent presence in his work with some unlikely authorities, I must say that this idea will be in the background for most of this study. My main concern is with structures through which perception circulates for Joyce's figures. The feeling of going beyond or getting outside oneself—the basis of knowledge of both the world and the self—has to involve the Other, but the Other is not perceived. What is perceived is a series of loops of language and the field these loops pass through. The discourses that fill this field generally serve as obstacles to what perception ultimately aims at, except when gaps or unclear points in these discourses reveal or suggest the Other behind them. My main concern will be the veil of words, but the operation of this tissue of signs involves the effect of a generative personal power concealed behind it.

Dialogue itself tends to be seen in Joyce as a textual veil, an obstacle. Spoken dialogue grows less important from one novel to the next. The most dramatic scenes appear early: "Ivy Day in the Committee Room" and the Christmas dinner in the first chapter of *Portrait*. By the middle of *Ulysses,* dialogue has become marginal in relation to interior or narrated monologue, or to experimental techniques that express what is not said. Stephen's Shakespeare lecture in "Scylla and Charybdis," while it is a great act of creation in Stephen's mind, garners no support and seems to be one of those externally dismal lectures in which the speaker is talking not to the audience, but to himself.

The main concentration of external dialogue in the second half of *Ulysses* is in "Eumaeus," the episode in the cabman's shelter. It seems to me that dialogue in the *Wake* is usually ritualized dream dialogue between parts of one mind, and seldom follows the logic of dialogue in which one speaker gives information to the other. In any case, "Eumaeus" presents the last direct dialogue in *Ulysses*. While a lot is said here, the theme of Odysseus in disguise is reflected in an emphasis on how inadequate the conversation is. The characters speak in cliché, periphrasis, and inadequate language because they are tired and shaken up by what has brought them together. Stephen disagrees with almost everything Bloom says in this chapter, and Bloom hardly understands any of Stephen's ideas. The following excerpt is not only typical, but is one of their closest moments of verbal contact in "Eumaeus":

> —What belongs, queried Mr Bloom bending, fancying he was perhaps under some misapprehension. Excuse me. Unfortunately, I didn't catch the latter portion. What is it you. . . . ?
> Stephen, patently crosstempered, repeated . . . , adding:
> —We can't change the country. Let us change the subject. (645/16.1166–71, first ellipsis Joyce's)

This is unusually close because Bloom comes close to realizing how different Stephen's mind is, whereas later, for example, he has no idea how repulsive Stephen finds his enthusiastic plans to make Stephen a semipopular singer (663–64/16.1820–66). About all they can talk about without disagreeing are trivial points like why restaurants turn their chairs over at night (660/16.1708–13). The non-exchange quoted above represents the gap in understanding or aporia which Lacan sees as the only sure sign of the unconscious (*Four* vii). Bloom and Stephen are having trouble talking because each is being confronted with something radically different, and this otherness has creative potential. The two men do communicate in this episode, but they do so *despite* the sense of their conversation.

The following episode, "Ithaca," in which Bloom brings Stephen home, describes what may be the most important dialogue in the novel. This final conversation, however, does not appear as external dialogue, but as a catechism between a questioner and an answerer who are invisible, and the turning of the conversation is displaced between these figures. This indicates that the most important circuits through which information is passing are not spoken.

The system of loops that is anatomized progressively throughout Joyce's canon has two aspects, speech and sight. Speech is a looping of language toward the object it addresses, an object that represents the Other from whom that language comes. The loop of sight circles around what is seen, but because sight is made up of signs and not things, both hoops are made of language. The revolvings of this articulation delineate its origin: its loopings not only develop the subject of Joyce's work, but constitute that subject. *Ulysses* is not about a day in the lives of some Dubliners insofar as such terms confine the subject to a realistic level. *Ulysses* is about the relations between this "day in the life" and something beyond it. If Bloomsday did not have this otherness, it would merely inhabit an ordinary novel without access to the subject of being. The world of *Ulysses* would not be alive without these loops that connect what can be expressed to what cannot.

The loops take many forms, but the basic model for them is the extension of sensation outside of conscious control. This takes place whenever a character hears, sees, or thinks something he does not understand, taking input from the Other. It goes on constantly because one never understands all that is attached to what passes through consciousness. When a character picks up a surprising turn of speech, a mythological reference, or a moment of inspiration, when he makes contact with an experimental technique from a later period, he is looping into the Other.

Circling also operates on a plot level when a character goes into an experience and what he finds returns to his mind. Such an ambit can take many pages. Lacan sees so many rounds and turns of signification in Joyce that in *"Le sinthome"* he draws a series of complex knots to represent the construction of the Joycean subject. I will not be developing such complexities, but will be mainly concerned with the circling of experience (sensation, thought, and action) from and to the characters—and with what this circling passes through.

The field of the Other that the cycle of experience swings around tends to assume certain structures that receive and concretize the looping of signification, and I will examine three typical ones. While not quite parallel in function, all three seem to represent the limits of maximum perception of the material world. These structures form a series that progresses through the three novels. Experience passes through a liquid flux in *Portrait* that (in effect) becomes a veil in *Ulysses* and then a wall in the *Wake*. The progress seems to increase impenetrability, except that the wall in the *Wake* is described as having a hole in it and is constantly being penetrated. Paradoxically, as the other side is further obscured, the external world on this side of the obstacle grows less real, more dependent on the unknown.

This aspect of my argument reflects the influence of phenomenology on Lacan, but in his structures, the transforming interchange between subject and Other gets a special dynamic from language. All three objectives—flux, veil, and wall—are designated as made up of words, so the whole system may be called a phonemenology. I argue that to run up against one of these fabrications is typical of the mode of perception in each novel. The most important and active of them is the veil of signs.[27] It has a more definite form than the flux, but it is more capable of moving and changing form than the wall, so its complex activity represents the material world effectively. The veil appears in all three novels (as the other two images do), but it is developed most strongly in *Ulysses*. Vicki Mahaffey, in *Reauthorizing Joyce*, examines the clothing imagery of *Ulysses* to richly elaborate many ways in which fabric constitutes the language of a world made up of veils (141–65).

Gender as Language

Mahaffey indicates here that the veil is linked to woman and that the genders are differentiated by clothing, but for Lacan, masculine and feminine are actually veils of language. The basic Lacanian principle in "The agency of the letter in the unconscious," that what psychoanalysis discovers in the unconscious is the "structure of language" (*Selection* 147), leads to the recognition that the sexes are linguistic systems. Juliet Mitchell indicates in her "Introduction" to *Feminine Sexuality* that gender is imposed in childhood, emphasizing that it is crucial to Lacanian thought to see that gender is not inherent in a person, but is a social construction (17).

If masculine and feminine are linguistic constructs, one of the main distinctions between these two modes is the opposition between words whose meanings are fixed, which are masculine, and words whose meanings shift or slide, which are feminine. The arbitrariness of these conventions supports Lacan's insistence that sexual identity is not authentic. Lemaire quotes Serge Leclaire's statement that the phallus is *"the signifier par excellence of the impossible identity"* (86); that is, it represents the idea of something equal to itself. This corresponds to the sharp definition of masculine language, while the feminine *jouissance* "which goes beyond" (*FS* 147) is the shifting from one signification to another. Such a shift matches Lacan's definition of desire as "a metonymic remainder that runs under" signifiers (*Four* 154). When one is clear about a word in one's mind, one is rational; when that word begins to get slippery, the feminine force of desire is loosening boundaries.

Feminine flow and masculine fixity interact in the formation of the subject. Lacan argues that the infant has a closeness to the mother in which feelings flow freely in imaginary language until the father imposes phallic authority, which separates the child from direct pleasure and forces it to use determinate symbolic language as a substitute (*R–S* 55–57). This is reflected in Chapter 1 of *Portrait,* as Stephen Dedalus is separated from his mother by the authorities (and Joyce), and struggles to understand words. As the authority that enforces language, the phallus stands for the firm center that controls the unclear shifting of meaning that Lacan associates with the feminine.

This linguistic division of genders is highly developed in Joycean texts. McGee approaches it in his discussion of *Ulysses* by arguing that whereas the father's name is fixed by society, the name of the mother changes and has no set position of its own (60–61). But the distinction between "woman formed mobile or man made static" (*FW* 309.21–22) is developed most extensively through ALP and HCE, the wife and husband of the *Wake.* She is a river that has no definite form and (verbally as well as in other ways) keeps going on, while he is a tower that tries to stand firm and take a definite position. As Colin MacCabe points out (146), both genders are described as involved in the act of writing, which expresses "the vaulting feminine libido," but is also "sternly controlled" by a "male fist" (*FW* 123.8–10).

These images suggest that the masculine function can no more exist apart from the feminine than writing muscles could contract without expanding. A basic observation of Freud's is that everyone includes both genders, as the *Wake*'s dreamer seems to include both HCE and ALP. Society, however, is organized to define people as either masculine or feminine. Lacan, in "The signification of the phallus" (*Selection* 281–91), emphasizes that the word *phallus* (unlike *penis*) refers to a symbol rather than an organ. The phallus is built on emptiness because it is an idea generated in the child by fear of castration. In Chapter 2 of *Portrait,* Stephen's interest in E——. C——. first appears in a scene that immediately follows one in which he is mistaken for someone called "Josephine" (68), so that his sexuality seems to spring from castration anxiety. For Lacan, the penis is only a sign used to validate something bigger, the power of significance claimed by men.

One value of Lacan's theory is that if masculine and feminine are linguistic categories used by all people, then we can stop worrying about being "real men" or "women" and be as masculine or feminine as we want at any time—if we can escape artificial social restrictions. McGee shows that the sexual excitement people feel in *Ulysses* usually is situated in an uncertain area between masculine and feminine, especially in the cases of

Leopold and Molly Bloom (117, 128). Joyce's main women all exert strong phallic powers, as Gretta Conroy, Bertha, and Molly do by having (or thinking of) their own men in opposition to their mates, and as ALP does by deciding to leave HCE. Each shows a will to fix on her own identity apart from the role given her by society. On the other hand, all the men whom Joyce respects have substantial feminine components. Despite his considerable anxieties, Joyce supports the mixing of genders in each person.

On the linguistic level, each of these figures has to use both the masculine and feminine modes to generate discourse that has both the firmness to be coherent and the vitality to be expressive. Lacan diagrams in a two-sided figure in *Encore* what he calls the "woman share of speaking beings" and "the share called man" (*FS* 150). This shows that though he distrusts the ideal union of man and woman, he values the interaction of masculine and feminine within the individual. Christine van Boheemen is correct in arguing that Joyce cannot escape the polarity of man and woman because that polarity is necessary to the representation of reality (38–42). On the other hand, while the polarity cannot be eliminated, it can be reduced to a linguistic game whose representational basis is questionable. This is a pattern Restuccia emphasizes, and it grows predominant in the *Wake*.

Thinking through the Veil

If all of us are covered by veils of sexual identity, and dialogue is also a veil, one is impelled to ask whether the veil can be penetrated and what is behind it, and Lacan's answer is paradoxical. Because we are constituted by language and can only see language, nothing can ever be identified behind the veil; but there is a temporary sense of passing through that is invaluable because it is the only way to see the unconscious. Lacan refers to this truth here as *ontique* (*Quatre* 33), which means 'having real being or noumenal': "What is ontic in the function of the unconscious is the split through which that something, whose adventure in our field seems so short, is for a moment brought into the light of day—a moment because the second stage, which is one of closing up, gives this apprehension a vanishing aspect" (*Four* 31).

"That something" that is glimpsed here is described by Lacan in the previous paragraph as the religious "illusion" of "oceanic aspiration." While it is illusion, its effect is to constitute the subject as a process. All of this is based on Freud, for the "oceanic aspiration," as Lacan states, comes from the opening of *Civilization and its Discontents,* and the two-stage looping is parallel to the *fort-da* game of Chapter 2 of *Beyond the Pleasure Principle.* Lacan goes on to take this game, in which a baby throws his spool away and then brings it back, as a model for the casting of the mind into new ideas: '... man thinks with his object. It is with his object that the child leaps the frontiers of his domain ... " (*Four* 62). The idea of the loop as a model for thinking gets expanded in Derrida's *The Post Card* (320-23).

The process of outgoing and return in the field of the Other that constitutes the subject is central to Joyce's work. The vanishing aspect, in the second stage, of what has been apprehended is parallel to the fading of radiance in Stephen's process of esthetic apprehension (*P* 213). We will see that *Ulysses* features a series of scenes involving the process of seemingly penetrating the veil to catch a glimpse of something that vanishes, and I hope to show that these are stages in the development of a Joycean subject.

First I examine the cyclical construction of *Portrait,* demonstrating how the action of each of its chapters presents a movement of Stephen's mind outward and inward that delineates the field of the Other. Stephen approaches the Other at the end of each chapter when he enters a feminine flux that gives him the power to reconstitute his identity. My second chapter explains how the author functions as the Other by providing his characters with a channel into the unconscious that they use whenever their language goes beyond their understanding.

My third chapter concentrates on the "Proteus" or strand episode of *Ulysses* and uses Berkeley's theories to indicate how Stephen sees the world as a veil of signs, a tissue he wants to penetrate. This veil fits in with Lacan's theory of the gaze, which is the other end of the loop of perception. In Chapter 4 I show how the gaze is depicted as operating between Stephen and Bloom, both when they are together and when they are apart. I indicate that each represents the Other or author for his opposite. My argument explains Lacan's statement in his seminar of 13 January 1976 that Stephen and Bloom are of the same substance (*Ornicar?* 7:15).

Chapter 5 examines a series of scenes in which Stephen and Bloom get fleeting senses of going through the veil late in *Ulysses* and considers how effective these feelings of passing through may be. My treatment of "Penelope" in Chapter 6 shows how Molly weaves the veil that Stephen and Bloom see because the movement of her thought as woman is the object of their perception through desire.

In the *Wake,* the subject of my seventh chapter, the interacting figures involved in perception are parts of one mind, and the perceptual process moves inward. I concentrate on a chapter of the *Wake* concerned with what the dreamer sees, I.4 (75-106). The figures of this chapter act out the formation of language as an interplay between levels of the subject. The plot of I.4, in which male conflict leads to a manifestation of the feminine, is such a common pattern in works and parts of works by Joyce that it may be called a prototypical structural unit of his canon.

Joyce's major works end focused on a woman's mind in an attitude of loss. The subject is known most completely in apprehending a woman's sense of loss because since infancy it has been created by feminine need. The man the final woman in Joyce is always longing for is more than an individual: as the lost object, he stands for the Other from whom one divides oneself in order to articulate oneself as conscious. I argue that the great loss in Joyce's work from which all other losses are derived is the loss of the author as Other.

What is lost, however, remains as the goal of desire. I conclude that the typical major narrative unit of Joyce's novels, while it begins with a sense that the veil cannot be penetrated, ends by enacting or envisioning the penetration of the veil in a moment of inspiration through the image of the kiss. The world of material reality that is in front of the veil and the realm of the unknowable behind it must interact to make the veil of the text tremble with life. The most harmonized form of this interaction, the kiss constitutes the identity that completes the work, an unstable, imagined identity that is a circulation between self and Other.

NOTES

1. "The Freudian Thing" (1955), in *Écrits: A Selection* 124. The line is spoken by one side in a debate Lacan imagines, but is typical of him. References to pages of this book will be preceded by *Selection* to distinguish it from the longer French *Écrits*. Lacan is influenced here by de Saussure's principle that the signifier is barred from the signified.

2. Lacan expands on the implications of Freud's idea in *The Four Fundamental Concepts* 176–79. References to pages of this work will be preceded by *Four*, and for the French text, by *Quatre*. One of the primary passages in Freud that Lacan refers to here is "The Libido Theory," in *Three Essays on the Theory of Sexuality*, *SE* 7:217–19. This is standard form for citing volumes of the *Standard Edition*.

3. In "The Space and Dialogue of Narration," in *Lacan and Narration*, ed. Robert Con Davis, 871–76, Ronald Schleifer sees Lacan's conversation with his desk as a Lacanian model of narration. Another essay in this collection, Régis Durand, "On Aphanasis: A Note on the Dramaturgy of the Subject" 860–65, also describes narration in terms of the loop of desire.

4. Ferrer, "Freudful Couchmare" 367–82, proves with quotes from a *Wake* Notebook that Joyce read two of Freud's case histories, "Little Hans" and "The Wolf Man," in 1925. For a survey of previous information on Joyce's knowledge of Freud, see my *Joyce between* 9–11.

5. Jean-Michel Rabaté discusses the problematic relation of Hegel to the *Wake* in "A Portrait of the Artist as Bogeyman" 126–32, and tends to see Hegel as an "embalmer" (127) who will not serve as a model of Joyce's thought. I argue that Joyce used the more dynamic aspect of Hegel's theories. This essay appears in *James*

Joyce: The Augmented Ninth, ed. Bernard Benstock, which I will hereafter refer to as *Ninth.*

6. I deal with another objection to the author's authority, the idea of the intentional fallacy, in *Joyce the Creator* 15–16, where I argue that if an author's intention is not represented in his work, it is because he has other intentions that he may not be aware of. From a Lacanian point of view, the author's intentions are always a group of different impulses in a variety of relations, including a good deal of conflict. The theory of the intentional fallacy, then, is correct in that a work cannot be seen as controlled by a single clear intention. But the theory is misleading if it is used to separate the work from its personal sources.

7. "...*soigneusement témoigné du sinthome de Dublin, qui ne prend âme que du sien à lui.* ..." "*Le sinthome, Seminaire du 16 Mars* 1976," *Ornicar?* 9 [1976]: 37. *Sinthome* is Lacan's term for Joyce's particular symptom, which will be explained below. All translation of Lacan's writing on Joyce is mine.

8. The idea that the language goes beyond the boy in this passage was suggested in conversation by Dan O'Hara.

9. Quoted in Budgen 257. Bloom is interested in astronomy, but the stylistic experience of becoming like a heavenly body is beyond his conception here.

10. One may say that the historical context of Joyce is the most relevant one, but this is only true insofar as it passes through Joyce's mind. He may go back to Vico or forward to Braudel, and he may have little awareness of some of the main historical events of his period, such as the shift in power from England to America.

If we consider Joyce's social position, we must ask what society he represents. Among others, he speaks for both Victorian Dublin and modernist Paris, two societies worlds and ages apart from each other. Likewise, Joyce was both a bourgeois and a revolutionary; and he was a paterfamilias preoccupied with projecting himself in feminine roles. These extreme contradictions indicate why the figure of Joyce is important in understanding the mix of Joycean discourse.

11. In his study of *Ulysses,* written under Joyce's supervision, Gilbert continually refers to "intermittent telepathic communication" (57) between Stephen and Bloom. See 26, 109, 149, 344, *et al.* A list of their verbal overlaps appears in my *Creator* 145–53.

12. See her Introduction to *Jacques Lacan and the école freudienne, Feminine Sexuality* 50. Page numbers from this collection will henceforth be preceded by *FS.*

13. Girard's use of the term *Other* is not Lacanian, but coincides partly with Lacan's term.

14. Joyce's use of this line of mysticism as it relates to Bruno is developed in Gose, *Transformation Process.*

15. The idea that a person can represent the Other for someone else appears in *Four* 218 and in "The direction of the treatment and the principles of its power," *Selection* 231, 237. Passages cited in the second section of this Introduction suggest that the Other may be brought into play by anyone with whom the subject speaks.

16. *FS* 147. Two of the main essays from *Encore* are reprinted with slight omissions in this collection.

17. *Joyce avec Lacan,* pages of which will be cited after *J avec L,* includes the

seminars of 18 November 1975 (apparently the first of the series *Le sinthome*) and 20 January 1976. Shorter versions of these as well as eight other seminars in the series appear in *Ornicar?*, numbers 6–11.

18. *"C'est l'avoir et pas l'être qui le caractérise. Il y a de l'avoiement dans le qu'as-tu?"* (*J avec L* 31).

19. To translate these writings, as Kevin Moore pointed out to me, one would need several lines of English vertically stacked in order to render the multiple meanings of each line of Lacano-Joycean "French."

20. *"Avoir, c'est pouvoir faire quelque chose avec. Entre autres, entre autres avisions dites possibles de ‹pouvoir› toujours être suspendues. La seule définition du possible étant qu'il puisse* ne pas *‹avoir lieu›: ce qu'on prend par le bout contraire, vu l'inversion générale de ce qu'on appelle la pensée"* (*J avec L* 32).

The second sentence is obscure. *Dites* as an imperative means 'say.' *Avisions* is an imperfect or subjunctive form of *aviser*, which can mean 'perceive.' Ragland-Sullivan informs me that it may combine *a* and *visions*. Little *a* (*autre*) is Lacanian code for the object of desire, as I will explain, so *a-visions* could mean 'visions of desire.' *Ne pas*, in italics in the original, could be a double negative.

21. Postcard of 16 April 1927, to Harriet Shaw Weaver, in *Letters* 1: 251.

22. The last idea appears, for example, in Bruno's *The Expulsion of the Triumphant Beast* 91. The *Wake* refers to Bruno's original name for the Church: *"Trionfante di bestia!"* (305.15).

23. Lacan's position is summed up by Catherine Clément, *The Lives and Legends of Jacques Lacan* 170: "If the father, present or not, fails to occupy the symbolic position assigned to him by our culture, disaster ensues." This disaster is usually insanity, as Lacan shows in "On a question preliminary to any possible treatment of psychosis," in *Selection* 199–220.

24. In "The Frame of Reference," in *Literature and Psychoanalysis,* ed. Shoshana Felman, Johnson refutes Derrida's attack on Lacan in *"Le facteur de la vérité,"* in *The Post Card* (413–96). She shows that Derrida simplifies Lacan and fails to acknowledge Derrida's debt to him (Felman ed. 465, 476–78, 501–2). Despite the opposition between the two thinkers, I believe that their ideas can be used to clarify each other.

Perhaps I should clarify my own position by saying a bit more about how Derrida is unfair to Lacan in *"Le facteur."* He begins by saying that Lacan favors the voice over writing and that this "phonematism" cannot be attributed to Freud (*Post Card* 463). This overlooks the fact that psychoanalysis has always been built on the living voice, and that many analysts fault literary criticism for analyzing writers without having their responses and the sounds of their voices to support the analysis.

Derrida's central charge is that in Lacan's circuit, the signifier returns to the place that sent it without any change or dissemination (464–65). This is untrue, for Lacan has the signifier follow circuits whose stages change its content, as I will indicate. The message always returns to the subject reversed and transformed, and it always changes the subject for the simple reason that it constitutes the subject. Therefore, Derrida's reduction is far from Lacan, who cannot be blamed for realizing that it is useful to posit a subject and an object in order to follow the course of thought between them even though he knows that these elements are always changing.

Finally, if Derrida accuses Lacan of trying to approach the truth, I doubt if Derrida himself ever escapes from the aim of truth, for it seems to me that he always returns to a movement of deferral that he invests with great transcendence and meaning.

25. Constantin-George Sandulescu presents a book about Joyce playing the role of Satan, *The Language of the Devil*. Of course, it is hard to imagine how the devil could exist without God, and the devil cannot represent Joyce more than partly, for Joyce was not fundamentally evil.

26. Kristeva explains the power of women over language in "Women's Time" (15–16) by arguing that "the permanence and quality of maternal love condition the appearance of the first spatial references which induce the child's laugh and then induce the entire range of symbolic manifestations which lead eventually to sign and syntax."

27. It may be argued that the title of my book should be *The Veil of Signifiers* because in the terminology that comes from de Saussure, a sign includes both a signifier and a signified; however, insofar as the veil appears to have substance, it gives the impression of including the signified.

PART ONE

_____

"In Outher Wards"

FW 285.22

1

The Portrait *Outward and Inward*

The Sign as Sin

The cycles of Stephen's progress in the *Portrait* are rites of sundering and reconciliation based on the pattern of sin.[1] The rhythm of separation from God and return to him echoes constantly through the Bible, and is built into the daily lives of Catholics through the mechanics of confession.[2] For Stephen, however, sin becomes an activity through which he develops himself by being shaken loose from an established context in order to enter a realm of semiotic shifting that expands his range of linguistic structure. Each time he repeats this pattern, he moves from masculine language into feminine. The more he possesses of language and its devices, the more mind he has. Stephen gains knowledge and control of this process throughout *Portrait*, moving toward an apotheosis in which he understands his life as a process of self-creation. Yet he suspects that he cannot create without the activity of another mind connected to all of his words. He tries to claim this mind as his own by foreseeing the artist who will give form to his life (Riquelme 84), but this artist must always remain beyond him.

As Stephen is recreated in *Portrait,* shaped by the self he will become, he is already beginning to understand in adolescence, at fourteen or fifteen, the process by which he is creating that self. A rich, seminal vision of this process appears at the start of the third chapter, when Stephen meditates on the algebra he is doing. This passage is central to my present treatment of *Portrait*, as the first in which Stephen recognizes the self-developing sequence that is the backbone of the novel. The plotting of his life results from sin, and the equation scene cuts in immediately after the voices of the prostitutes he has begun to frequent: " . . . another equation began to unfold itself slowly and to spread abroad its widening tail. It was his own soul going forth to experience, unfolding itself sin by sin, spreading abroad the balefire of its burning stars and folding back upon itself, fading slowly, quenching its own lights and fires" (*P* 103).

As the equation is factored, the figures on each line increase in number, so that the terms that were implicit in the original figures are expanded. The description renders this expansion as a positive stage, whereas the contraction of the figures toward resolution is presented as fading and quenching. The emphasis is on unfolding or dissemination.

The steps by which the new terms are added are referred to as sins. Sin is therefore seen as a process of division that separates the factors of the soul. And it is not only in his debauched phase that Stephen sees sin as the model for self-creation. When he finds his artistic vocation in the fourth chapter, he vows "To live, to err, to fall, to triumph, to recreate life out of life!" (*P* 172). Even when he re-creates himself by religious conversion in Chapter 3 the driving force is a terrible sense of sin. In his essay "Oscar Wilde: The Poet of 'Salome'" (1909), Joyce, paraphrasing Yeats, refers to "the truth inherent in the soul of Catholicism: that man cannot reach the divine heart except through that sense of separation and loss called sin" (*CW* 205). While *separate* comes from the Latin for 'apart—set,' it looks like *se parere,* which could mean 'make oneself appear, fulfill oneself, or give birth to oneself.' As for *sin,* Skeat says it was originally derived from the Greek for 'being,' and so it is cognate with *sein.*[3]

Lacan's seminar on Joyce, *"Le sinthome,"* refers to Joyce as a man of sin, a man made up of sins, as well as a saint of man. Here Lacan argues that Joyce's art, or use of words, always "supplied his holding of the phallic." For Lacan, all that we can perceive or possess of things has to appear in words that refer primarily not to external objects, but to the linguistic systems in which they are enclosed. He says here that creation was divine solely because God named things. Therefore the primal sin of Adam and Eve was to use language. When Adam named the animals, though he was following God's orders, he was doubling God's creation; and this led to the serpent, who, as a phallus, represented the assumption of the patriarchal power of naming (*J avec L* 38–40).

Stephen moves toward clarification of himself by expanding into language, multiplying the words in which he is expressed—and he does so by falling, by going wrong, by being threatened. One can trace this development of self-language through self-division from the start of the book as Stephen learns about things through words and learns words by being uncertain about them. The way to generate or receive a new word is to be confronted by a situation for which one does not have a word. This position, threatening but filled with possibilities, touches the essential subjective experience of sin, which is to lose control of one's feelings, to have them overflow the boundaries of reason. Therefore every sign involves a sin.

Wordflow

Glancing at a few of Stephen's most marked questions about words, I notice how deeply their elusive undertones relate to his fundamental anxieties. By his struggle to understand the different ways by which words mean, he aims to protect his identity not only against specific threats but also against a general one: the separation from God involved in not knowing. One of Stephen's earliest interrogations of words occurs as he is feeling insecure on a football field, a field that is threatening not only because it represents male aggression but because it involves an unpredictable shifting of patterns (not to mention interceptions):

> He kept his hands in the sidepockets of his belted grey suit. That was a belt round his pocket. And belt was also to give a fellow a belt. One day a fellow had said to Cantwell:
>
> —I'd give you such a belt in a second. (*P* 9)

The meanings of *belt* are as far opposed as they can be: it either refers to a warm feminine enclosure for the hand or to a sudden male attack by the hand. And if the same word can present such different actions, then very different words can mean the same thing, as with the mysterious, multilingual name of God (*P* 16), which represents total knowledge. The relation between sound and meaning is raised by the word *suck*, which makes the sound a liquid hole makes and has disturbing "queer" overtones" (*P* 11).

Such linguistic uncertainties appear continually: how can a woman be like a Tower of Ivory or a House of Gold (*P* 35)? What is smugging (42)? Nor do they involve only writable words. Stephen wonders what colors roses can have (*P* 12), what a kiss means (*P* 15), and whether all white things are cold (*P* 13). He considers that the same "pock" sound is shared by drops of water and cricket bats, and wonders if different sounds of flogging can be linked to different kinds of pain (*P* 41, 44, 45, 59).

Every kind of sign that makes up the world Stephen perceives must be drawn into the network of his associations, and he struggles with little success to find an order that will hold them all together. If he cannot understand *belt, suck,* or God's name by putting them into a system, he will be vulnerable to something terrible. This is partly because these images have disturbing associations, partly because uncertainty is painful—and the most terrible possibility is that he may be to blame. By learning the different operations of the signifiers, he protects himself by articulating himself. But a kind of sin or separation creeps into his assimilation of these functions as his focus shifts from fitting them in to expanding himself with their multiplicity.

Stephen depends on the rule that "by thinking of things you could understand them" (*P* 43). His way of standing under things, however, is neither to put them into a clear order nor carefully to examine their external referents, but to work them into his mind until he can play with them easily: "Words which he did not understand he said over and over to himself till he had learned them by heart: and through them he had glimpses of the real world about him" (*P* 62). He loops out to the world in words in order to take it in as words, and although he may tell himself he is being logical, he values these words less for their stability than for their fluid mobility.

Derrida, in a discussion of memory, argues that the essential distinction between outside perceptions and inside ones is really a distinction between words with fixed definitions and words that shift: "The 'outside' does not begin at the point where what we now call the psychic and the physical meet, but at the point where the *mnēmē* ['memory'] instead of being present to itself in its life as a movement of truth, is supplanted by the archive, evicted by a sign of re-memoration . . . " (*Dissemination* 109).

When we see something clearly, we see it as outside. This explains the psychological interior effect of the blurred images of impressionism, a term that is generally accepted as describing the technique of *Portrait*. We cannot feel the border between psychic and physical, but we do sense the difference between clear and unclear words. Clear words with fixed meanings are objectified and dead, while unclear words, with associations that keep changing, produce, through their flux, the effect of the interior. Stephen's investigations of words consistently focus on questions of meaning that are unresolved, and so he brings words into the flow of his mind, or puts his mind into the flow of words. He may not know this yet, for he seems rather to think that he will somehow solve all the ambiguities he keeps focusing on. But he later realizes that what he values in language is its expression of the internal world rather than the external one (*P* 166–67).

From the first page of the novel, where Stephen creates the image of the green rose, he is driven to create his own dynamic language by focusing on displacements of the existing structure: "But you could not have a green rose. But perhaps somewhere in the world you could" (*P* 12–13). The point is not that you could, but that you could not. Stephen is absorbed in the possibilities of language, "The sole definition of the possible," as Lacan put it, "being that it is not able to 'have a place'" (*J avec L* 32, alternate translation). Stephen wants to make a mental world freed from the external world corrupted by the father. He aims to return to his sense of the inner chamber of his own fertility, an internalized mother that he later refers to as "the virgin womb of the imagination" (*P* 217).

Seeing in Cycles

Again and again Stephen is driven to turn away from what he knows and to open up the meanings of words. The main movements of his mind follow this procedure to make up the plot of the novel. Senses of separation and loss expand his language at turning points in the action of each chapter. I mapped out the structure of *Portrait* in *Joyce between* as a series of cycles motivated by Stephen's inner dynamics. I argued that his mind moved back and forth between an attractive maternal image and a threatening paternal one. Paternal images make him flee to the image of the mother, but when he approaches her attraction, guilt makes a father arise.

At the start of each chapter of *Portrait*, Stephen finds himself in a new world in which he strives to move toward a maternal goal around which this world is organized. Early in the first chapter, for example, he is sustained at school by daydreams about his mother and going home (*P* 9, 10, 15, 20, 23). As Stephen settles into a stable relationship with this maternally oriented environment, he perceives a male figure as threatening him and this forces him to set off in a new direction to find a new world involving a transformed maternity.

Figure 1: Cyclical Structure of a Portrait

	Chapter 1	Chapter 2	Chapter 3	Chapter 4	Chapter 5
New World	School	Family homes	Nighttown	Church	College
Maternal Goal	Mother (& alma mater)	E— C— as ideal	Prostitutes	Virgin	Irish Muse
Paternal Threat	Wells & Dolan	Heron & father's collapse	Arnall's sermon	Director's offer	Cranly (as conventional Ireland)
Wandering	To rector	To whore	To confession	To beach	To Europe
Triumph	Lifted by boys	Kiss	Eucharist	Vocation	Flight
Nursing Image	"the brimming bowl" (*P* 59)	Kiss	Taking wafer	"The earth that had borne him . . . to her breast" (*P* 172)	"The white arms of roads, their promise of embraces" (*P* 252)

Figure 1 represents only the main versions of the cycle.[4] There are numerous lesser rhythms of desire and anxiety in every chapter. In fact, every sign tends to be apprehended through such a cycle. Joyce may have had something like this in mind when he wrote, in The Pola Notebook of 1904, "Now the act of apprehension involves at least two activities, the activity of cognition or simple perception and the activity of recognition."[5] When one moves toward seeing the object, one is motivated by desire for what is attractive. But one reaches the sign or finds its reality when it resists one's desire, and the conflict between actuality and desire makes one aware of one's desire as sin, as separation. In reaction to this resistance, one takes the sign back to oneself and rearranges or re-cognizes it to understand and accept it, to make it accord with desire. In the largest sense, the whole movement of the *Portrait* consists of Stephen seeing this cyclical pattern and learning to understand it, to make it his own.

The earlier versions of the recurring threat in the diagram seem inevitable: Wells, Father Dolan, and Vincent Heron all attack Stephen physically, while his father's repeated failures in Chapter 2 overwhelm Stephen with aching guilt because his sense of competition with Simon is so strong. But the later threats are more individualized. Father Arnall's sermons are shown to be laughed off by some of the other boys (*P* 125). And the figures who threaten Stephen in the last two chapters are trying to help him. He plays an increasingly active role in perceiving these threats.

There seems to be no compelling reason for Stephen to be threatened by the director's offer of the priesthood, though he is under pressure to accept. His superior education was intended by his mother to prepare him for this possibility, and after realizing he will not accept it, he feels "a sudden instinct of remorse" on going home and seeing the misery of the brothers and sisters whose welfare was sacrificed to his (*P* 163). But his sense of responsibility for his resistance to priesthood is his own; and it is this highly personal opposition that makes the director's offer threatening enough to terminate his religious career.

Similarly, when Cranly advises Stephen to pray for his mother and to conform outwardly rather than go into exile, his advice is considerate, intelligent, and pragmatic. Stephen can only see him as a threat by a strong assertion of will, by expanding himself into what he will become. The artist has to reject this sensible compromise or he will continue to be surrounded by the forms of repressive authority.

In every chapter, if Stephen were not forced to move out of the world in which he has become established, his mind would be enclosed by its forms. Instead a threat arises, and it is increasingly obvious that this threat is caused at least partly by his own volition, though the will involved may be unconscious. The threat always causes him to wander off in a direction he has never gone before. Here he finds himself in an area outside boundaries, an area swarming with the shifting of language. This shifting expands his perception into a new world of images that not only becomes a new wing of his mental development, but in fact constitutes him as a new person.

The linguistic flow, imaged as moving liquid or maternal embrace, that Stephen makes contact with at the end of each chapter gives him great potential for language. The prostitute's kiss at the end of the second chapter is a strong example: "He closed his eyes, surrendering himself to her, body and mind, conscious of nothing in the world but the dark pressure of her softly parting lips. They pressed upon his brain as upon his lips as though they were the vehicle of a vague speech; and between them he felt an unknown and timid pressure, darker than the swoon of sin, softer than sound or odour" (*P* 101).

The "vague speech" she presses directly on his brain is a powerful medium of communication, and is described in transcendent terms. The word *vague* and similar words like *dim* recur in later passages of estheticism to suggest mysterious potential: " . . . from cloud on cloud of vague circumstance confused form was veiling softly its afterglow" (*P* 217). Such words are linked to potential because they present what is not defined. The "unknown and timid" pressure is the feeling of another being who is as far as possible from being mediated by words.

Psychology, by Michael Maher, which was evidently Joyce's textbook, says that touch is a powerful medium of perception though it is vague, that it has little variety, yet "delicate sensibility to differences."[6] Its small vocabulary and fine nuances bring it close to the unconscious. Sight, the clearest of the senses, is obliterated as Stephen surrenders to a *jouissance* less conscious ("darker") than sin itself. In the delicacy of a touch "softer than sound or odor," the demarcation between self and other dissolves, allowing him to reshape the bounding lines that distinguish his body, his language, and his mind. Because give and take mingle so plentifully, the touch of lovemaking is the most vital model of the linguistic loop that embodies a person. And because touch is so wordless, it reaches an openness from which new words will come.

The prostitute expresses Stephen's own soul and body through her maternal fusion with him, and the life she transmits is what gives him the ability to see himself creating himself in the scene with the equation thirty lines later. Every ending in Joyce is the beginning of the next stage, and the accession of vitality that Stephen receives at the end of each chapter of *Portrait* leads directly to a new vision and a new system of language at the start of the next one. The assertion of manhood that makes him feel the overflowing of the "brimming bowl" that ends the first chapter leads to the end of latency and the stirring of thoughts about girls and sex in the second.

The Eucharist that ends the third chapter, which is closely parallel to the prostitute's kiss at the end of the second, conveys the word of mother church into Stephen. This magic word is formless (for the wafer is only accidental), yet it contains an entire language. Not only does it lead Stephen to the system of piety he engages in at the start of Chapter 4, but the church gives him a spirit, as well as a series of symbols that will be essential to his art, a point to which I will return. When he gets his artistic vocation, he has a liquid reverie after "the earth that had borne him" has "taken him to her breast" (172): "His soul was swooning into some new world, fantastic, dim, uncertain as under sea, traversed by cloudy shapes and beings. A world, a glimmer, or a flower? Glimmering and trembling, trembling and unfolding, a breaking light, an opening flower, it spread in endless succession to itself. . . . "

Everything in this underwater world is shapeless and changes constantly. The range of "A world, a glimmer, or a flower" indicates how extremely diverse the form of the whole may be. This follows the famous visionary lines that open Blake's "Auguries of Innocence": "To see a World in a Grain of Sand/ And a Heaven in a Wild Flower." Apparently, Stephen's trembling eyelids pick up a gleam of light from outside and distort it into moving patterns inside the lids.

As the strongest positive vision of his art, this endless unfolding generates the drive behind the esthetic theories Stephen elaborates in the fifth chapter, and at the end of that chapter, he flies toward the sea. Every chapter, then, ends with Stephen energized by contact with a maternal flux. Immersed in this shifting environment, his imagination is free to follow the flow of his "inner" feelings into new configurations of language out of which he will generate a world of signs. Yet in every case Stephen would not reach this womb of imagination unless he was deflected toward it by the disturbing appearance of a male threat that was partly external.

Liquid Letters

Another way to describe the change at the center of the action in each chapter is to say that Stephen's mind stops moving forward and begins to move laterally. At the start of each chapter he is trying to consolidate his position within an established social subsystem: (1) to be like the other boys, (2) to be a good son, (3) to save money for prostitutes, (4) to save up religious grace, or (5) to work within the Irish University. But then the threat that he focuses on stops him in his tracks, making him move to the side, in fact to several sides at once. He passes into a field of metonymy, a field in which signs are connected not hierarchically or causally, but rather by nearness on the chain of associations. In "The agency of the letter,"

Lacan argues that the chain of signifiers in the unconscious is not merely linear, but a polyphony extending in many directions (*Selection* 153–54).

Stephen's forward movement may be associated with masculinity, and his lateral shift, with femininity, by extension from Lacan's linguistic theories. "The agency" modifies Roman Jakobson's idea that the difference between metaphor and metonymy is basic to language. Lacan associates metaphor with the substitution of one word for another, which he ties to Freud's *Verdichtung,* the concentration of meaning; while he defines metonymy as connecting one word with another, or displacement (*Selection* 156–60). I associate metonymy with any shift through a series of words connected by closeness rather than meaning, and in Joyce this frequently takes the form of sound shifting (as in *ivy-ivory*), rather than metonymy itself.

The difference between metaphor and metonymy seems to me to parallel the distinction between the masculine fixation of language, which equates one thing with another, and the feminine flow beyond each signification to the next. All people use both, and this chapter shows how Stephen passes through masculine and feminine phases at different stages of his cycles when his environment changes, hardening and softening his language to reveal different levels of his subject.

When Stephen enters the feminine field of metonymy or wordshift, a new language and a new world can be shaped. Thus, for example, when he is confronted by the need to decide about priesthood, "a din of meaningless words drove his reasoned thoughts hither and thither confusedly" (*P* 161). At this point he remembers Clongowes, and the pattern of being thrown into a senseless streaming that he passes through here is descended from the scene in which Wells shouldered him into the square ditch, recounted early in the book (4). The male threat tends to send his mind flying in all directions and drives him to seek an isolation or enclosure that will allow him to look into his mind (or his language) to see the new possibilities there. Stephen grows more skillful at immersing himself in flux as the novel proceeds, but feelings of terror continue to be associated with the experience of abandoning the self, and this is why he has to be jarred into it.

Wells's aggression in Chapter 1 seems to cause Stephen to get a fever, thus generating the semicomatose vision Stephen has while lapsing into a dream in the infirmary. As Stephen's mind moves toward projecting an "inward" space, this vision establishes that there is a permanent level of verbal fluidity that he feels as deep inside himself. Indeed the fluidity may be the crucial constituent of the sense of inwardness, or even of dream. At the start of this paragraph, Stephen is awake, looking at his room; at the end he is asleep, dreaming of the dead father figure Parnell being borne in a ship across the harbor:

How pale the light was at the window! But that was nice. The fire rose and
fell on the wall. It was like waves. Someone had put coal on and he heard
voices. They were talking. It was the noise of the waves. Or the waves were
talking among themselves as they rose and fell.
　　He saw the sea of waves. . . . (*P* 26–27)

This passage introduces a frequent motif of voices murmuring as waves,
or what the *Wake* refers to as "say water" (50.34). It indicates that a substratum of shifting signification is always present in Stephen's subconscious,
and when his consciousness sinks toward dream, he will approach it. But if
this generative swarming is in Stephen's mind, so are the threats that propel
him toward it. And as Stephen moves through his cycles, he plays a more
active role in controlling and understanding both the threats and the flux.
In Chapter 4 he decides that the defeats and alienations of his life were
necessary to lead him to "the end he had been born to serve" (165). As he
approaches becoming the author of the book, he begins to see the cyclical
structure that constitutes both the *Portrait* and his identity.

Insofar as Stephen can stand under the way in which his own conflicting
needs shape the crises of his life, he assumes the position to which he
ultimately aspires: "The artist, like the God of the creation, remains within
or behind or beyond or above his handiwork . . . " (*P* 215). Whereas fate is
traditionally attributed to external power, Stephen has intuitions that his
fate is shaped by his own compulsions; and so he decides that he is ready to
err and fall again (172). But the forces that drive him can neither belong to
him nor be appropriated by his consciousness. For the process to continue
to work, the threats must remain external and terrifying, and the flux,
quite incomprehensible. So Stephen is attached to something beyond
himself that will not be domesticated. The artist must remain invisible,
other.

One image Stephen uses to represent this something beyond himself
that is also within is the Paraclete. Church doctrine holds that the Paraclete,
or Holy Ghost, dwells in the souls of the just. Being inherent in man, it is
intimate, but as part of God, it is distant and unattainable. Stephen emphasizes the strictest doctrine on the subject by mentioning twice that a sin
against the Paraclete cannot be forgiven (*P* 149, 159).[7] Stephen's insistence
on the need to follow one's inner spirit is crucial to his devotion to art, and
even after he leaves the Church behind, the Paraclete continues to operate
in his belief in himself.

The Paraclete appears among men early in the Acts of the Apostles, at
Pentecost, when it descends on Jesus's followers: "And they were all filled
with the Holy Ghost, and began to speak with other tongues, as the Spirit
gave them utterance" (Acts 2:4, King James Version). It is manifested as a

confused din of multiple voices that come from within and yet are "other." Therefore the Paraclete resembles Stephen's images of linguistic swarming within, such as the "din of meaningless words" that drives his thoughts confusedly as he is deciding to reject the priesthood (161). In this scene Stephen hears his personal Paraclete, and he tends to immerse himself in such shifting at moments of crisis. Joyce evidently regarded speaking in tongues as a feature of his writing. In three of his early notebooks, he wrote "Art has the gift of tongues" (Scholes and Kain, *Workshop* 70, 86, 97). Beryl Schlossman argues that Joyce talks in tongues through foreign languages in the *Wake,* and that the artist brother "Shem's writing forms a Pentecost of language" (166). In a 1904 letter to Constantine Curran, Joyce refers to his forthcoming *Dubliners* stories as "epicleti" (*Letters* 1:55). Ellmann explains that *epiclesis* is Greek for an invocation of the Holy Ghost (*JJ* 163).

The voices of the Paraclete, however, can be terrifying to Stephen (or Joyce) insofar as they represent an incomprehensible, alien presence within. Such a presence tends to appear to Stephen as demonic possession. We find its voices when Stephen is overcome by lust in the second chapter and feels a dark "presence subtle and murmurous as a flood . . . like the murmur of some multitude in sleep" (99–100). And after the sermons on hell, he hears the "murmurous voices" of demons outside his room (*P* 136). Around 1909 Joyce bought a pamphlet by C. G. Jung, *The Significance of the Father in the Destiny of the Individual,* which showed how demonic possession represents the presence of the father, and the aggressive demons in *Portrait* seems to represent the Other as the paternal harshness of the superego.[8]

On the other hand, when Stephen feels himself enclosed by maternal protection, as he does at the end of each chapter, the inner flow of voices is exquisite because its free movement is the source of the creative vision that he sees as the truest reality within him. An outstanding example occurs at the creative peak when Stephen is completing his villanelle and imagines E—. C—. sharing his consciousness: "Her nakedness yielded to him . . . enfolded him like water with a liquid life: and like a cloud of vapour or like waters circumfluent in space the liquid letters of speech, symbols of the element of mystery, flowed forth over his brain" (*P* 223).

The depth of Stephen's immersion in fluidity here allows him to discern that all of the signs that swirl by are only symbols of a primal mystery beyond expression. This Brownian movement of intelligible matter in the formless form of "liquid letters" corresponds to what Freud called primary process thinking, the indiscriminate flow of associations in the id.[9] It is the same neutral flux whether the organization of Stephen's mind is oriented toward the father or toward the mother, whether the flux appears negatively or positively. Like the Lacanian subject, it has no innate character, but constitutes itself as the effect of the interaction of opposing forces.

While these opposing forces are environmental, they are arranged by the author's cyclical interpretation of his memory. From the 1904 essay, "A Portrait of the Artist," Joyce believed that personality was not static, but a succession of phases (*P* 257–58), and such Joycean theories shape Stephen's life. Because the different modes of Stephen's thought react to his environment, the arrangement of plot is already an arrangement of technique, for different situations entail different rhythms and modes of thought. The nature of Stephen's existence or the shape of his character always depends on the other end of his thinking, and that is why he is preoccupied with this otherness.

Divining

For Stephen, as a product of his culture and his development, the flux he runs into, as we have seen, tends to appear either as terrible or sublime. The combination of these two extremes is uniquely indicative of God, a powerful term in Stephen's thinking. After Stephen as artist is no longer devoted to God as such, he continues to be impressed by godlike psychological effects. His constant attempt to perceive the truth of his life, to put together the system of signs in which he is enclosed, is always striving to see an inner pattern, and that pattern reveals the pregnant void beneath it.

The 1904 "Portrait" gives as the artist's aim "by some process of the mind as yet untabulated, to liberate from the personalised lumps of matter that which is their individuating rhythm" (*P* 258). The major form this individuating rhythm takes in the final novel is the alternation of attraction and threat that shapes the book's cycles—and by seeing this rhythm one can sense the indifferent totality that generates it, the subject of the narration. Insofar as Stephen is fixed on what shapes the course of his individuation, he seeks constantly for his author. The inevitable and unknowable extremes between which his experience is suspended—the surprising threat and the incomprehensible drift—attach him to something beyond himself. This something he finally objectifies, worships, and even dreads as the artist he will become.

The aim of seeking what creates one is suggested among Stephen's announcements of his objectives in the last chapter:

> . . . to express, to press out again, from the gross earth or what it brings forth, from sound and shape and colour which are the prison gates of our soul, an image of the beauty we have come to understand—that is art. (207)

> . . . to express myself in some mode of life or art as freely as I can and as wholly as I can. (247)

The image of "prison gates" in the first quote refers to Blake's recurring conception of "the five senses, the chief inlets of Soul in this age" (*Poetry of*

Blake 34). Stephen here presents the senses as limits to seeing the soul. The beauty the artist understands is beyond the senses, which only give an image of it. Stephen will soon define this beauty as corresponding to the stages his mind goes through in esthetic apprehension (*P* 209). The second quote shows that the beauty he expresses in art is the nature of his own soul, which he strives to express wholly. He does this best by representing its individuating rhythm, the interplay of opposing forces that reveals the dynamism between them. This generative opposition is the truest function of himself, the process that calls forth all the particular images, and so creates him. Essentially contradictory in its need for positive and negative, this interaction cannot be portrayed directly. Even the lyrical passages of flooding are only approximations, secondary effects in one phase. The most active and personal way Stephen can represent this identity of rhythm is by focusing on his interaction with the projected artist as a mature man who looms behind the narrative.

If all of Stephen's words are charged with a conflict that points to an absent narrative authority he strives to encompass, this aim accords with Derrida's theory of the origin of language, a deconstructive version of Plato. Derrida says that the use of signs to represent truth is based on the disappearance of an original direct knowledge of truth, a childish cognizance that for Derrida is represented by the face of the father: "The disappearance of that face is the movement of differance which violently opens writing . . . " (*Dissemination* 167). That is, it creates the distinction between absence and presence, which is the basis of the other oppositions that make up language through what Derrida calls *differance*.

This pattern is parallel to the Lacanian one in which the signification that constitutes personality starts with loss (*Four* 23). On the first page of *Portrait*, Simon Dedalus's face appears "through a glass," with divine overtones suggested by this biblical phrase (1 Cor. 13:12), and by magnification and hair: "His father told him that story: his father looked at him through a glass: he had a hairy face." This countenance is left behind at this point, never to regain its direct magnitude. Stephen's thoughts take over in the third person the narrative begun by his father, an account that leads him on this page to the creation of an original image ("green wothe"), and to the distinctions between warm and cold, mother and father.

Derrida sees writing as a parricidal supplanting of the authority of the father because it imitates a prior creation (*Dissemination* 164). He sees the subversive devotion to writing as a replacement of the father by the god of writing, Theuth or Thoth (*Dissemination* 84–94), the god to whom Stephen devotes himself in the last chapter of *Portrait*. It is not clear that Stephen's image of Thoth is derived from Derrida's source, Plato's *Phaedrus* (274c–76), yet Stephen's Thoth, like Plato's, is an illegitimate god opposed to social solidity: "But was it for this folly that he was about to leave for ever the house of prayer and prudence into which he had been born and the order of life out of which he had come?" (*P* 225).

The orthodox God is replaced by a ridiculous one, but Stephen is not joking: he believes in a power of Thoth's that goes far beyond the god's bird-headed image. In the *Wake* Joyce identifies himself with Thoth or Hermes when he calls the autobiographical Shem "the first till last alshemist" (185.34–35), for Hermes is supposed to be the first alchemist, and if he were immortal, he would be the last. The ironic portrayal of Thoth does not eliminate a claim on divinity.

Just as writing always strives to destroy the father, it always strives to recreate him, neither aim being abated by its impossibility. If Stephen is seeking to grasp the force that creates him all through the novel, then all of his perceptions are aimed at and shared with an invisible narrator. I can give an idea how this works by looking at one of the unusual and vivid words for perception in *Portrait,* the verb *divine,* which appeared in the 1904 version (*P* 259). In the second chapter of the novel, the figure of Monte Cristo "stood forth in his mind for whatever he had heard or divined in childhood of the strange and terrible" (62). Divination means perception beyond the senses. It includes foretelling the future and discovering obscure things by the aid of deities or rites.

Stephen seems to think that such perception in conjunction with a higher power is a necessary part of being fully percipient. In Chapter 2 at Belvedere College his nature is "smarting under the lashes of an undivined and squalid way of life" (78). This way of life in which the system of the school has enclosed him is "undivined" in that it does not use perceptions that are beyond immediate conscious sensation.

Moreover, the word *divined* may serve to describe the way Stephen is written. Phrases like "divined" and "smarting under the lashes" are typical of much of *Portrait* and *Ulysses* in that they express both the character and the narrator. Such sharings are usually referred to as narrated monologue because the character's thoughts are told in the third person, so that his language speaks of him. But these phrases, while they express Stephen precisely, are beyond his verbal capability. This is especially obvious at this point, when Stephen is an adolescent, but it continues to be prevalent in Joyce's novels. I believe that people seldom think in such well-wrought prose as Joyce's; and even if we recognize Stephen's precocity and Joyce's skill in capturing the rhythm of thought, anyone who does think in such prose is subject to an organization far beyond his kenning.[10]

Bakhtin accounts for such effects by arguing that all novelistic discourse involves at least two languages because the character is spoken by the author (*Dialogic* 44–47). What we get throughout the book is not Stephen's language, but the image of Stephen's language. Because this language is written by another, it combines whatever language Stephen may have at this point of his life with other languages that focus the image. For example, "divining" throws in some theology, and "smarting under the lashes," a touch of psychoanalysis. While a phrase like "in childhood" may seem to come more from Joyce's end, and "strange" may seem more like Stephen, in fact both voices are joined in every word. Bakhtin says that the voices speaking simultaneously are engaged in a dialogue, which means that they go back and forth.

What Stephen sees is "divined" by being shared with and influenced by an author who sees beyond him. This technique uses the artist to re-create the actual conditions of perception, which is always dependent on a complex prior self established in language. In this case there is also a meta-self linked to vocation: the narrator selects, emphasizes, and shapes those perceptions of Stephen's that will lead to art. C. H. Peake shows that in transforming *Stephen Hero* to *Portrait,* Joyce left out elements that did not contribute to the development of the artist (69), and in doing so, he changed Stephen's nature.

Divination also means searching for water, and in the scene on the beach in which Stephen receives his artistic vocation, he picks up a pointed stick and wades up a rivulet to find himself surrounded by drifting. The creative perception he seeks must be found by immersing himself in a flow, and in this sense he is seeking water whenever he divines an impression that takes him beyond the conventional.

Stephen's Random Rites

My tumble . . . is my own.

FW 154.33–34

The transcendent level of perception, its co-operation with a higher level of consciousness, is confirmed by Stephen's specification of the only way in which his soul can actively approach the external world. This passage occurs during Stephen's religious phase, but the attitude it indicates remains a permanent part of his makeup: "In vague sacrificial or sacramental acts alone his will seemed drawn to go forth to encounter reality: and it was partly the absence of an appointed rite which had always constrained him to inaction . . . " (*P* 159).

This prefigures the later esthetic theory in which Stephen will enclose the perception of the object within a three-stage ritual form articulated through Aquinas (*P* 212–13). The ritual apprehension ends in a luminous stasis of pleasure during which the mind feels itself glowing. One of the main purposes of religious ritual is to free the mind to look inward by protecting it within a framework of prescribed acts.[11] By arranging Stephen's life as a series of cycles, the artist transforms the crises in that life into a series of self-generated rituals that force him to look inward or into the flux of language and to develop himself. As he grows increasingly aware of imposing these rituals on himself, he becomes his own church and the forces in his mind become the objects of his faith. The structures of his rites as priest of the imagination are increasingly selected to fit the laws of his mind rather than being determined by tradition.

Stephen's name refers to the idea of a religion not enclosed by any form. The eleventh *Brittanica,* in its article on St. Stephen says that this was his major advance over the Apostles: "His special 'wisdom' lay in greater insight into the merely relative nature and value of the externals of Israel's religion, and particularly those connected with the Temple." As St. Stephen is defending himself against the Jews who are going to stone him, he says, " . . . the Most High dwelleth not in temples made with hands; as saith the prophet" (Acts 7:48). He argues that he is not wrong to violate the rules of Judaism because the forms of religion are not essential.

St. Stephen is paraphrasing Isaiah here, and he goes on to repeat Isaiah's argument that God cannot value any particular Temple because he made everything. Isaiah carries this attitude further by adding that God looks only "to him that is poor and of a contrite spirit, and trembleth at my word," and rejects the sacrifices of those who have "chosen their own ways" (Isaiah 66:2–3). This may refer to idolatry, but it seems to suggest that God can be reached neither through religious structure nor through conscious choice but only through the feelings of insecurity and unhappiness that our later Stephen finds so generative. St. Stephen omits the last point from Isaiah, but he may exemplify it by being the first Christian martyr.

One of the Jews who condemned St. Stephen was Saul of Tarsus (Acts 8:1). Afterwards, Saul converted, took over Stephen's leadership of the church, and became St. Paul. He has been accused many times of introducing fanaticism, authoritarianism, hatred of the body, and antisemitism into the church.[12] Joyce probably saw St. Stephen as the free aspect of the church destroyed by its repressive aspect.

Stephen's Dedalus's rejection of religious structure is linked to his name saint's denial of the Temple on the two occasions when Dedalus is seen performing rituals in temples made of air in Chapter 5. In the first of these he practices augury with a group of swallows "circling about a temple of air" (224), while in the second he remembers trying to pray "to the sombre nave of the trees" (232). The more arbitrary the frame of Stephen's devotion becomes, the more he reduces it to the laws of his own mental activity, but those laws turn out to involve another mental activity behind his.

Stages of Dialogic Dialectic

I have suggested that this other mind is the artist who creates Stephen and that his rituals and divined perceptions aim at this mind. But the image of Stephen's religion as without boundaries suggests that the teleology of *Portrait* is not so simple. Rather than aiming at a particular goal that remains constant, Stephen's ritual perceptions aim at a series of goals that shift through a continuing process. In the first chapter, his perceptions lead him to the truth to himself that he finds as a student at Clongowes, while in the second, he finds his truth in sex, and in the third, in religion. While his vision is leading him to the goal of each chapter, he has no knowledge of the goal of the following one. He will not begin to develop toward the next goal until he has reached the present one, and the goals may be extremely opposed to each other. Moreover, there is no reason to believe that the image of the artist he attains in the last chapter is final. Presumably he will stay an artist, but he will go through other cycles, and his image of art will change. We may say that each stage includes the previous ones, and also that each earlier stage has to be gone through on the way to the later ones; but at each stage Stephen aims at something different.

The kind of shifting teleology described here is best expressed in Hegel's dialectics, which presents the development of the mind as a series of stages, each with its own characteristics, but all necessary to the ongoing progress of the spirit. Hegel's theories are especially effective in describing Stephen's relation to his environment as a function of this dialectic.

The characteristic mode of Stephen's volitional involvement with the world is one in which, having organized his language and prepared his ritual, he releases his consciousness toward the world by seeing it expressing him; then he brings his consciousness back mixed with the world by seeing himself expressing it.[13] The crowning model of this looping is the vision Stephen attains of himself as artist. By projecting himself outward as a narrator, he generates a creative power that returns to expand the mind that sent it. Insofar as he creates his object by shaping his story, he creates himself.

This model controls all points of his perception in the sense that on some level of his being among the ongoing stages, whatever he perceives either supports or opposes the expansion of his mind. Of course, opposition, as we have seen, may be helpful, while encouragement (such as his father's) may weaken him, but he is always moving toward the goal of creativity by sending his mind toward the object before him and mentally returning from it. Hegel's phenomenology captures the vital, complex interplay of this process.

The idea that the self is formed by a movement outward followed by a movement inward, and even the idea that it consists of these movements, were available to Joyce in the famous preface to Hegel's *Phenomenology of Spirit:*[14]

> The realized purpose, or the existent actuality, is movement and unfolded becoming; but it is just this unrest that is the self; and the self is like that immediacy and simplicity of the beginning because it is the result, that which has returned into itself. . . . (12)

> . . . the True is Subject. As such it is merely the dialectical movement, this course that generates itself, going forth from, and returning to, itself. (40)

If the self is made up of the going out and coming back of intelligence, then it is a signifier because it operates to communicate between two parties. Hegel's phenomenology, while it is not informed by linguistics, presents patterns of interaction that Lacan builds on to describe the operation of the signifier. The Other whom Stephen engages in dialectic has to give him a unified goal to aim at, and this corresponds to the goal-oriented aspect of Hegel; but the goal also has to keep changing to sustain his development, and this matches the dividing phase of dialectic that Lacan emphasizes. The goal of *Portrait* may be identified with the ungraspable idea of the "mature artist," who is Stephen's creator insofar as Stephen believes in him. Every image Stephen interacts with tends to lead him toward this goal, though it may lead him first through being a whoremaster or the prefect of his sodality.

Stephen's movement of mind outward and inward repeats itself in many forms throughout *Portrait*. Early in the first chapter he writes his name on top of a column of expanding locations that ends with the universe. First he reads down this column, "Then he read the flyleaf from the bottom to the top till he came to his own name" (16). So he follows the list outward and then selfward. To recognize the generative power of this, notice its parallel to the scene in the garden of Bloom's house, when Stephen and Bloom think about the vastest spaces and then about the tiniest particles (*U* 698–99/17.1043–69).

Stephen tends to see E——. C——. in a similar pattern as characteristically moving away from him and then moving back again (*P* 69, 219, 222). His relation to the souls of the masses of the Irish people is expressed through Davin: " . . . the rude Firbolg mind of his listener had drawn his mind towards it and flung it back again . . . " (*P* 180). And in Stephen's esthetics theory, the artist's mind goes out to the object and then returns with a glow because the object corresponds to the mind's own phases.

Stephen's awareness of the loop of desire is strongest in adolescence:

" ...all day the stream of gloomy tenderness within him had started forth and returned upon itself in dark courses and eddies..." (77). And the most elaborate statement of such dialectical movement is the equation passage with which I began:

> The vast cycle of starry life bore his weary mind outward to its verge and inward to its centre, a distant music accompanying him outward and inward....
>
> ...another equation began to unfold itself slowly and to spread abroad its widening tail. It was his own soul going forth to experience, unfolding itself sin by sin, spreading abroad the balefire of its burning stars and folding back upon itself, fading slowly, quenching its own lights and fires.
>
> ...At his first violent sin he had felt a wave of vitality pass out of him and had feared to find his body or his soul maimed by the excess. Instead the vital wave had carried him on its bosom out of himself and back again when it receded: and no part of body or soul had been maimed but a dark peace had been established between them. (103)

The chief benefit of this turn of the cycle is a rapprochement established between the soul and the body, both of which gain by knowing each other. This is very much in line with Hegel's dialectic of development, and in representing Stephen's thoughts as Hegelian, the passage is a solid example of how his perceptions are constantly augmented by the author beyond him. But then the logic of Hegel's dialectics is built on the dependence of the mind on something beyond itself. An entity cannot exist in itself because it has no identity except in relation to something else, so that the position of this first line is untenable: "The Thing is posited as being *for itself,* or as the absolute negation of all otherness, therefore as purely *self*-related negation; but the negation that is self-related is the suspension of *itself;* in other words, the Thing has its essential being in another Thing" (*PS* 76).

It can only define itself relative to otherness, and this is why Hegel says that consciousness is not a discrete entity, but "this whole process itself, of passing out of itself" and appropriating an object (*PS* 144). Consciousness is always shared with another.

The dialectical movement Stephen defines in the equation scene remains fundamental to his activities for the rest of the book. He echoes the image of his "soul going forth to experience" from that scene at the very end of the novel when he says, "Welcome, O life! I go to encounter for the millionth time the reality of experience..." (253). The process he has engaged in countless times before is a movement out into the world that will loop back to create his soul.

All the cycles on the structural diagram represent this process. At the beginning of each cycle (chapter), Stephen is moving toward an object constituted by the world he is established in. The threat that arises in the

middle defines the limit of his perception. It is the aggressive function of
the object, the father as reality principle. It is the author, who is the essence
of what he has to meet, that turns his perception back upon himself. The
wandering Stephen takes up at the end of each chapter is a movement
toward self because it abandons existing goals. This return movement
becomes evident at each ending when Stephen, having passed through
deep uncertainty and immersed himself in the flux, is uplifted by a strong,
unexpected sense that he has found his real self. It is unexpected because
he gains something from a new object that speaks for his author. But the
teleological force of all this is undercut by the author's awareness that the
new self will not last.

Hegel recognizes the instability of the self in the definition cited above:
" ... it is just this unrest that is the self" (*PS* 12). At his best, as in this phase
of his theory, Hegel avoids the synthetic tendency for which Derrida faults
him. Derrida holds that Hegel's theory of synthesis (sublation) overlooks
the fact that when you combine two agents, there is always something left
over (*Dissemination* 15). While Hegel's phenomenology aims finally at complete self-knowledge, the self as a movement outward and inward cannot
be completed, so that complete self-knowledge would lack a self.

The contradiction in Hegel is also in Joyce. As Stephen's desire to
"express" himself as "wholly" as he can (*P* 247) suggests, Joyce aims at
complete self-knowledge, but he does not want to lose personality. He
approaches such knowledge by projecting a series of selves, and of others
with whom these selves interact. This project is already rolling through the
series of Stephen's *Portrait* selves. But the knowledge that could bind these
figures together is perpetually deferred, outside-created reality in the place
of the invisible god. Self-development requires such an unattainable goal, a
goal essentially other.

The contradiction is between the self and the other that knows it, for
self-knowledge requires an outer view. This contradiction was already
implicit in Plato's early version of dialectics, to which Stephen refers in the
dialectic "Scylla and Charybdis" (190/9.235). Derrida points it out: "To seek
'among yourselves' by mutual questioning and self-examination, to seek to
know oneself through the detour of the language of the other, such is the
undertaking presented by Socrates. . . . " Derrida highlights the contradiction by adding that dialectic was conceived of as a passage between the
human and the divine (*Dissemination* 121–22).

Joyce follows the method of knowing oneself through the language of
the other, and if his dialectic is divided into distinct stages, these have the
advantage of filling the mind he creates with more richness, depth, and
complexity than a simple process could yield. It is through the transitions
from one Stephen to another that the model is established of communicat-

ing with his future self. None of the versions of himself among whom he seeks could resemble him without this unknown level, so every discrete identity is incomplete.[15]

As I mentioned, Stephen's meditation on his equation emphasizes the phase of unfolding and describes the return as fading and quenching. The least important thing about this equation seems to be the fact that one thing equals another. Joyce does not forget the loss that is inseparable from growth. In the dialectic of Stephen's developing vision of himself as an artist, there is always a substantial residue of his mind that remains fixated on prerational obsessions, and this unsynthesized margin causes the triumph at the end of each chapter to be followed by a downfall. Such a downfall is predicted when Stephen speaks as Icarus, addressing Daedalus as his father, on the last two lines of the novel. The artist is beyond him, and even when he grows as an artist, the creative force of otherness that the artist represents must always be beyond him.

One way Joyce undercuts the possibility of synthesis in *Portrait,* the possibility of Stephen becoming his own creator, is by focusing on the field involved in the dialectic between subject and object. In the first phase of the movement that fills this field, the subject-in-formation goes out towards the object, and in this phase the perceiver is moved by his alienation from the object. In the return phase of the movement, perception coming back from the object is alienated from the self, if only because it returns to form a new self, different from the one it left. In Lacan's terms, the dialectical movement out and in reappears as the loop of the path of desire, and this movement has the effect of causing the division that constitutes the subject.[16] One application of this is that every new identity Stephen takes on through the latest cycle alienates him from the self he formerly had. He is divided from himself as he grows conscious of himself.

In each cycle what Stephen perceives, which corresponds to his mind, has two distinct phases, a phase that attracts him and one that repels him. I have already associated these phases with an attraction to mother and a fear of father that are built into Stephen. But these forces are capable of changing and dialectically engaging Stephen only insofar as they are objectified as exterior, active in their otherness. And so, divining an agency behind the tumbling of experience, Stephen moves toward identifying the complex force that is creating him with the author he aims at. Therefore the author must operate through these primal oppositions: he enters his work as a group of opposed forces that constitute Stephen's personality as a division.

Stephen's elaborate effort to understand artistic creation in the last two chapters is a transfer of religious paradigms to esthetic psychology that aims to know and join through art the Other that is creating him. If his effort to

be his own creator is bound to fall short of full self-knowledge, nevertheless
he can create himself prodigiously insofar as he succeeds in assuming this
role.

A good indication of the intensity of Stephen's devotion to the Other is
the increasing sophistication of his style. Here, for example, are thoughts
he has in his physics classroom in Chapter 5: "O the grey dull day! It
seemed a limbo of painless patient consciousness through which souls of
mathematicians might wander, projecting long slender fabrics from plane
to plane of ever rarer and paler twilight, radiating swift eddies to the last
verges of a universe ever vaster, farther and more impalpable" (*P* 191).

While it is impossible here, as often, to say to what extent Stephen's
thoughts are supplemented by the artist as narrator, it is likely that he
thinks in something like these terms. But anyone whose consciousness
takes such an estheticized form is not living his experience, he is writing it.
Such perception is augmented by language that strives to fulfill the artist in
the future.

The elaborate nature of Stephen's discourse shows how hard he is
continually working for the Joycean Other. He has replaced the authority/
alterity of society with that of art. In Lacan's Rome Discourse, he characterizes the obsessive as a slave working for an internalized master who can
never be satisfied (*Selection* 99–100). Stephen's sense of beauty arises out of
his service to this master, and he can only gain a sense of freedom from the
Other by confronting and understanding its great power in constituting his
mind.

Contact with the Other is presented as the goal of Lacanian analysis by
Shoshana Felman in *Jacques Lacan and the Adventure of Insight.* Felman
points out that Lacan finds *Oedipus at Colonus* an advance on *Oedipus Rex*
because Sophocles has the older Oedipus accept his fate. She says that the
aim of Oedipus's life is to know the discourse of the Other as represented
by the oracle. To assume one's history is to take responsibility for the
discourse of the Other, and Felman says that psychoanalysis derives its truth
from passing through the Other (129–33, 152). Felman emphasizes the
paradox that at the end, Oedipus cannot understand the knowledge he
represents, but he has to go on telling his story to convey the truth of his
myth to others (142–43). I see the fact that Oedipus can give truth without
grasping it as parallel to the way in which Joyce can play the role of the
Other in his work without filling that role in life.

NOTES

1. Shari Benstock speaks of a play between "sin" and "sign" in the *Wake* in her
"Nightletters: Woman's Writing in the Wake" 230–31.

2. James King West points out in *Introduction to the Old Testament* that the Hebrews go through a cycle in which prosperity leads to apostasy, which leads to oppression, which leads to penitence, which leads to deliverance, which leads back to apostasy (179). This pattern is repeated many times throughout the Bible.

3. In "Joyce and Skeat," Stephen Whittaker shows that Joyce must have used one of the first three (similar) editions of Walter Skeat's *Etymological Dictionary* rather than the fourth (1910), which is the one most commonly available.

4. This diagram appears in *Joyce between* (59), which explains in detail how it works (20–83). I bring it back because I want to expand its implications in new directions.

5. Scholes and Kain, *The Workshop of Daedalus,* 81. The context of this discussion tends to align perception with desire.

6. Pp. 67–68. Michael Gillespie suggests that Maher was Joyce's textbook and describes Joyce's markings in it in *Joyce's Trieste Library* 159.

7. Gifford, *Joyce Annotated* 206, lists the sins against the Holy Ghost and says that while they were thought of as unforgivable, it was possible to obtain forgiveness by special measures for all of them except final impenitence.

8. "The Significance of the Father . . . " appears, with the original text of 1909 distinguished from later additions, in Jung's *Collected Works* 4:301–25. Ellmann says Joyce probably purchased this and other early psychoanalytic works in his Trieste library around the time that they were published in *The Consciousness of Joyce* 54.

9. Psychic energy is free to circulate in the primary process, which is unconscious, while it is bound to images in the secondary process, which is rational. See "The Primary and Secondary Processes," in *The Interpretation of Dreams, SE* 5:588–609. In *Television* (13), Lacan says that primary process "implies" *jouissance.*

10. Scholes and Corcoran notice this in "The Aesthetic Theory and the Critical Writings" 695: "In *A Portrait* Stephen achieves in casual conversation what Joyce himself could not accomplish when he was Stephen's age. He is able to do this because the older Joyce is behind him like God in his creation, guiding his thoughts and gilding his tongue."

11. Jung recognizes ritual as contact with otherness in "Transformation Symbolism in the Mass," *Collected Works* 11:249: "In the ritual action man places himself at the disposal of an autonomous and "eternal" agency operating outside the categories of human consciousness . . . in much the same way that a good actor does not merely represent the drama, but allows himself to be overpowered by the genius of the dramatist."

12. The charges against Paul are summed up in Hyam Maccoby, *The Mythmaker: Paul and the Invention of Christianity.*

13. Ragland-Sullivan says of Lacan (90), "He concluded that because of the fashion in which identity is formed, human beings do not perceive by contemplating objects—that is, objectively—but through a subjective filter of representations through an emptying out of representations onto the world.

14. The Preface ends on 45.

15. Joseph Buttigieg, in *A Portrait . . . in Different Perspective,* argues that Joyce condemns Stephen for having a faulty ideological position. Buttigieg overlooks the

constant change in Stephen's position and the likelihood that Joyce never intended
to portray anyone with a solidly correct position. Such a position leaves little room
for growth, and personality in Joyce consists of conflict between different positions.
A parallel, but more flexible criticism of Stephen is given by Kershner, who sees
Stephen as trapped by images of romantic egoism from popular ideology (165–90).
I think Kershner underestimates the complexity of Stephen's irony, and at times
overlooks Bakhtin's argument (*Problems* 73) that the dialogic character should never
be finalized.

I'd like briefly to respond here to the argument that Stephen is an esthete with a
negative relation to history. Stephen's view of politics is sharp, though Joyce decided
not to expound socialism explicitly after *Stephen Hero*. In *Portrait*, Stephen is
probably correct in realizing that in his Ireland socialism cannot avoid being
subordinated to a nationalism that is attached to the church. He is also probably
right in believing that he can do more for humanity by developing an understanding of the mind through self-exploration than he could do by restricting himself to
a narrowly political aim. The point at which Stephen in *Portrait* and Ursula
Brangwen in Lawrence's *The Rainbow* (1915) declare that one should define oneself
apart from family, church, or state may be a step forward for human history.

16. Lacan refers to the outward movement as alienation and says that it
condemns the subject to appearing only in division (*Four* 210).

2

The Author as Other

My position is that the subject has to emerge
from the given of the signifiers which cover him
in an Other which is their transcendental locus. . . .

Jacques Lacan[1]

The Barred Subject as Multiplicity

As Stephen discerns behind the text of his life the mind on which his mental activity depends, he struggles to define and join the artist who is creating him. Throughout *Portrait* he delineates how his thinking and seeing are shaped by the rhythm of his interaction with this otherness, and the delineation is extended further in *Ulysses*. It serves to reveal the psychological ground of his experience as authorial activity. Turning from Stephen's development to the role of his author, I hope to show that the shape of Stephen's dependence reveals what he is attached to as the shape of Joyce's involvement in his work, a shifting shape of multiplicity and conflict.

Every author must provide depth for his figures from a source beyond consciousness if they are to resemble people, for people constantly receive and send impressions and images that they can neither understand nor predict. Joyce re-created this psychic flux with phenomenal success: his characters and objects are constantly being bombarded with surprising phrases and turns of style. To generate this vitality, Joyce projects himself as a series of authorial agencies designed to interloop with each other within, above, and below the discourse of the text. By doing so, he synthesizes the complex structure of the unconscious.

The basis of the narrative agencies that Joyce projects in his work is the Joycean personality that is withheld from his creatures and so constitutes the unreachable otherness out of which they spring, the unknown that defines and energizes them. This authorial otherness is connected to the work by a generative transformer that uses the structure of the author's unconscious to arrange the personality of the work (what Kenner calls "the mind of the text")[2] as a group of interacting forces that are expressed as circuits of character, theme, and technique.

To understand the operation of the Joycean Other as a framer of narrative, we must see the mind of the text made up of several forces that interact as distinct personalities. Lacan reminds us in "The subversion of the subject and the dialectic of desire in the Freudian unconscious" that Freud subverted the traditional unity of the subject by showing that the mind is made up of opposing forces. Lacan translates Freud's concepts into linguistic terms, and when he speaks of "The signifier" here, he refers not only to the spoken word but to all of its unconscious determinants, so that the term is his equivalent for personality: " . . . the signifier is constituted only from a synchronic and enumerable collection of elements in which each is sustained only by the principle of its opposition to each of the others" (*Selection* 304).

Personality can only exist as a group of opposed forces, and Lacan diagrams such groupings in the form of four graphs in this paper. Moreover, he sees the interacting functions of these graphs as fictional characters when he identifies them with Shakespeare's figures in "Desire and the Interpretation of Desire in *Hamlet.*"[3]

Stephen argues in the "Scylla and Charybdis" episode of *Ulysses* that Shakespeare's personality is defined in his work by a familial pattern of connected characters, the oedipal triangle of usurpation. Because for Stephen the subject is constituted by a dialectic of desire, the connections between his Shakespeare's characters are relations between parts of the mind of the creator "consubstantial" in his work (*U* 197/9.481). A similar pattern applies to *Ulysses* itself, in which Stephen, Bloom, and Molly, as I will show, express parts of Joyce's mind and add up to a Joycean subject that cannot quite be put together.

Lacan's *subject,* which is comparable to Freud's *unconscious,* is barred from consciousness as a primal level of constitution of the self at the root of speech. It differs from Freud's internal unconscious by being external and an effect of language. Yet "The subversion of the subject . . . in the Freudian unconscious" suggests that Lacan regards his unconscious as equivalent to Freud's. An externality that operates as internal, the barred subject is the individual form of the Other. Just as this subject can never be made conscious, so Joyce's authorial subject is barred from perception by his characters. Nevertheless, each fictional personality or signifier is defined by the Joycean circulation out of which it comes and into which it returns.

Lacan maintains that the unconscious is generated by an interplay of the situations of personal relations, culture, and language, and cannot have any inherent content. This view seems to conflict with Joyce's providing of the unconscious for his characters. The depth he provides, however, is not a fixed entity but a process, as his authority is not monistic, but multiple. He summoned extraordinary awareness of the linguistic lives of his figures on both personal and cultural levels to synthesize an interplay that dazzled Lacan. Joyce's version of this linguistic context, however divided, is the maximum expression of his individuality, for no one else exerted these particular powers of verbal creation, or spoke with this range of unspoken voices.

Joyce projects a sense of knowledge beyond what is knowable in Bloomsday Dublin, where no one knows why 16 June 1904 is significant, why Homeric images keep popping up, or indeed why anything one does has the meaning it has as part of the book. This knowledge, however, can never be reached,[4] so the reader's sense of Joyce as a definite authority behind the veil of language is an illusion. For Lacan, however, the illusion of the artist's authority is essential to art. He says that when we look at a painting, we seek the gaze of the master. And because the artist constructs his personality into the picture, our looking attains the effect of the master looking at us, even if the picture has no eyes and the effect is unconscious. Lacan says that this effect is "perhaps merely illusion" (*Four* 101), but according to his theory we could not see the picture without it, for perception is motivated by desire, and desire needs to sense a response.

If the presence of Joyce is an illusion, this need not prevent it from having strong effects. The Other is also an illusion, but its structure controls our lives and we cannot exist without it. Lacan's concept of the Other, in fact, is based on Sartre's idea of "Being for Others," but Lacan changes this idea. While "Being for Others" is a limited state in Sartre, for whom the Other tends to be an invidious force of social censure (221–302), Lacan holds that there is no consciousness that does not depend on the Other. Because Lacan believes in the unconscious, he develops the Other into a more complex and vital entity than it is in Sartre. The illusion of Joyce as artist in the role of the Other is central to the coherence of the fictional world. This coherence is as strong as Joyce's deconstructive incoherence and inseparable from it, for the two aspects revolve around each other.

Does the status of Joyce's printed presence as illusion mean that that presence cannot speak for him? Rather than thinking so, we should remember that all identity is illusory in Lacan. One reason for this is that the self is always composed of language, and the reality behind language can never be reached because words can refer only to other words. Therefore, even if I stand directly before you, my presence is an illusion made of language. In this view, Joyce's presence in his work is as authentic as any actual person's can ever be.

Self as Loss

Because the signifier refers to an object that cannot be reached, the central feature of the self is a sense of loss. Freud argues that the ego is made up of a series of identifications, each triggered by a sense of loss of the object taken in (*Ego and Id, SE* 19:28).[5] Similarly, in Lacan the self is constituted in language as a sense of separation from a lost object, for language is a substitute for parental presence (*R–S* 57). If the withdrawal of another person—which may range from stepping out of the room or disagreeing to dying—adds to the child's mind by causing him to introject the other's image, then Joyce's method of withdrawing behind his text is a gift of mental activity from him to us.

The pattern of discourse fundamentally structured as an address to a lost object appears throughout *Portrait*. As I have demonstrated elsewhere (*Joyce between* 37–41), the ideals at which Stephen aims are based on the mother, from whom he was separated at Clongowes Wood. Similarly, the goal of artistry toward which he orients his life is based on lost memories of an ideal image of his father. On the last lines of the book he finally addresses (in writing) the master he serves: "Old father, old artificer, stand me now as ever in good stead." The phrasing indicates that the "old father" he symbolizes as Daedalus has been with him all along, overlapping with him or standing in his stead. This artist within, behind, and beyond his experience fits Ragland-Sullivan's definition of the Other as including repressed parental images.

Joyce's interior monologues turn from the tradition of narrative spoken or written to another person, so they illustrate the idea that discourse begins by being addressed from one aspect of the mind to another. This shifting other to whom thought is addressed has to be external to justify the communication of speech, but it cannot be seen in definite form. It is lost because the stream of consciousness motivates itself by re-creating loss. In *Ulysses*, interior monologue is motivated most immediately by Stephen's loss of his mother and by the Blooms' partial loss of each other. These crises indicate some of the main identifications being addressed, but everyone who speaks in his mind addresses someone who is not there.

Bloom, in "Sirens," thinks, "Thou lost one. All songs on that theme" (*U* 277/11.802), and Stephen, in *Portrait*, defines the lyric as "the simplest verbal vesture of an instant of emotion" (*P* 214), or the most direct speech of the feeling self. The two statements add up to indicate that the purest expression of the self always takes the form of a sense of loss. Thus Joyce implicitly anticipates the theories of Freud (*The Ego and the Id*, 1923) and Lacan that the self is built on a sense of loss.[6]

This anticipation has a theological basis, for in the world Joyce came from, the most essential loss was supposed to be separation from God. People were supposed to talk to God frequently and to take him into themselves, and Joyce, as *Portrait* indicates (240), did this passionately as an adolescent. In the world he went into, the wordworld of his work, the great loss on which existence is founded is the loss of Joyce. No matter what relatives, friends, enemies, spirits, abstractions, or self-images the characters may address in their minds, they are always ultimately talking to Joyce, trying to explain themselves to him. He represents the power of the unconscious that hears what they say to themselves (and what we say to ourselves). They approach this power through gaps in their discourse, contradictions formed by the added accents with which Joyce's narrative agencies supplement their thoughts. Lacan presents a structure for the process by which the unconscious conveys itself into language; and Stephen, in the "Proteus" episode of *Ulysses,* has a vision that resembles this structure as he is thinking about where his speech comes from.

The Anchoring Point

Ragland-Sullivan says that the Lacanian analyst listens for incongruities in the patient's speech that reveal the discourse of the Other, which appears through knots of verbal connection in the patient's unconscious known as *points de capiton* (R–S 114, 229). The *point de capiton* ('upholstery tack' or 'anchoring point') is the elementary cell, the first graph presented in "The subversion of the subject," the simplest form of the major Lacanian structure for articulating the unconscious as discourse. Lacan says this diagram shows "where desire, in relation to a subject defined in his articulation by the signifier, is situated" (*Selection* 303). If desire comes from the Other, the *point,* by defining the source of desire, shows how the Other articulates itself in language. It has a special fitness for Joyce as the writer of the unconscious.

This Lacanian model is delineated when Stephen writes a poem in "Proteus" that focuses on the image of a male vampire kissing a woman: "He comes, pale vampire ... mouth to her mouth's kiss" (48/3.397). This has overtones both of the death of Stephen's mother at God's lips and of the primal scene of sex between father and mother. Stephen elicits the poem from the stream of his consciousness by halting the flow of his thoughts: "Put a pin in that chap, will you?" (3.399). The writing of the poem is thus parallel to "the 'anchoring point' (*point de capiton*), by which the signifier stops the otherwise endless movement (*glissement*) of the signification" (*Selection* 303).

Lacan's first graph of the forces that articulate discourse, like his other, more complex versions of the graph, consists basically of two opposed

Graph I

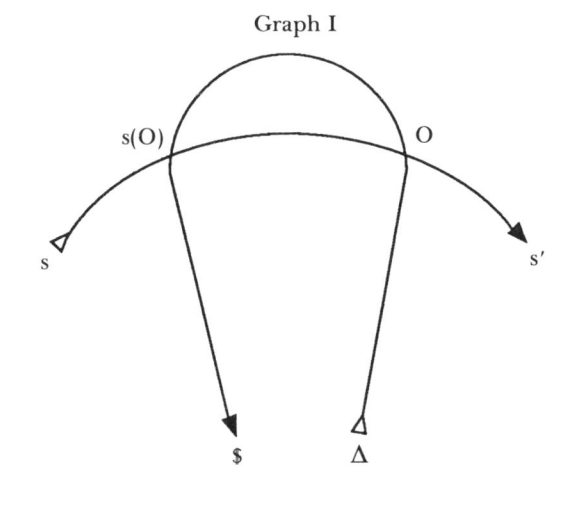

Figure 2: Lacan's first graph from "The subversion of the subject" (303).

movements. I have modified the diagram in figure 2 by adding the labels "O" and "s(O)" for the two crossing points although they do not appear until Lacan's *"Graph II"* (306).

There is an arc-shaped vector moving clockwise and a hook-shaped one moving counterclockwise and crossing the arc at two points. The arc represents the sliding of signification on "the signifying chain" (303), originally *"la chaîne signifiante"* (*Écrits* 805). Jacqueline Rose defines *signifiance* as the "movement in language against, or away from, the positions of coherence which language simultaneously constructs" (*FS* 51), and I see the arc as the metonymic flow of words in the unconscious. The hook goes in the opposite direction indicated by Rose's last eight words. On the second version of the graph, the first point at which the hook crosses the arc is labelled "O," while the second point of crossing is called "s(O)." Lacan says of these points: "The first, connoted O, is the locus of the signifier's treasure. . . . The second, connoted s(O), is what may be called the punctuation in which the signification is constituted as finished product" (304).

I believe this means that the hook moves from the locus of the Other (O), which is so rich with suggestion that it cannot be expressed or perceived, to the punctuation that pins the Other down into a statement, reducing it to an inadequate representation.[7] The arc moves toward uncertainty, and represents the tendency of language to express the ineffable. It corresponds to Eco's idea of unlimited semiosis, in which any signifier refers to a series of other signifiers that multiply without end (68–69). Lacan's hook, on the other hand, moves toward certainty and represents the tendency of language to trap or enclose meaning by enunciation.

If Lacan links shifting meaning to the feminine and stable meaning to the masculine, then the arc and the hook of the elementary cell may conceivably be compared to the flowing of the mother and the fixity of the father respectively. But a clearer correspondence that seems useful is between the two movements of Lacan's cell on one hand and on the other, the movements of perception outward toward the object and then back toward the subject. Lacan suggests that the system he begins to elaborate here is an extension of the loop of desire when he says, "The subjection of the subject to the signifier, which occurs in the circuit that goes from s(O) to O and back from O to s(O) is really a circle . . . " (304). The other that stands for the Other is perceived in the circling of signification: " . . . the other, appears in so far as the drive has been able to show its circular course" (*Four* 178).

Such movement occurs every time Stephen finds a new word or sees something new. Lacan says in an unpublished seminar that at the *point de capiton* "something new is invariably produced."[8] He implies that to see the new signifier involves a phase of drifting into chaos. Sheridan's "otherwise endless movement" of the arc does not do justice to Lacan's *"glissement autrement indéfini"* (*Écrits* 805), with its overtones of "indefinable otherly sliding." The outward phase of the loop is a dissemination, and Lacan sees it as enacting a division in which the subject is revealed (*Four* 210).

After Stephen's cognition expands to take on a new possibility, it contracts to fix that possibility in a formulation, as in the factoring of sin: "the eyes opening and closing were stars being born and being quenched" (*P* 103). Each new word-cycle he goes through adds to his being. Lacan uses the word *parlêtre* ('speechbeing') to indicate that being can only exist as speaking (*Ornicar?* 7:9). When a word is active in and beyond Stephen's mind, it is filled with the complexity of movements and relations that make the signifier constitute the subject.

The expansion of Stephen's mind at the end of each chapter moves toward a new object as his wandering takes him someplace he has never been. The new sense of identity he reaches at the end, always saturated with receptivity toward the object, is not clearly formulated. It is a pre-identity still moving outward, and at the beginning of the following chapter, he defines this identity by practice, enclosing himself within a definite signified as sinner, saint, or artist; thereby he actualizes the vision the first phase of which he entered into during the previous ending. Between chapters the narrative circles outside itself and through a Joycean Other that turns it around from centrifugal to centripetal.

In the new chapter, once Stephen is enclosed within his new identity, the vitality of his expression is gone. Language is fixed in a definite meaning by the law of the Father, whereas the free flow of signifying is feminine. Stephen submits to the law of the Father by filling a definite place, so the male threat of castration that arises always represents the fixation of the word. All of the men who threaten Stephen are conformists: Heron, for example, attacks him for liking the rebel Byron (*P* 81). Once the word is formulated or enunciated, its potential for expressing reality is mutilated and a new word must be sought—so Stephen, to stay alive, always has to aim at a signification he can never reach.

The vampire and the woman in Stephen's "Proteus" poem may be seen respectively as the hook and arc of Lacan's graph. When the signifier, which Lacan equates with the symbolic power of the phallus, makes contact with and fixates the flowing of signification, the latter dies. This suggests that the mistake Stephen's mother made was to accept her position in a patriarchal order. But the signification of this arrangement is also the soul of the artist, which Joyce consistently represents as a woman (anima). And in the final, written version of the poem, it is Stephen whom the vampire desuscitates: *"Mouth to my mouth"* (132/7.525). The soul of the artist dies by being transformed into the signified of the work. But the soul is not fully transformed: it remains alive behind the text as a verbal illusion (which may be all it ever was for Lacan) insofar as it remains unattainable.

Opening the Sentence

... another would finish his sentence for him. ...

FW 288.4

Stephen tries to escape the consequences of his morbid vision of a sex act that is also an act of writing, just as Joyce tried to bring what had been lost in the work back to life in that work. One way Stephen does this, with Joyce's help, is to concentrate on the sliding chain and the phase of going forth. He identifies his soul with his mother in "Proteus" by meditating on his soul as a "shamewounded" woman clinging to him (48/3.422), who soon turns to May Dedalus when he says, "What is that word known to all men?" (435). Stephen strives to keep both his soul and his mother alive by presenting language in the process of issuing forth, language that has not yet been finished or even really heard. This language in process is *jouissance,* Joyce's symptom.

Lacan gives the elementary cell two kinds of function. Its synchronic function is hidden and leads to the source. I take this to mean that when its parts are put together at once (synchronically), it defines the root of the self. On the other hand, "The diachronic function of this anchoring point is to be found in the sentence..." (*Selection* 303), so that every sentence is a circuit of issuance and return, a loop. Roy K. Gottfried's *The Art of Joyce's Syntax in Ulysses* argues that most sentences in the novel reveal a balance between the utmost freedom of arrangement and the order needed to make sense (12–27). These two sides are so polarized in Joyce's mature writing that the anchoring points of many sentences are opened up and their opposing forces shown in contrast.

The sentence Stephen puts his pin into illustrates such Joycean de/con-structure: "He comes, pale vampire, through storm his eyes, his bat sails bloodying the sea, mouth to her mouth's kiss" (48/3. 397–398). The first two words of this very loose sentence are the main clause, and the following four parts all modify it. Each part involves a twist that violates standard form. At the start, the normal order of "the pale vampire comes" is reversed to put "he comes" first, making the appearance of the vampire-God both more sudden and more inevitable. In the second part, reversal makes the eyes pierce more effectively because the storm comes first. Part three uses "sails" and "bloodying" in surprising ways that may be called expressionistic or hysterical.

Perhaps the biggest shock in the sentence after the vampire himself is the unanticipated appearance of "mouth to her mouth's kiss." The kiss image does have an antecedent: it refers to a line of Douglas Hyde's that Stephen calls forth here to complete his preceding meditation on the woman who "trudges" (47/3.392) across the world to come to God. But within this sentence the kiss makes a jump from what preceded, not only because it is unexpected, but because the scale changes from distant to close up as the vampire who seemed to be approaching is suddenly on her. Like other gaps in this disconnected string of images, the jump to the kiss expresses the urgency of the unconscious. It concludes the sentence resonantly and leads to Stephen's poem because the attachment of the soul or woman to phallic authority is the oedipal heart of Stephen's alienation, equivalent to the dependence of the signifier on a prior signifier.

This sentence is better written than the poem Stephen makes from it, which is derivative of Hyde:[9]

> *On swift sail flaming*
> *From storm and south*
> *He comes, pale vampire,*
> *Mouth to my mouth.* (132/7.522–525)

The superiority of the prose to this poem suggests not only that Stephen will never feel at home in the finished language of poetry, but that he could not write the prose sentence. Nor could he speak it intentionally. He can feel it, but it may be a decade before he develops the technical resources to express its free movement. It is written in the style of 1915–17, not that of

1904. Stephen can only express this sentence in conjunction with an agency beyond his knowledge that hears the first movement of his feeling. This agency is played by Joyce as the Other taking apart the anchoring points of Stephen's sentences, opening their constructions. The process will lead to the prevalence of fragments in many passages of Bloom's thought.

It is commonly assumed that there is no narrator for the stream of consciousness. Gérard Genette says in *Narrative Discourse* that Joyce's interior monologue should be called "immediate speech" because it is "emancipated . . . from all narrative patronage" (173–74). This overlooks the elaborate machinery that frames interior monologue, as well as the fact that different writers, such as Joyce, Woolf, and Faulkner, write interior monologue in different ways. The style of each of these writers is apparent through a range of his/her different characters. I once wrote some interior monologue, and found it a laborious process: I started with logical discourse and slowly stripped away connections in order to give the language the natural movement of thought. It is extremely difficult to create such free movement, and Joyce was known to write deliberately.

Lily Briscoe, in Woolf's *To the Lighthouse,* wants to capture in her painting "that very jar on the nerves, the thing itself before it has been made anything" (287). She struggles for years to do so, and only after a decade does she succeed in representing this "immediacy." Both Joyce and Woolf had to work over their experiences for years (sometimes unconsciously) before they could understand them well enough to give the impression of penetrating life. The vast effort behind interior monologue constitutes a narrative agency at the other end of the characters' thought, and it includes the range of cultural and personal elements in the Other.

The quality of the vampire sentence that keeps Stephen from being able to express what he means, a quality of otherness indicated by its gaps, is the inspiration he tries to follow in his poem. This otherness leads him on to a series of lines that seem even further from anything he could write or speak: "Mouth to her moomb. Oomb, allwombing tomb" (48/3.401–402).[10] Hearing these lines is more a matter of feeling than of understanding: they are the discourse not of the self, but of the Other.

As a writer, Stephen is devoted to the other world of literature. Not only are his thoughts controlled by the artist he aims at, but they draw on diverse background influences that loop into his discourse from the wide cultural context of the Other. These sources must have passed through Joyce's mind in some way, though he need not have been conscious of it. The otherness of Joyce's position keeps us from knowing many influences from his personal memories, and forgetfulnesses. In this case, we can recover a source that makes it understandable that Stephen, with his interest in literary experiment, should be able to conceive the word "moomb." I will treat this influence, Rimbaud, in my next chapter. Stephen Dedalus never explicitly mentions Rimbaud, so we must turn to biography here. Stephen Daedalus does speak of Rimbaud in *Stephen Hero,* but it seems unlikely that Joyce intended this early novel, part of which he destroyed, to survive. So our knowledge of Joyce's interest in Rimbaud may be called accidental. Joyce must have intended his work to have, as it does, an invisible background, much of which could never be traced, and this blackground corresponds to the Other.

Gaps in the continuity or clarity of the text, such as "moomb," reveal the discourse of the Other as a voice coming from outside the established context. Such a voice always involves biographical references, at least to Joyce's experimentation of a period subsequent to the action. "Moomb" also refers to Joyce's 1904 interest in Rimbaud. Only through a route that loops away from Stephen's discrete identity can the language-before-language that extends his identity be expressed.

Stephen and Joyce's other characters in *Ulysses* are connected to such external language not only when composing, but at moments of feeling that resonate often throughout the day. In a sense they are virtually always composing. Here, for example, is what some part of Bloom thinks while listening to Ben Dollard in "Sirens": "Croak of vast manless moonless womoonless marsh" (11.1012). Bloom, who could certainly not write this, is influenced by music here. But all of the narrative techniques that inform the episodes of *Ulysses* have the effect of adding external layers of discourse (such as those of sciences, myths, and symbols) in order to express added levels of the characters. Some of these extra fields of signs are present in the action, like the singing Bloom is listening to here—and some have to be spoken by figures external to the action, like the scientific catechism of "Ithaca." All of them cause the languages of the characters to revolve around those of the author.

Stephen is aware that inspiration means that something speaks or blows through him, something he identifies with the artist. Lacan's Other, as the unknowable source from which desire always speaks, is the source of inspiration. Stephen's references in "Proteus" to the womb/tomb at the other end of his breath (48/3.402) refer to the mystery of going into the Other and coming out of it, a passage through language. When discourse is given added accents from beyond itself, the conflict between coherence and alterity brings out the opposing principles in the elementary cell to suggest the complex intention behind language.

The Superego

Further indications of how the unconscious reaches consciousness through opposition, and of how Joyce gives depth to his figures, may be gained by the use of Freud's concept of the superego. While the correspondence

between Freud and Joyce will be my main concern in this section, I believe
that Freud's concept is analogous to Lacan's ideas. The combination of
streaming and capture in the *point de capiton* suggests that the Other
reaches the individual through an opposition that is parallel to the genders.
A major reason for this is that in personal history the earliest and most
fundamental images of the Other develop out of images of the parents, as
Ragland-Sullivan indicates:

> The formulation (m)Other is meant to express the idea that the human
> subject first becomes aware of itself by identification with a person (object),
> usually the mother.
> Later the Other (A) [*Autre*] refers to the Symbolic other, or to the real
> father. . . . (16)

The forming of the subject by identifications with mother and father is
parallel to the development of Freud's superego. This agency first internal-
izes a mother imago (the ego ideal) and then adds to it a paternal authority.
Freud uses the terms *superego* and *ego ideal* interchangeably in *The Ego and
the Id,* and says that the superego contains paternal and maternal identifications *"in some way united with each other"* (*SE* 19:34, Freud's italics). Because
the superego continues to include not only authority but ideal, it remains
the voice not only of severity but of all beauty, spirituality, and humor (*SE*
19:27–36, 21:164). Otto Fenichel says that the two sides of the superego stay
"as intermingled as were the protecting and threatening powers of the
parents" (106). One cannot protect without potentially threatening, and a
threat usually offers conditional protection. Yet the superego has generally
been simplified as an oppressive figure because people have trouble
grasping that in the unconscious, where opposites are inseparable, it
cannot be the source of oppression without being the source of liberation.

The same paradoxical combination of oppression and liberation is
reflected among critics who concentrate on the Other as an external social
agency. Kimberly Devlin, in " 'See ourselves as others see us': Joyce Looks
into the Eye of the Other," emphasizes that the gaze of the Other causes a
shameful sense of being watched and censured by society. But McGee, in
Paperspace, uses the term *Other* for an ideal "collective subject" in which everything will be shared (196). They are both right, for the social Other, like the
personal one, cannot wield the power to repress without controlling the
power to free. So we unconsciously derive both from the same source, and
it is often the appeal of the social ideal that keeps people in bondage.

Freud diagrammed the superego as the only channel leading from the
id to the conscious in his *New Introductory Lectures* (*SE* 22:78–79). As a link
between unconscious and conscious, the superego is parallel to the *point de
capiton,* which links the Other to articulation. The superego tends to

appear as a voice, and is credited with special power over language (Fenichel 107). Through the interaction of its maternal and paternal aspects, it shapes the formlessness of the id to make language, just as the *point* originates language through the interaction of its sliding arc and its hook of enunciation. Both systems represent the author who mediates expression and repression.[11]

Lacan speaks of the Other as showing two faces based on the parents. He interprets "one face of the Other, the God face, as supported by feminine *jouissance,*" and adds, "And since it is there too that the function of the father is inscribed in so far as this is the function to which castration refers, one can see that while this does not make for two Gods, nor does it make for one alone" (*FS* 147). The reference to deity has its irony, for Lacan realizes that the opposition between masculine and feminine shown by the appearance of the Other (the Other itself is neutral) is not biological or inherent, but a product of the cultural organization of signifiers that creates the roles of mother and father. In Freud's system, the basis of every personality includes images of both genders in active relation to each other. I believe this is also true in Lacan, but in Lacan, the genders are linguistic structures.

The feminine and masculine sides of Stephen's superego constantly push and pull him through the cycles of *Portrait*. For a close-up of how this process operates, let us look at one of his main actions. In Chapter 2, this is what drives Stephen to lose his virginity: "He felt some dark presence moving irresistibly upon him...a presence subtle and murmurous as a flood filling him wholly with itself. Its murmur besieged his ears like the murmur of some multitude in sleep; its subtle streams penetrated his being. His hands clenched convulsively and his teeth set together as he suffered the agony of its penetration" (100).

Both aspects of the superego are active here: while the maternal images of the prostitute draw Stephen toward them from the front, the masculine aspect attacks from the rear. The pattern not only recurs in *Portrait* and (as I'll show) in *Ulysses,* but also in the *Wake,* as in this description of HCE: " . . . light leglifters cense him souriantes [Fr. 'smiling'] from afore while boor browbenders curse him grommelants [Fr. 'muttering'] to his hindmost" (130.1–3).

Stephen's anxiety about lacking manhood (castration) gives him a sense of homoerotic passivity here, and his guilt over his father's weakness in this chapter makes the dark paternal incubus more threatening. Stephen would not be driven to the sex act without a terrible sense of being passively feminine, and I submit that this is not because he is abnormal, but because he is (with Joyce's help) more aware of the dual nature of sexuality than most men. The Lacanian McGee points out that sexuality is neither mascu-

line nor feminine, but somewhere in between (98, 117). The fantasy of
being raped by the Father is an extreme but not inaccurate version of the
anxiety that drives men, whether to manhood or morality.

Assuming that Joyce, by playing the role of the unconscious, is in the
position of the Other, he can see a lot more from there about what is
involved in these images than the adolescent Stephen can see—so he can
give the scene an immediacy that can only come from beyond. Stephen's
speechbeing is always suspended between opposites in the Other, which
reveals itself through the gap in discourse created by any opposition. In this
case the gap is accompanied by a murmur from under the surface of
speech, the sliding of signification. If Lacan sees the Other (as Freud sees
the unconscious) as the ground of desire and consciousness, then by this
light Joyce has to enact this role in order to give his figures human speech.

Lacan's system indicates that no one can fully be or know the Other (*FS*
32–33), but he says that people can represent it or produce its effects. For
example, he says that in obsessional neurosis, the role can be "held" best by
the dead father (*Language* 146n.). There is a parallel between the dead
father and the author who creates his word child and then passes away. In
one of his last seminars, "The Other is Missing" of 15 January 1980, Lacan
says that he will "be Other" when he dies "after a lifetime spent being it in
spite of the law" (*Television* 133). While he is alive, Lacan can only be the
Other when he speaks from outside his consciousness, the field of rational
language (the symbolic) controlled by phallocentric law. Lacan's desire to
go outside this field led him to imitate Joyce.

If Joyce plays the role of the unconscious or Other who enters his work as
a series of opposed psychic forces, this suggests that he constructs his subject
into the work, so that it revives the question of whether he is present.
Kristeva takes a positive view in "Joyce 'The Gracehoper' or the Return of
Orpheus," where she says that he "lives on physically in his works, which
form his true filiation" (*Ninth* 174), and that he enters *Ulysses* through an
opposition between masculine and feminine that resembles the superego:
"Love's two forms—which are two variants of identification, the one paternal and symbolic, the other maternal, having to do with the drive—are
united in the artist's experience, leading him to transmute "consubstantially"
his psychic life into his characters and their adventure" (*Ninth* 178).

The "paternal and symbolic" is the aspect of language that involves the
definite meanings of words, while the "maternal, having to do with the
drive" involves the shifting of signification in the dynamic of feeling. So the
Kristevan use of Lacanian terms here can be taken to indicate that the
gender division in the superego is parallel to the linguistic division of the
point de capiton. What Kristeva seems to overlook here is that Joyce can only
enter his fiction by being transformed into language through such mecha-

nisms of linguistic opposition as the superego and the *point*. Therefore his actual identity is hidden behind a veil of words and can only be apprehended through signs whose connection to their origin is permanently indeterminate.

Lacan's system, however, finds the same linguistic obstacle in everyone, in print or in person. The basis of my subjectivity, my barred subject, can only reach me transformed into the oppositions of language. So I can only approach my real self, what motivates me, through contradictory interpretations, and I misrecognize myself as inevitably as I misrecognize Joyce. We are both hidden behind veils of text. In designing a model of the subject that was so far withdrawn behind linguistic complexity, Joyce recognized the reality of living in language and expanded depth psychology to anticipate Lacan. If the subject of Joyce can only be approached through the veil, we must consider how the veil works, and as a first step, we will have to see things as words.

NOTES

1. Cited in *The Language of the Self* 106n.49, Anthony Wilden's enriched edition of Lacan's Rome discourse. I will refer to this edition as *Language*. The quote is from Lacan's *"Remarque sur le rapport de Daniel Lagache,"* in *Écrits* 655–56. Wilden's translation continues: " . . . through this he constitutes himself in an existence where the manifestly constituting vector of the Freudian area of experience is possible: that is to say, what is called desire."

2. Kenner, *Ulysses* 112. Kenner says he got this idea from Bruce Kawin, author of *The Mind of the Novel*.

3. Early in this essay, trans. James Hulbert, in Felman, ed., *Literature and Psychoanalysis* 11–23, Lacan identifies Hamlet with the pure signifier, Gertrude with the Other, and Ophelia with the object. He says little about the role of the elder Hamlet, which I will take up below.

4. Phillip F. Herring, in *Joyce's Uncertainty Principle,* consolidates as a general rule what many of us suspected: Joyce's works are designed to render the crucial questions of meaning unresolvable.

5. Ragland-Sullivan points out that Freud modified this view by saying that the healthy ego should go beyond identification, but Lacan argues that Freud should not have retreated from making, in her words, "identification the means by which an ego . . . is formed" (R–S 35).

6. Lacan refers to "the central defect around which the dialectic of the advent of the subject to his own being in the relation to the Other turns—by the fact that the subject depends on the signifier and that the signifier is first of all in the field of the Other" (*Four* 204–205).

7. A good explanation of this diagram appears in Clément, *Lives and Legends* 175–78.

8. Cited in "Lacan and the Discourse of the Other," Wilden's long essay in *Language* 274.

9. Don Gifford points out in *Ulysses Annotated* 62 that Stephen's poem follows "My Grief on the Sea," in Douglas Hyde's *Love Songs of Connaught*. Gifford first wrote this book with Robert J. Seidman, but he revised it alone, so I will simply use his name. Future references to Gifford will usually not need page numbers because his notes are geared in order to the text of *Ulysses*.

10. The word "moomb," which appears in the manuscript and in the Gabler edition, is given as "womb" in the 1961 edition, an indication that Gabler's text is generally better, despite occasional lapses.

11. A more detailed discussion of the superego and its relations to the Other and the author appears in my "The Other of *Ulysses*," which presents Freud's topological diagram of the superego. Although Freud's concept of the superego parallels Lacan's dialectics of the signifier, Lacan actually uses the term *superego* in the usual, simple sense to refer to a masculine agency of censorship. Lacan's superego separates the child from the maternal object of desire. The ego ideal that is thus repressed enters an unconscious element called the *moi* (*R–S* 53). Ragland-Sullivan describes the *moi* as divided between maternal and paternal agencies (56), and as mediating between conscious and unconscious (105)—features of Freud's superego. I feel that the phallic agency that represses desire must retain the power to express it, and Lacan sees the superego as "an equivalent of language" (*R–S* 57) and says that it speaks for the Other (*Television* 87).

While revising, I found a passage in the seminar of 18 November 1975 in which Lacan speaks of Joyce playing the role of the Other (though Lacan's *a* is lowercase) in *Ulysses*. While this passage focuses on the paternal aspect, it seems that the feminine role of Joyce as *jouissance* would also pertain to the Other:

> This other which is in question is what manifests itself in Joyce by this, that it is in short charged with father. This father, it so happens, that Joyce must sustain in *Ulysses* so that it may subsist. By his art—art which is always the something that, from the foundation of the ages, comes to us as born of the artisan—Joyce not only makes his family subsist, but he makes it illustrious (*l'illustre*), and by the same stroke he makes illustrious that which he calls *my country* [English in the original], the uncreated spirit of his race. It is this by which the *Portrait of the Artist* ends, and there is where he gives himself his mission. (*J avec L* 46)

PART TWO

The Veil of Signs

3

"*This weaving of earth
and of air*"

Berkeley and the Veil

In *Ulysses,* both Stephen and Bloom are preoccupied with defining for themselves the operations of their own perceptions, and for each the ongoing inquiry into the sources of knowledge includes experiments. Sensory experience for the two men involves striking parallels of what they see and of how they see it. For each in his way vision operates among signifiers rather than among things signified, and it involves the construction of forces interacting in space, in a complex that seems to both men to have an inaccessible intelligence on the other end. To establish that the things seen in *Ulysses* are made of words—for characters as well as readers—I will examine Stephen's observations in the "Proteus" episode as they relate to Berkeley. De Saussure's principle that the signifier is barred from the signified, which influenced Lacan (but evidently not Joyce) was anticipated by Berkeley early in the eighteenth century.

In his essay on Blake (1912), Joyce included Berkeley on a short list of innocents who would be slaughtered "if we must accuse of madness every great genius who does not believe in the hurried materialism now in vogue" (*CW* 220). The foremost modern Irish philosopher, Berkeley was a superb prose stylist.[1] He eventually settled in Cloyne, a town on the Bay of Cork, the city John Joyce hailed from and brought his son to visit.

Berkeley's piety would have alienated Joyce, for the Bishop's arguments against materialism aimed to promote the importance of God. John Oulton Wisdom, however, argues in *The Unconscious Origins of Berkeley's Philosophy* that Berkeley's early work sprang from an impulse to rebel against the establishment by dismantling the existing world; and he made up for this by increasing emphasis on devoutness in his later work (180–82). But Berkeley's prescriptions for the religious use of knowledge are vague and platitudinous. Such attempts to promote social causes as his campaign to build a college in Bermuda in order to teach idealism to the Indians were often unrealistic and ineffectual. The inspired part of Berkeley's work was his taking apart of the known world by anatomizing the conventions behind perception.[2]

Wisdom says that Berkeley's tendency to see the world as a product of his mind was a projection of himself into the role of God. If God is the absolute Father, then replacing God is the absolute form of parricide. One of the strongest versions of parricide in the *Wake* is the story of how the Irish soldier Buckley shot the Russian general, a story with overtones of killing a deity (*FW* 338–55, and elsewhere). Berkeley, whose clearest identity in the *Wake* is as the archdruid Balkelly (610–12), also tends to blend with Buckley, as in "Berkeley showed the reason genrously" (423.32) and *"Burkeley's Show's a ructiongetherall"* (346.11–12). Thus the *Wake* repeatedly links Berkeley to the demolition of the establishment.

Stephen is investigating the relation of language to reality in "Proteus" with the aim of going beyond what is given, and Berkeley helps him here to consolidate a necessary realization. What Stephen sees himself seeing on the beach is language, a field of coded signs whose surface he searches in hope of finding the truth. The key to this is in Stephen's description of Berkeley's achievement: "The good bishop of Cloyne took the veil of the temple out of his shovel hat: veil of space with coloured emblems hatched on its field. Hold hard" (48/3.416). The image of Berkeley as a wizard deriving the field of appearances from his head excites Stephen to say "Hold hard" because he sees that the idea of the veil is crucial to his quest.

The multicolored veil of the Temple in Exodus (26:31–35) separates the part men can see from the holy of holies. The figurative usage of this veil to refer to the appearance of the material world seen as symbolizing and concealing a transcendent world behind it was found by Joyce in Yeats, who got it from Mallarmé. In his essay "Crisis in Poetry" (1895), Mallarmé says that his period is witnessing "a fluttering of the temple's veil" (34), meaning that the boundary between the physical and the transcendent is shifting and growing uncertain. This evidently describes the influence of the Symbolist movement, which sought a magic language behind appearances. Yeats, in "The Adoration of the Magi" (1897), a story Joyce was absorbed in around the turn of the century, refers to "that inquietude of the veil of the Temple, which M. Mallarmé considers a characteristic of our times" (309).

Another possible influence on the veil image is suggested, if not embodied, by *The Candle of Vision* (1918), by George Russell (AE). Joyce completed the *Little Review* version of "Proteus," with the Berkeley passage, by December of 1917 (*JJ* 441), but he read the *Candle* before completing the "Circe" episode, probably to review the ideas of his character AE. He might have encountered Russell's velations elsewhere. In *The Candle*, AE describes a youthful vision: "The tinted air glowed before me with intelligible significance like a face, a voice. The visible world became like a tapestry blown and stirred by winds behind it. If it would but raise for an instant I knew I would be in Paradise. Every form on that tapestry appeared to be the work of gods. Every flower was a word, a thought. The grass was speech; the trees were speech; the waters were speech; the winds were speech" (5–6).

This passage shows that the idea of a world made of language has antecedents in mysticism. Though Stephen links the idea to Berkeley's logical arguments, there are mystical overtones in the *Wake* when Balkelly confirms the equation of the veil with the world of appearances. He refers to "all too many much illusiones through photoprismic velamina of hueful panepiphanal world spectacurum of Lord Joss" (611.12–13). These lines include *velamen,* Latin for a drape or heavy veil; and the Greek-based coinage *panepiphanal,* which means 'showing everywhere.'

If the Temple veil is the panorama of visible objects, then it is congruent with the edge of the diaphane, Aristotle's term for the surface we see when we see color. In anglicizing Aristotle's *diaphanes,* usually rendered as "transparent" or "translucent," Stephen uses a word that suggests a veil. And in transforming the static diaphane into a veil, Stephen emphasizes its movement, which in the most direct terms, is simply the way in which colors appear to move closer and further away as objects do so, so that the veil of living vision trembles and swirls perpetually. Later this veil will be seen in Bloom's vision in "Oxen of the Sun": " . . . winding, coiling, simply swirling, writhing in the skies a mysterious writing" (414/14.1107). Here its movement ("writhing") is writing in the air, which tends to suggest a writer.

Ultimately, the movement of the veil suggests more than surface: as the Symbolists noticed, it implies something beyond. Movement blurs outlines, makes boundaries unclear, and suggests activity behind itself; and when the object takes a new position, one sees it as contingent. This is one implication of Stephen's recollected thought from Aristotle in "Nestor": "It must be a movement then, an actuality of the possible as possible" (25/2.67). Movement renders potential actual by presenting something on its way. It is a powerful tool in Stephen's use of language, and its effects begin with making things seem unreal, in circulation.

The "coloured emblems hatched" on the field of Stephen's veil follow Berkeley's theories in being distinct from the external reality they represent, as signifier is sundered from signified. Emblems are miniature symbolic devices, such as a picture of a peacock representing pride, or a saint holding a bleeding heart. The emblematic image is highly conventional and far removed from what it stands for. "Hatched" also refers to indirect representation. In heraldry, to hatch is to draw with lines or dots to indicate the tincture of heraldic devices (O'Shea 158). Even something as sensual as color can be reduced to a code, and Stephen is almost definitely aware that colors are actually degrees of vibration, subminiature lines and dots. This idea is developed in Maher's *Psychology* (80–84).

The emblems of color on the field are parallel to the poem Stephen has just written, which he describes on the previous line as "Signs on a white field" (3.415). One of Berkeley's central arguments is that we never see anything but the structures of language, signs that stand for different physical features only by comparison with other signs. For example, he starts *A New Theory of Vision* (1709) by showing that distance is not something we see, but an effect we construct into our visual impressions by imposing a conventional system. As Stephen puts it, "Flat I see, then think distance . . . " (3.418): " . . . what we immediately and properly see are only lights and colors in sundry situations and shades, and degrees of faintness and clearness, confusion and distinctness. All which visible objects are only in the mind; nor do they suggest aught external, whether distance or magnitude, otherwise than by habitual connection, as words do things" (*Works on Vision* 57).

Berkeley proceeds to go through all the other categories of what we "see" to demonstrate that color, movement, form, number, and identity are all defined and created by systems that operate like language. The quality of any point of perception only exists in relation to other members of the chain that defines it. We put together different impressions into conventional assemblages or clusters that we call objects and persons (108–17). Berkeley's thinking here anticipates Lacan, poststructuralism, and semiotics, all of which agree that language goes beyond words into physical impressions —and that words and signs refer primarily not to external objects, but to the systems of other words and signs that delineate them. Derrida, for example, insists that there is nothing outside the text but writing (*Grammatology* 158).

Berkeley uses the phrase "the curtain of words" (*Principles* 21), and Alexander Fraser's study *Berkeley,* which was in Joyce's Trieste library, refers to "the mist and veil of words" (13), a phrase from the commonplace book Berkeley kept in his teens at Trinity College, Dublin. These phrases, like Madame Blavatsky's *Isis Unveiled,* use the veil image mainly to refer to concealment, but Stephen's imagery shows that Joyce derived from Berkeley the image of the world of appearances as a veil of signs.

Current scientific theory tends to agree with Berkeley that what we see are words and not images. R. L. Gregory argues that there are no images in the brain; instead, the eyes feed the brain "information coded into neural activity": "We may take an analogy from written language: the letters and words on this page have certain meanings, to those who know the language. They affect the reader's brain appropriately, but they are not pictures. When we look at something, the pattern of neural activity represents the object and to the brain *is* the object. No internal picture is involved" (9).

Such analysis indicates that what passes through a person's mind is a neural code that he has no access to, and it is translated to consciousness by a linguistic order he is not aware of. These two forces may correspond to the chain of signifiers or arc and the punctuation or hook of Lacan's elementary cell. Here is a physiological basis for the famous Lacanian principle that the structure of the unconscious is the whole structure of language. In the *Four Fundamental Concepts,* Lacan observes that the optical layers that separate perception from consciousness are "the place of the Other" where "the subject is constituted" (45).

Language as the unconscious of sight is the subject of "Proteus" that is designated in the first sentence: "Ineluctable modality of the visible: at least that if no more, thought through my eyes." The last four words show Berkeleyan thinking involved here, but so may "modality." It means primarily that the visible is imposed as a mode, method, or way, or as a series of modes. Hermann von Helmholtz, a scientific authority on perception of the late nineteenth century, used the term *modality* to refer to the mode of each sense as opposed to the other senses. According to Susan Sutliff Brown, Stephen is referring to Helmholtz's use of the term "to describe the 'involuntary' and 'inevitable' mechanisms by which the senses perceived 'signs' such as color" (228). On a related level, *modality* in logic refers to the qualification that distinguishes a proposition as asserting or denying the possibility, impossibility, contingency, or necessity of its content. This level shifts the emphasis onto the structure that supports the content of visual reality, a linguistic structure according to Berkeley. Stephen is probing the verbal underpinning of sight.

The first Symbol listed for "Proteus" in the Linati schema is "Word" (*"Parola"*), and the Science of this episode is "Philology."[3] The technique, with its constant shifting into different languages and dialects, foregrounds the concrete nature of language as the object seen. Making word choices arbitrary, it focuses on the invisible agency behind the choosing, as if we could see a wind rippling the veil with sudden displacements. Surprising alternative words reveal linguistic possibilities concealed by the usual assumption that a word corresponds directly to a thing, an assumption on which the world's idea of reality rests. Berkeley characterizes this kind of linguistic reality as ineluctable:

> No sooner do we hear the words of a familiar language pronounced in our ears but the ideas corresponding thereto present themselves to our minds; in the very same instant the sound and the meaning enter the understanding; so closely are they united that it is not in our power to keep out the one except we exclude the other also. We even act in all respects as if we heard the very thoughts themselves. So likewise the secondary objects . . . only suggested by sight, do often more strongly affect us, and are more regarded, than the proper objects of that sense.
>
> (*Vision* 42)

When Berkeley says that we act as if we heard thoughts, he recognizes the gap between clear words and the flow in the mind. The clarity that makes external reality masterful is a function of the "secondary objects" in the last sentence, which include the stability and continuity of form. These objects are secondary because they are not seen directly: what we see changes constantly. We build constructions of stability by applying elaborate systems and codes to the "coloured signs" (*U* 3.4) that flash across our visions. And though we never know them outside our minds, we are trapped in these mental structures. As Lacan puts it, "It is the world of words which creates the world of things" (*Language* 39).

Externality

Stephen is attracted to Berkeley's theory because it suggests the possibility of escaping from the network of concretized language that encloses him, but he has his doubts. The phrase, "at least that if no more," following the "modality" of the opening sentence, suggests that there may be something out there beyond language. And in the first paragraph he says that Aristotle was aware of bodies before colors because he knocked his head against them. This prefigures later images of the protagonists struck by the physical solidity of the world: Stephen hit by a British soldier in "Circe" and Bloom knocking his head against the recently-moved sideboard in "Ithaca" (705/17.1275ff.). Such points remind us of Boswell's anecdote about Johnson kicking a stone to refute Berkeley (Boswell 333).

How does Berkeley explain people bumping into things? He says that in order to give people security, God made the principles of the language of perception regular and constant. Problems of physical situation arise because the reification of the language of the senses into material reality results in prejudices that entrap man destructively (*Principles* 53–56). Berkeley's thought here almost prefigures Lacan's analysis of the hidden powers of language that shape and disturb us. In effect, Berkeley argues that language operates as the unconscious that causes our concrete predicaments, but he does not develop the idea of the unconscious beyond the notion of ingrained, systematic error.

In "Nestor," just before "Proteus," Stephen recognizes that a system projected by one's mind can attack with unexpected violence. He says here that history "is a nightmare from which" he is "trying to awake" (34/2.377), that it is made by the mind and that he participates in its imagined world. As he hears the cries of hockey players on their nearby field of conflict, he thinks, "What if that nightmare gave you a back kick?" (2.379). Rather than expressing doubt about the status of history as nightmare, this statement implies the terrible power of dreams over reality: they can not only kick you, but give you a back kick, an unconscious one.

Joyce need not accept Berkeley's ideas as strongly as Stephen does here to see their great force in revealing hidden truth. When Stephen is punched by Private Carr or when Bloom bangs into the sideboard Blazes Boylan moved, they are certainly being struck by areas of their own minds that they have denied—and also by the languages of male aggression in the culture that encloses them. They are struck internally and externally by the Other, by the unconscious concealed behind the veil of appearances.

Stephen is in dread of an obscure gap in his mind from which thoughts come that he cannot predict: "... in my mind's darkness a sloth of the underworld ... shifting her dragon scaly folds" (26, 28/2.72–74, 171). He recognizes that this powerful, unknown, feminine area of the mind is traditionally under God's control when he reflects that the shadow of Christ lies over the hearts of men and on his own (26/2.84–85). This field controlled by a hidden author is the darkness in which his language and desire are formed, and so it is also the source of his apprehension of physical reality.

The scope of Stephen's dread emerges as he keeps his eyes shut on the first page of "Proteus": "Open your eyes. No. Jesus! If I fell over a cliff that beetles o'er his base ... " (37/3.14).[4] I have driven by Sandymount Strand, and there is nothing resembling a cliff on that flat expanse, so Stephen must fear that his mind will change the topography utterly as he walks "into eternity" (3.18).

Everywhere Stephen sees writing that implicates an unknown writer as he tries to read the "signatures of all things" (3.2): "These heavy sands are language tide and wind have silted here" (3.288). This line takes a military undertone from its iambic septameter, the meter not only of Blake's prophecies, but of "The Battle Hymn of the Republic." Under the control of church and state, the material world goes marching on as a linguistic juggernaught in which Stephen is enclosed. He trudges through a sediment of words like the "heaps of dead language" that offended him late in *Portrait*. Then, as now, his reaction against the deadness of ordinary language led him to a vision of wordshift, his meditation on "ivy." But the encrustation of false language was localised then by the corruption of the city. Now everything is covered with a veil of misusage, and his own mind is implicated, so that he struggles to break through in order to free himself.

The various forms of language that Stephen runs through are all corrupted dialects, so that the most refined discourse of intellection is no better than the alien criminal slang of Gypsies: "Language no whit worse than his [Aquinas's]. Monkwords, marybeads jabber on their girdles: roguewords, tough nuggets patter in their pockets" (47/3.387–88). In both cases words reduce the potentiality of perception to dead, compacted residue. Yet concealed behind the veil is the intelligence that articulated it; the solidity of the world is "made by the mallet of Los demiurgos" (3.18). As Los is Blake's figure for artistic imagination, it seems that Stephen hopes to have access to the creative intelligence.[5]

Whereas Berkeley's God, as source of the langworld, manifests himself positively by the constancy of his rules, Joyce's artist supports life by breaking rules, by lifting discourse out of ordinary understanding. In the ceaseless transformations of "Proteus," Stephen is constantly generating new terms and images that stretch or violate the limits of language. In doing so, his mind loops beyond itself to join with and separate from otherness, and therefore to participate in imaginary activity beyond Stephen's prior limitations. He does this by unique images and usages, such as a woman who "trascines" her load (47/392) and a dog "vulturing" the dead (363). By capturing vivid moments of these objects, he expands the range of images he was given, changing himself as he recreates his world.

He can do this as well within his mind, as when he turns Swift into a Houyhnhnm, "his mane foaming in the moon" (39/110). As far as I know, this image had not been used before, and it adds to Stephen's vocabulary, reappearing as a new word in "Circe," "moonfoaming" (573/15.3975). Thus the otherness can be internal. Stephen also speaks to otherness when he uses foreign words. There are four languages he uses frequently in this episode, and three more he dips into occasionally.[6]

The strongest means of breaking out of linguistic structure in "Proteus" is the creation of new words. These begin with rare and obsolete words like "westering" (47/393) and combinations like "brightwindbridled" (38/56); but they soon come to include portmanteau words such as "abstrusiosities" (45/320), the original pair "moomb. Oomb" (48/402), and "hismy" ([two words on 50]/487). "Hismy" is especially indicative of Stephen's joining with otherness. ness. The cultural context that all of these words fit best is the context of the artist.

"Proteus" switches rapidly from one language or perspective to another, and Stephen eradicates the conventional contexts of each verbal unit with the intention of penetrating the veil. He says of his soul, "Now where the blue hell am I bringing her beyond the veil?" (48/3.424–25). If the veil is made of language structures that allow us to see things in recognizable forms, then new verbal constructions, what Fritz Senn calls dislocutions (202–12), create gaps in the veil, breaching its ability to cover. As I have indicated, Lacan regards such gaps as sources of truth. Here a split in the signifier shows a division in the subject, making one aware that one is dispersed in a larger context.

The newness of the dislocution is what seems to split the veil, so what is glimpsed is unclear and has to fade when really seen. As a temporary disorientation rather than a full perception, it may be called a ripple of the veil rather than a puncture. It is, however, the goal of Stephen's quest, which is designated by the terms Proteus and *primal matter. Prima materia,* which Joyce gives as the Sense of this episode on the Linati schema, is the streaming of matter before form (see *Creator* 40–42). When Stephen reaches the protean level of primal matter, he joins the creative power of the artist. As in *Portrait,* he opens himself to a new identity by contact with flux, but this newest identity will involve Bloom.

The Artist as Rimbaud

Yeats derived the trembling of the veil from Symbolism through Mallarmé, and Stephen's effort to achieve vision by transforming language, disorienting his senses, and focusing on the magic power of words is substantially parallel to the ideas of Arthur Rimbaud, though Stephen is more concerned than Rimbaud with social reality. Mallarmé is the Symbolist Stephen refers to most in *Ulysses,*[7] but *Stephen Hero* says of an earlier Stephen, "He read Blake and Rimbaud on the values of letters and even permuted and combined the five vowels to construct cries for primitive emotions" (32).

We can see the effects of these early experiments in lines like " . . . mouth to her moomb. Oomb, allwombing tomb" (48/402). Therefore such experimental language could appear in Stephen's mind on Bloomsday; yet Joyce was not capable of integrating such language into a narrative in 1904, or when he wrote *Portrait.* His later mastery shapes the line as part of a larger continuity. For example, Bloom is thinking about the womb and the tomb in "Hades," when he attends a funeral at the same hour as "Proteus." As Bloom in a carriage passes an old man selling bootlaces, what he hears is "Oot," which is repeated (93/6.229–30). Bloom is thinking about death at this point, and "Oot" evokes a hollowness similar to that of "Oomb," so Bloom is also involved in the signification of vowels.

Phillip Herring was first to point out the importance of Rimbaud's influence on Joyce, but Herring's view of that influence is too narrow. Herring focuses on the sonnet "Voyelles," which equates vowels with colors and feelings, and which Joyce liked to recite from memory (Curran 29). Herring blames Rimbaud for turning Stephen toward estheticism (*Uncertainty* 141, 158–59), but Rimbaud made an invaluable contribution by guiding Joyce toward visions of the opening up of words, so Stephen follows a fruitful path. Catherine Millot says that Stephen uses a method of repeating words until they are emptied of their sense in order to reach the heart of signification (*J avec L* 90). Stephen practices this technique in the "Ivy" meditation of *Portrait,* and once his words are "emptied" of their "sense," he can see their movement as they "band and disband" (178–79), a step toward confronting the veil.

Stephen's view of the dynamic reality behind words may partly derive from the nonsensical repetition and word play of such Rimbaud poems as *"Le Coeur Volé"* ("The Stolen Heart," my translation):

> *My sad heart slobbers at the poop,*
> *My heart covered with shag.*
> *They're squirting it with jets of soup,*
> *My sad heart slobbers at the poop:*

To give an idea of the wordplay involved in this poem, I will quote two of its middle lines: *"Ithyphalliques et pioupiesques./Ô flots abracadabrantesques"* (Rimbaud 130). Compare the verses Stephen improvises as he watches the looping of his words:

> *The ivy whines upon the wall*
> *And whines and twines upon the wall*
> *The ivy whines upon the wall. . . . (P 179)*

Such looping and unlooping of words is frequently evident in "Proteus," in such later episodes of *Ulysses* as "Sirens" and "Oxen of the Sun," and in the *Wake*. Rimbaud seems to have provided the Joycean artist with a fundamental attitude linked to techniques for playing with language, taking apart and recombining words to observe their movements and connections.

Stephen may allude to Rimbaud when he envisions his medieval ancestors cutting up a school of stranded whales: " . . . a horde of jerkined dwarfs, my people, with flayers' knives, running, scaling, hacking in green blubbery whalemeat. . . . Their blood is in me, their lusts my waves" (*U* 45/3.304–306). This seems to refer to the first page of the "Bad Blood" section of *A Season in Hell* (1873), the work in which Rimbaud speaks of the "Alchimie du Verbe." In *"Mauvais Sang,"* he visualizes his barbaric ancestors by saying, "The Gauls were the clumsiest flayers of beasts . . . ," and adds that he inherits from them every vice and luxury (Rimbaud 301). There may also be an allusion to "Rinbad the Railer" (*U* 737/17.2325)—who was not only a railer, but at one time a sailor—in "Telemachus." There Stephen visualizes his mother: "Her shapely fingernails reddened by the blood of squashed lice from the children's shirts" (10/1.268). Her shapely nails may owe something to the "sovereign nails" (*"ongles royaux"*) of Rimbaud's sisters in "The Lice Pickers," his poem about the sensual experience of having his lice picked by them (Rimbaud 142–43).

If Stephen becomes Rimbaud at the same time that he becomes a medieval Celt, this exemplifies another important mode of transformation in "Proteus." Just as Stephen passes outside of the order of known language, he tends to pass outside of his own identity. He is disturbed to realize that he tends to be most aware of himself at moments when he imitates others:

My two feet in his [Mulligan's] boots are at the ends of his legs. . . . (31/3.16–17)

God, we simply must dress the character. (41/174)

Other fellow did it: other me. (41/182)

Proudly walking. Whom were you trying to walk like? (41/184)

That is Kevin Egan's movement I made . . . (49/439).

The life of Stephen's identity is most active when it takes on other identities, even while it loses itself. This pattern resembles Freud's idea of identity as a series of identifications, and as a Lacanian signifier, identity stands for something else. Like the phallus in Lacan, it is a claim to fulness that is based on emptiness. Stephen's "other me," as Herring indicates (156) may refer to a famous line from one of Rimbaud's letters, *"Je est un autre"* (Rimbaud 6), or 'I is an other,' with faulty agreement.[8]

What Stephen is being ironic about here in the largest sense is the principle that any definition or sample of his identity will have to appear in the disguise of words or signs. And so it will always be a falsehood, substituting an inert detail for the living whole. Stephen, however, is not fully aware of the implications of his feelings of shared identity. Like most thematic material, these ideas, which involve Bloom, have to be augmented by the author, supplemented beyond any particular consciousness in the book, to reach their fulness.

Stephen can only exist in words or signs, and when he leaves himself behind to join the otherness of a new image, identity, or gesture, he returns from what is writing him enriched by a new signifier. Derrida points out that writing, as an imitation, is neither present nor absent (*Dissemination* 103). If Stephen imitates Buck Mulligan, as he often does, he is not Stephen and he is not Buck. His truest identity lies in the principle of change, the dialectic between self and Other.

A similar suggestion within Joyce's ken is found in Berkeley's distinction between "ideas" and "spirit." Ideas, the images we perceive, are passive for Berkeley, while spirit, the source of all creation and action, can never be known by the senses. If what I see is idea and what sees it is spirit, the terms tend to be equivalent to object and subject: " . . . we do not see a man—if by "man" is meant that which lives, moves, perceives, and thinks as we do—but only such a certain collection of ideas as directs us to think there is a distinct principle of thought and motion, like to ourselves, accompanying and represented by it" (*Principles* 96).

The inner self is entirely other, Lacan's barred subject. Nor can we see ourselves behind the signs much better than we can see someone else, so

Stephen is as alienated from every particular image of himself as he is from those of others. He searches among the flotsam and jetsam of his being for an animating principle, mysterious as the movement of the sea, that has cast off these signs.

Kissing the Other

In *Portrait,* Stephen says, "The personality of the artist passes into the narration itself, flowing round and round the persons and the action like a vital sea" (*P* 215). When the characters are independent or dramatic, the artist disappears behind the action (*P* 215), but when they feel dependent on something larger, which is often, the illusion of the artist tends to be there in oceanic form until it is time to withdraw again.[9] Proteus, like Mananaan Maclir, another sea-god of transformation, may be seen as embodied by the incomprehensible shifting of the sea, the principle of flux. When Stephen tries to comprehend such movement through language (the only way), he is trying to understand the principle of creation outside and inside himself.

The impossibility of apprehending the creative principle of formlessness that the sea represents is seen in theological terms as Stephen imagines William of Occam: " . . . the imp hypostasis tickled his brain" (40/3.124). Hypostasis, or 'lower standing,' which also tickles Stephen's brain, is the process in which Christ's spirit comes down into a physical body. Stephen here imagines a series of priests making Eucharists: "And at the same instant perhaps a priest round the corner is elevating it. . . . And two streets off another locking it into a pyx. . . . Down, up, forward, back. Dan Occam thought of that, invincible doctor" (40/120–24). As Gifford points out, Occam said that Jesus was not present in the host in quantity and therefore could appear in any number of hosts simultaneously. Stephen specifies the shapelessness of the spirit by positing its appearance in a series of separate locations moving in different directions. The Eucharist thus resembles the sea, which moves in an infinite number of directions and spreads everywhere, including the saline solution inside of one's body. The meditation on woman that leads to Stephen's poem says that she contains "tides, myriadislanded, within her" (47/393–94). Similarly, Joyce, as an omniscient narrator, is everywhere within Stephen and can expand his smallest features to vastness; yet Joyce is also, like the Other as source of the Subject, actually as external and unreachable as the heart of the sea.

Stephen imagines the formlessness of the Other as coming from within as he focuses on his breath. He is composing a poem here, so his lips are thought of as a source of heightened language. Yet he is also kissing the air, an extension of the kiss of death God gives his mother in the poem, which, as I have suggested, tends to stand for the mortal hypostasis of living feeling into dead words. But though the poem is an abortion, the fertility behind it appears in the prose. In the gap of Stephen's writing, when he pauses, his potential is heard: "His lips lipped and mouthed fleshless lips of air: mouth to her moomb. Oomb, allwombing tomb. His mouth moulded issuing breath, unspeeched: ooeeehah: roar of cataractic planets, globed, blazing, roaring wayawayawayawayaway" (48/401–4).

As this is narrated monologue, Stephen mixes with Joyce here in the sense that it is not possible to tell whether any image comes from the narrator or the character. In its decomposition of words, this may be the most linguistically free passage in "Proteus," and I think it is the heart of the vision Stephen aims at. He senses here that the gap in the veil expands to an echoing vastness of open space. Without the forms of speech imposed on it, his breath becomes an interplanetary roar. This tiny sound, amplified, is like the prostitute's kiss in *Portrait,* which was so subtle it was almost beyond the senses. That kiss conveyed a revelation, and the feeling that urges Stephen to write here (the next word after the ones quoted is "Paper") is one of reshaping the universe. The cataractic planets, a violent waterfall of heavenly bodies, suggest not only cataclysm, but cosmogony. The wombing tomb of everything is the source of creation. Stephen is kissing the Other.

As he writes, he feels that the individual contains the potential of the universe before he puts it into form. Bending over rocks, he imagines projecting his shadow into outer space: "His shadow lay over the rocks as he bent, ending. Why not endless till the farthest star?. . . . I throw this ended shadow from me, manshape ineluctable, call it back. Endless, would it be mine, form of my form?" (48/408–14). His expansiveness is curtailed by the reality of his shadow. If it did not end, it would be cosmic, but it would not be his. No matter where it happens to end, and the locus seems arbitrary here, it is ended and called back by Stephen. He shapes it, but its "manshape ineluctable" is as subject to the conventions of language as everything else he sees. As the impression Stephen makes on the world, the shadow is equivalent to his writing, the "signs on a white field" of the following line. Yet the shadow is also the world writing on Stephen, for it can only mirror his form when intercepted by the world. The toss and catch of the shadow thus enacts the *fort/da* of perception, so that it becomes a model of the signifier. The endless casting of the shadow is the sliding of signification anywhere, and what returns it is the hook of punctuation.

The image of Stephen writing himself on and with the world leads directly to Berkeley's veil of emblems (48/416), suggesting that the veil is written. In his perceptive treatment of the veil imagery in *Ulysses,* McGee equates the veil with the text and says that in "Circe," "Each word is a thread . . . " (186). The veil is written with loops of perception, so that every point of which it is woven is a *point de capiton* or some more complex knot of psychic language forces.

Eco says that a sign is "the meeting ground for independent elements (coming from two different systems or two different planes . . .)" (49). In this case, the signs that make up the veil are nodes of intersection between the perceivable Bloomsday world and the Other beyond it. Many of the complex knots that Lacan elaborates in his seminars on Joyce seem to represent the knots of signification in Joyce's writing as symptoms of Joyce's subject. In the seminar of 17 February 1976, for example, Lacan says that *le sinthome,* which he had described earlier as Joyce's symptom, is what holds the functions of the knot together (*Ornicar?* 8:15). This suggests that a knot in the veil may have Joyce's personality encoded on the other end.

Stephen makes a typical reference to his potential authorship here when he asks someone (Joyce?), "Who ever anywhere will read these written words?" (48/414–15). But he cannot see where his maximum extension could lead; he sees only darkness and obstruction. The shadow projects a darkness within him, the part of his mind that is under the control of the Other, as opposed to the part that seeks to confront the Other. The shadow also images the obscurity and materiality of the signifiers that make up the world.

Stephen cannot consciously reach the other side of the veil, but his verbal techniques give him a sense of passing through. He can ripple the veil by shifting meanings, or make a gap in it by creating or framing a word (such as "oomb") separate from meaning. Moreover, as he moves into deeper levels of the meanings of words, he gets the effect of lifting layers of veiling, though the veil always returns as soon as the next level gets coherent. As he pushes the organization of language and perception backward, his author withdraws into further levels of obscurity, so that the freer he is, the more sophisticated his Other has to be to draw him on.

Another way Stephen approaches what is beyond or within is by focusing on signifiers of the incomprehensible basis of life, and he has been thinking here about such enigmas as the sea, death, breath, and darkness. These mysteries have often been projected on women, and the meditation that combines them leads Stephen to envision his soul as a woman and then, when the woman becomes his mother, to ask her for "that word known to all men" (49/435), another obscurity. His dialogue with this other in himself elicits a need for humanity that will draw him to Bloom. He begins to relate to Bloom through things at the end of "Proteus," when he is captivated by an object he finds incomprehensible. Through this incomprehensibility, he confronts himself in the Other.

Shiprelation

The final confrontation begins with Stephen's discovery that he has forgotten his handkerchief (498–99), and so has no place to put what he has picked from his nose. The handkerchief parodically represents the veil of appearances encrusted with excretions of language. "Cyclops" rubs our noses in this fact by a long description of a well-used handkerchief as a panorama of Irish landscapes, with about thirty-five picturesquely green "scenes depicted on the emunctory field," and "rendered more beautiful . . . by the rich incrustations of time" (12.1447–64).[10] If Stephen has left his dirty handkerchief behind, it may indicate that through his analysis of language, he has gained a sense of passing beyond the veil. He has penetrated the ineluctable modality to the point where he can see not the residue of language he projects, but otherness itself, something quite inexplicable to him.

Without a hanky, Stephen has to put his snot on a rock, and because this action falls outside the fabric or veil of social propriety, he dreads being seen: "Behind. Perhaps there is someone" (51/502). The sense of being watched by someone signals the presence of the Other, and when Stephen turns, he sees a ship that transfixes him inexplicably:

> He turned his face over a shoulder, rere regardant. Moving through the air high spars of a threemaster, her sails brailed up on the crosstrees, homing, upstream, silently moving, a silent ship. (51/503–5)

The lifted sails suggest revelation, for veil is derived from *uelum*, the Latin for 'sail'; and the cords that tie the sails suggest an unseen language, braille. The ship that ends the episode is an epiphany toward which "Proteus" has been leading, and it connects with the next episode, "Calypso." Virtually all of the episodes of *Ulysses* end with images that wrap up this section and lead to the next. For example, the word "Usurper" (23/1.744) at the end of "Telemachus" leads to a view of the unfairness of history in "Nestor." "Nestor" ends with a veil image: "On his wise shoulders through the checkerwork of leaves the sun flung spangles, dancing coins" (36/2.448–49). This leads to the fluctuating multiplicity of "Proteus."

One way in which the end of "Proteus" leads to "Calypso" is that Stephen speaks of devouring "a urinous offal" late in "Proteus" (50/479), while Bloom's taste for kidneys "faintly scented" with "urine" appears in the first paragraph on him (55/4.4). But the ship has also been seen as prefiguring Bloom. Harry Blamires (18) observes that the sense of someone behind him that the ship gives Stephen—"Behind. Perhaps there is someone" (51/3.502)—is parallel to what he later feels when Bloom passes by him at the end of "Scylla and Charybdis": "About to pass through the doorway, feeling one behind, he stood aside" (217/9.1197). I have shown that the force of the father tends to appear behind Stephen.

D. B. Murphy, the sailor who appears in "Eumaeus" as "Odysseus Pseu-
dangelos" (Linati schema) or Odysseus in disguise, is on the Rosevean.
So the ship that confronts Stephen-Telemachus contains a version (if an
ironic one) of Odysseus returning, and it signals the arrival of Bloom,
who fills the episodes that follow immediately. Bloom, whose name, like
the ship's, refers to a flower, is later opposed to Stephen by being classified
as "centripetal" (703/17.1225) because he is so firmly homebound. The
"homing" ship comes from the sea, the great symbol of otherness in
"Proteus."

Stephen does not realize that these implications attend the ship, but the
way in which the description of the schooner shifts into a neutral-sounding
third person seems to indicate that his self-consciousness recedes and he is
taken out of himself by this imposing object. For there is no doubt that the
description speaks for Stephen. "The black arms of tall ships" appealed to
Stephen at the end of *Portrait* with "their tale of distant nations" (252), but
he is uneasy here.

In fact the last sentence of this quote resembles the vampire sentence
that inspired Stephen's poem. It is even looser and more disorganized in its
similar rhythm, for it is a fragment without an active verb, so it shows that
Stephen is taken aback. Like the vampire sentence, it describes something
high that appears suddenly in the sky, moving from the sea. Both sentences
emphasize that the thing appears "through" the air, and the vampire is
curiously given "sails." An underlying pattern of uncanny dread appears
here that seems linked to the ideas of God and Father. It recurs when ALP
reaches the sea at the end of the *Wake:* "If I seen him bearing down on me
now under whitespread wings . . . (628.9–10). It is relevant here that Bloom,
as I will show, inspires dread in Stephen throughout *Ulysses*. But while this
underlying dread is marked, Stephen's main reaction to the ship seems to
be puzzlement, not knowing what it means.

The margin on which the ship impresses Stephen though he cannot say
why is the margin on which it speaks for the Other beyond the veil: he has
no language adequate to it. What strikes him most about it is its silence, and
this suggests that he wants it to speak. It must be speaking, for it is
significant, but he cannot hear it. What it is saying, or what he is saying
through it, will return later in his day. What the ship has to say to Stephen
beyond what he can hear constitutes the potential in him that is expressed
by fate, the dramatic form of the unconscious.

It is Joyce in his persona as author who is speaking through this vessel,
and the message of the returning voyager that will come back to Stephen
from this image is designed by Joyce. Yet this message can never be made
conscious. Stephen says of Shakespeare that he speaks to his work as "the
sea's voice, a voice heard only in the heart of him who is the substance of

his shadow" (197/9.479–80). A voice heard only in the heart is not heard consciously. The sea's voice may seem anonymous, but it is as intimate as the roar of Stephen's breath or blood.

NOTES

1. George Saintsbury, *A History of English Prose Rhythm,* which Joyce depended on extensively for "Oxen of the Sun," referred to Berkeley as "almost the greatest *writer*" of the Augustan period (252, Saintsbury's italics).

2. The most substantial treatment of Joyce's use of Berkeley is Pierre Vitoux, "Aristotle, Berkeley and Newman." But Vitoux seems to me to go astray by trying to accommodate Joyce to Berkeley's piety.

3. The schema for *Ulysses* that Joyce sent to Carlo Linati, together with his other major plan of correspondences for *Ulysses,* the Gilbert-Gorman schema, appears in Ellmann, *Ulysses on the Liffey* after 187.

4. A reference to *Hamlet* 1.4.71.

5. Los the blacksmith, who creates forms with his hammer, is explained in Northrop Frye, *Fearful Symmetry* 251–53.

6. The frequent ones are French, German, Latin, and Italian. The occasional ones are Gypsy, Greek, and Hebrew.

7. David Hayman, *Joyce et Mallarmé,* the standard work on the connection, does not deal with the veil image. But Joyce's use of Mallarmé's idea of the veil of illusion is treated as an image of the difficulty of marriage in the *Wake* in William Carpenter, *Death and Marriage: Structural Metaphors for the Work of Art in Joyce and Mallarmé* 175–222.

8. Lacan cites this line as an anticipation of his ideas in *Book II* of his seminars (7).

9. In "The Sea of Joyce," Chapter 5 of *Creator* (84–102), I argue that all images of the sea in Joyce's novels are images of Joyce's mind.

10. An even more debased version of the veil of signs appears late in "Joyce *le symptôme* II," where Lacan says that one purpose of Joyce's writing is *"crever dans le papier hygiénique"* ('to split the toilet paper'), *J avec L* 36.

4

The Gaze

The Field of the Gaze

To situate the veil of signs within the structure that supports it, further layers of Stephen's system of visual relation to external objects and to the Other can be revealed at this point by the use of another theory of Lacan's. Moreover, this theory applies also to Bloom because Bloom's system of seeing is parallel to Stephen's—parallel despite differences so serious that the two systems can be described as moving in opposite directions. They both accord with Lacan's influential theory of the split between the eye and the gaze, which appears in *The Four Fundamental Concepts.*[1] This theory can help us to see how perception is organized both for the protagonists and between them, how they see the world and each other—and how they see the world through each other. At the climaxes of their visual careers Bloom and Stephen have experiences of passing through the veil, experiences that match Lacanian models for the formation of the subject.

The key principle of Lacan's gaze theory is that one can only see something by imagining that it is looking at one: "... this is the essential point—the dependence of the visible on the regard of that which places us under the eye of the seer."[2] One's perceptions, even of landscapes and still lifes, must be motivated by being drawn toward its objects by desire, and desire is always based on an imagined response. On an aural level, as I have indicated, Joyce's characters interloop with him dialogically as self relates to Other. In vision, the imagined response is called the gaze and comes from a locus built into the structure of visuality, and of being.

As perception in Lacan depends on being gazed at, so does existence. If what we see is language, then being is being seen in language, and seen more completely than one can see oneself: "... I see only from one point, but in my existence I am looked at from all sides" (*Four* 72). The point from which I see is the eye and the surrounding watchfulness is the gaze that constitutes me as the subject of a larger consciousness. The totality behind the gaze is the Other. This view is an extension of Lacan's theory of the mirror stage, which holds that one's personality is formed by the way others see one, that a child's image of himself is a reflection.

The idea of being seen from all sides suggests God. As Lacan puts it, "The spectacle of the world ... appears to us as all-seeing. This is the phantasy to be found in the Platonic perspective of an absolute being to whom is transferred the quality of being all-seeing" (*Four* 75). While Lacan does not think that such a being can be found in life, Joyce's decision to play such a role in relation to his creatures was dictated by the compelling logic of his creation. He had to assume the perspective of the gaze to give his characters fullness. Joyce remarked to Frank Budgen that one of the prime aims of his modern version of the story of Ulysses was to create a figure who would be complete because he was seen from every perspective: "I see him from all sides, and therefore he is all-round in the sense of your sculptor's figure. But he is a complete man as well—a good man" (Budgen 17). Joyce recognized his responsibility for the visual apparatus described by Lacan.

This apparatus, however, is more complex than I have indicated. What the eye sees is a field in which the eye itself is an invisible center, and this field is seen by focusing on a particular point. At the same time, the subject maps himself in the picture, so that I project myself as a formal composition onto the field seen before me. Near the center of the visual field is a blind spot or hole, a reflection of my pupil, and behind this blind spot is situated the gaze. I cannot see what is regarding me in all of my perceptions any more than I can see the consciousness of a person looking into my eyes. Conventions lead me to believe that through a certain code of lights and movements, I am seeing the other person's thought, but all I see is a screen of signs. Lacan says, "You never regard me there where I see you."[3] The center that covers the gap corresponds to what Lacan calls the *objet petit a,* with the lower case *a* standing for *autre.* As opposed to the Other (*A*), which can never be seen, this little point of otherness is the focal point of desire.

Le regard is the term generally translated as 'the gaze,' and this suggests some typical problems of translating Lacan. The prefix *re* gives *regard* a sense of returning something; this is lost in the Scandinavian word *gaze.* In fact, Lacan's system is often based on the French language. For example, the idiom *cela ne vous regarde pas,* which could be literally translated as 'that does not look at you,' is used to mean 'that does not concern you.' Moreover, *objet* is used without any modifier in Racine to mean "loved one" (*Phèdre* lines 636, 1117). I will try to keep such differences in mind in my effort to apply Lacan's theory of vision to an Irish writer.

The point that is the object of desire in Lacan always stands for an absent phallus. In fact, as I have suggested, the Lacanian phallus is absent by nature, a symbolic organ defined by negation because we first become aware of it through the sense of castration. The hole or lack that is the object of desire stands for the flaw through which the Other seems to show its need for one. Desire, as the desire of the Other, always comes from a source one cannot locate, and the center of any pictorial composition is always the desire of the Other to show itself, behind which is the power of the Other to create one's being (*Four* 115). The phallus, a presence that cannot exist without implying absence, is invisible in its fully realized state. Joyce describes the actualized phallus as invisible when Joe Hynes asks about Bloom, "I wonder did he ever put it out of sight" (338/12.1655): the question implies that if he hasn't put it out of sight, he doesn't have it, risk being essential to manhood.

What can actually be seen is neither the gaze nor the subject, neither the Other nor the self, but the image or screen that mediates between them as they create each other. In Figure 3 Lacan diagrams the eye and the gaze as overlapping cones pointing in opposite directions.

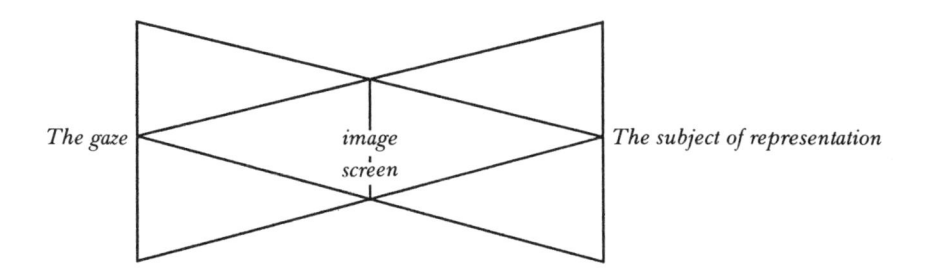

Figure 3: The structure of the gaze, from *The Four Fundamental Concepts* (106).

One cone widens out from the point of vision of the eye to extend to the picture, while the other returns from the point of the gaze to form the field of vision in which the subject sees himself. This field of vision is the plane you see when you open your eye, and the point from which you see is completely lost in it, but your subject is expressed in it. There is a tendency for the two ends to interchange. What you see is the screen, which appears at the point where the intersecting cones—the widening one and the narrowing one—coincide by having equal diameters. This screen, or the surface that is seen, corresponds to Stephen's diaphane or veil of appearances. Derrida points out that to *appear* is both to show and to hide (*Dissemination* 211), and the screen indicates something behind it even while it conceals. We can get an idea of the construction of the gaze as a field of depth by looking at what lies behind the diaphane according to Stephen's view of

Aristotle. Moreover, examination of Stephen's visual constructions will soon suggest Bloom's.

The Adiaphane

On the first page of "Proteus," Stephen conceives of the diaphane, or transparency, as having an adiaphane or darkness behind it. The diaphane can be passed through, but the adiaphane is impenetrable: "Diaphane, adiaphane. If you can put your five fingers through it it is a gate, if not a door" (7–9). When Stephen closes his eyes to escape the veil of appearances, he hopes and fears to pass beyond the field of light into the impassable darkness on the other side of it: "If I open and am forever in the black adiaphane?" (26).

The darkness on the other side of light corresponds to outer space and the void on which the world according to Stephen is founded (207/9.841–42), but also to the darkness within Stephen that he finds when he closes his eyes. This is the creative otherness with which he communicates in *Portrait*, the force that will yield his destiny. In fact, the adiaphane, what is below the surface, stands for potentiality according to Aquinas. His *Commentary* on Aristotle's *De Anima* holds that while light is the activity of transparency, the "potency" of the diaphane is in darkness (273). Stephen, by a meditation that subordinates the specific articulations of language to the protean flow that underlies them, tries to pass through the light of actuality into the darkness of potential behind it. If Stephen aims beyond the veil, at the flux that precedes words, we will see that Bloom aims *at* the veil through his constant pursuit of material objects.

Stephen makes an extensive effort to understand where the thought of distance comes from, recognizing that it involves two stereoscopic points of view. And as he has this recognition of the alterity of his own vision, he divides into two viewpoints, addressing himself in the second person and in the first plural so as to recognize another within: "You find my words dark. Darkness is in our souls do you not think? (48/3.420–21). The universal tendency to address oneself as another person expresses the darkness within that I have linked to potentiality and otherness. Stephen is divided by the thought of depth because he sees it in conjunction with the Other.

As he strives to comprehend the source of depth and thinks of the darkness behind light, he apparently sees a pair of gypsies watching him, and this leads to a series of feelings of being watched. He thinks, "If I were suddenly naked here as I sit?" (47/390), and wonders, "Who watches me here" (48/414). He also refers to himself in the third person (which is rare) and as an object of potential perception: "Me sits there with his augur's rod . . . unbeheld" (48/410–11). In accordance with Lacan's model, his effort to understand and penetrate the visual field is accompanied by a sense of being observed, and this pattern is acted out on a more physical level by Bloom.

In "Calypso," at the butcher's shop, when Bloom's senses are first stirred to excitement, the text describes "his soft subject gaze" (59/4.163). Bloom is impotent because his desire and its vision are constantly connected to a sense of being watched by the authorities who are finally manifested in "Circe." Two of the main representatives of authority in Nighttown are referred to as "the watch" (453/15.674). Bloom's sex life is a parody of the theory of the gaze because as a voyeur he likes to have the women he watches watching him. Gerty Macdowell knows what he is up to in "Nausicaa" (365ff./13.700ff.), and when he unconsciously imagines himself watching through a keyhole in "Circe," Blazes and Molly know that he is there. In fact, one reason he asks about Molly's letter from Boylan in the morning (63/4.310) is that he needs to know that Molly knows that he knows about Blazes.

Bloom's need to be seen watching something he should not see is a need for shame, and shame may be a strong feature of all desire. It corresponds to what Lacan calls the invidious aspect of the gaze.[4] The other end of Bloom's discourse has to include both the mercy of beauty and its severity, and he sees this Other through the *objet a,* the image that attracts. The Other that watches Stephen is repeatedly envisioned as a woman embarrassed by his vices, whether she be his mother or his *anima:* "Our souls, shamewounded by our sins, cling to us yet more, a woman to her lover clinging . . ." (48/3.3.421–23).

Bloom's continual reflections on the senses are filled with equivalents to those of Stephen. For example, in "Lestrygonians," he thinks of experimentally depriving himself of eyesight, as Stephen does when he closes his eyes. But whereas Stephen tries to leave the sensory world behind, Bloom wants to feel what sensory experience would be like for someone else, a blind man: "They say you can't taste wines with your eyes shut . . . ," he thinks, and in another context, "Want to try in the dark to see" (181–82/8.1123, 1142). One of his main experiments with perception occurs in this episode when he tries to see a clock on top of a bank:

> Can't see it. If you imagine it's there you can almost see it. Can't see it.
>
>   .   .   .   .
>
> The tip of his little finger blotted out the sun's disk. Must be the focus where the rays cross. (166/562–67)

Though Bloom's experiment is no more successful than Stephen's, he supposes here that perception and depth are both subjective, influenced by mental operations. He also recognizes an arrangement that dominates his life—that vision is focused on a screen that conceals an unbeholdable reality behind it.

Bloom Enveiled

Bloom's visual field of desire is perpetually driven toward images of material objects, especially voluptuous women. While Stephen wants to pass beyond the veil of natural appearances, Bloom is powerfully attracted toward this very veil. "His brain" typically is "yielded" to a profusion of "sunwarm silk" (168/8.637, 634), and many images that attract him are presented as veils. He does want the veil to move, or to suggest the life principle behind it, or even, in a parody of the ideal, to fit snugly. When it hangs loose or shows no signs (of life), it becomes pure or repressive, an obstacle to contact with the material world, the living veil. But what bothers Bloom most is generally what is behind the veil.

Bloom's need for a curtain is illustrated by the picture of the Nymph that hangs over his and Molly's bed. This picture is itself a sort of veil over Molly: Joyce identifies it with Calypso in the Gorman-Gilbert schema, implying that this ideal image tends to supplant Molly in Bloom's mind. The name *Calypso* in fact derives from the Greek *kalyptra,* 'veil.' Moreover, the Nymph herself testifies in a fantasy of "Circe" that Bloom felt a need to cover her: "And with loving pencil you shaded my eyes, my bosom and my shame" (546/15.3265). As a covering for the vagina, the veil is linked by Derrida to the hymen, which preserves potentiality while denying it (*Dissemination* 212–15).

Yet Bloom's tendency to conceal the source of life can be counteracted by an agent that will shake or dislodge him, in effect confronting him with the Other behind the veil, and in *Ulysses* Stephen serves such a function. Bloom also plays the role of a revealer to Stephen, but the men see each other through two different structures of the gaze (not as two ends of the same structure), and the veil Bloom lifts reverses the orientation of Stephen's. While Stephen in "Proteus" pierces the veil of decaying matter to approach spiritual truth, Bloom, in "Circe" and "Ithaca," lifts the veil of spirit to find a physical reality that is debased.

The characteristic use Bloom makes of his equivalent for Stephen's diaphane appears when he daydreams in "Lotus-Eaters" about meeting a girl with a veil in church (81/5.376). A few pages after this, he visualizes Molly, her dark mystery and her gaze partially covered by a linen veil: " . . . the darkness of her eyes. Looking at me, the sheet up to her eyes, Spanish, smelling herself . . . " (84/5.494–95). Here he enacts the gaze by putting himself into her mind as she is looking at him. When he projects Molly in her most authoritative form in "Circe," she is heavily veiled with a "yashmak" (439/15.300) and he is terribly self-conscious.

In the *Odyssey* Penelope wears a veil when she appears before the suitors (Books 1, 16, and 18). This suggests that Homer's Achaeans followed the rules we associate with the purdah. The metonymy that equates woman with veil or fabric seems to be well distributed. In America women used to be referred to as "skirts," and in *Ulysses* the word *shawl* is used repeatedly to mean 'prostitute' (314/12.803–9). Mahaffey develops the powers women derive from their connection to fabrics, which affords them special insight into and control over the textual textile of life (161–65, 187–91).

The correspondence of Bloom's veils to Stephen's diaphane is made clear through the most immediately effective (and tightest) form of the veil, the semitransparent hose that Bloom is watching on Gerty MacDowell in "Nausicaa," when he gets his strongest physical satisfaction of the day: "O, those transparent!" (381/13.1262). The third love of Bloom's day is Martha Clifford, the secretary with whom he corresponds, and she never appears to him except in the form of "signs on a white field."

For someone as thoroughly enveiled as Bloom, veils can take many forms that are not directly velar. The description of Molly quoted above reflects Bloom's strong interest in smells. In "Nausicaa," the episode in which he is most aroused, he analyzes the sense of smell extensively, seeing it as a tissue of particles projected by women, a point Mahaffey notices (156): "Suppose it's ever so many millions of tiny grains blown across. . . . It's like a fine fine veil or web they have all over the skin, fine like what do you call it gossamer, and they're always spinning it out of them, fine as anything, like rainbow colours without knowing it" (374/13.1017–21).

The first line suggests a veiling function of language that Joyce was well aware of, rhythm: "ever so many millions of tiny" reinforces the sense of profusion through the rapid rippling of $'--'- \; / \; '--'-$. One of the veils that everything described in words has to pass through is the veil of sound. In this passage Bloom sees the veil or web as something women naturally secrete and project "without knowing it." It is a field of tiny signifiers spread floating across the whole "panaroma" (*FW* 143.3) of sensation.

However attractive the veil may be to Bloom in its more dynamic manifestations, its primary function is to cover and obscure. Therefore all obstacles that keep Bloom from seeing what he wants to see are by extension part of a veil of circumstances spread through the world. In "Calypso" Bloom is prevented from following a woman servant by the need to pay for his pork kidneys (59/4.173). And in "Lotus-Eaters" a tram slews between as Bloom is trying to watch the silk stockings of a lady boarding a carriage (74/5.131). The interruptions draw Bloom back from a tighter fabric (skirt or stocking) to a looser one, the network of material accidents in which he is enmeshed. He is absorbed in the looser one because its stirrings can lead to tighter ones. Every part of the system of accidental veils is seen by Bloom as derived from the ultimate authority of his world, Mother Nature.

Bloom venerates the veil itself, linking it to the magic powers of the East. In "Sirens," after thinking how mysterious a yashmak makes a woman (281/11.943), he reflects on the mystery of vocation: "Seems to be what you call yashmak or I mean kismet. Fate." (289/11.1232). The slip is no accident, for every mystery is a veil, and because Bloom sees desire as the primary force (or unified field) of the physical universe, he sees fate as caused by physical appearances.[5] In a fantasy in "Circe," as he is about to be flogged by three society ladies, he explains, "It was your ambrosial beauty. Forget, forgive. Kismet" (468/15.1108). Beauty is fate. Bloom is not conscious of his equation of yashmak and kismet; nor is he capable of using the word "ambrosial" with such facility. All of the ideas in this paragraph are completed for him by Joyce to express him better than he could express himself.

Molly is at her most aggressive when she appears in a yashmak, and in traditional psychosexual terms, veils, like stockings are fetishes: they symbolically conceal the absence of a penis, and so they imply a phallic power. Insofar as the veil covers a gap, fetishism is the basis of all attention to material objects and the signs through which they are known. In the theory of the gaze, the object of focus (*objet a*) always conceals a phallic power, so that woman always possesses such power insofar as she attracts man.[6] The image of Molly that draws Bloom is built into a structure that conceals a power manifested by Blazes Boylan. Molly would not attract Bloom as she does if she did not have the will to seek satisfaction beyond what he can provide.

Because the Other behind the gaze has both maternal and paternal aspects, Bloom not only has Molly on his mind all day, but also the demonic Boylan, who must in effect be perpetually berating his weakness. While Boylan's image might seem to deter Bloom from what he does, in fact this image is part of the mechanism that keeps him on his course. His desire cannot resist the dynamism of evil. In "Hades," he thinks of Blazes, "Fascination. Worst man in Dublin" (92/6.202). He uses the word "fascination" to criticize Molly, but there is another voice speaking in the word that feels that fascination, which is expressed by a breakdown of syntax throughout the paragraph, as typified by the single-word sentence "Fascination." The ideal cannot exist without the threat, Bella without Bello.

Just as the penis represents the phallus for the male, Blazes represents Molly's phallus, her will, that which Stephen calls "woman's invisible weapon" (196/9.461). It is invisible not primarily because of woman's anatomy, but because man shapes the veil of signs surrounding woman to cover over the power behind her gap. In fact, the sequence of observations that leads

Bloom to his thoughts about the fascination of Blazes in "Hades" is one that locates Boylan exactly where he should be in Lacan's scheme: in an invisible center. As Bloom is riding with others in a carriage, thoughts of Boylan suddenly occur to him, starting a new paragraph, and then he turns to distract himself by considering a nearby statue:

> He's coming in the afternoon. Her songs.
> Plasto's. Sir Philip Crampton's memorial fountain bust. Who was he?" (92/6.190–91).

When the others point out that they are passing Boylan, Bloom finds it a coincidence: "Just that moment I was thinking" (92/197). He has no idea that the reason he thought of Blazes was that he saw him subliminally. Boylan has been the center of Bloom's perception, but Bloom has not seen him, and it is common for the objects Bloom focuses on to screen what is really on his mind. Often this is obviously Blazes, but it is also Molly watching him from behind her veil, for the Other includes both parents. Lacan argues that the center of the visual field is a screen over desire, and that external reality is marginal to this screen and can only appear after the screen has been constructed (*Four* 108).

Stephen's equivalent to Molly in *Ulysses* is his mother, and his preoccupation with her involves the dark powers of father and God, to both of whom she has given herself. This mental structure is active in what he sees. In the first episode, he strains to see the beauty of the world, but his vision is dimmed by the thought of his mother's violation: "Sea and headland now grew dim" (9/224). When he tries to see the "great sweet mother" Mulligan speaks of, he soon perceives the "dull green mass of liquid" as a bowl of his mother's vomit (5/1.108). His mother's wound is the unbearable gap at the center of his vision, an anti-image that carries with it the paternal force that removed her vitality from everything. When May Dedalus appears in "Circe," she wears a bridal veil, and one thing it indicates is that she is beyond the veil. It is the death of the primal object of desire, her union with the Father, that causes Stephen's world to be covered with a veil between *Portrait* and *Ulysses*.

Stephen and Bloom at Gaze

Extensive parallels in what Bloom and Stephen see and in how they see it, such as are shown by their experiments and by the images of violated women that condition their perceptions, suggest that they are designed to complement each other. It is hard to deny that the protagonists are created for the purpose of meeting, though it may be said that their meeting is ironic, in which case their purpose is. Insofar as they are created to meet, each is the source of creation for the other. The action of *Ulysses* may be described as a process in which Stephen and Bloom see each other through their reciprocal structures of the gaze. Each of the two represents the Other for his opposite by standing for the rest of life. Indicating that a person encounters a series of figures in his life that represent the Other, Lacan refers to "the first Other he has to deal with, let us say, by way of illustration, the mother" (*Four* 218).

The activity of otherness that the two men exert on each other appears in images of optical reciprocity that extend from their meeting to their parting. Even before they meet, as I have indicated, Bloom may be suggested by the ship that seems to stare at Stephen at the end of "Proteus." Stephen's feeling that something is watching him is a vivid enactment of the gaze. Moreover, the sense of defensive looking back involved in Lacan's *le regard* appears here as Stephen is described in heraldic language as "rere regardent" (51/3.503). The English *regard*, while it is still commonly used for affection, is not common for visual fixation, which is why *gaze* is the best translation of Lacan's term. But our *regard* can still denote gazing in extreme and old-fashioned usages such as Stephen's fixation on the ship and Mulligan's ironic reaction, in antique, occult dialect, to Bloom's visual fixation in "Oxen of the Sun": "Any object, intensely regarded, may be a gate of access to the incorruptible eon of the gods" (416/14.1166–67).

Here is the sentence in which Bloom first sees Stephen in "Hades": "Mr Bloom at gaze saw a lithe young man, clad in mourning, a wide hat" (88/6.39). The primary meaning of "at gaze" seems to be that Bloom is simply staring, but the word *at* suggests that he is being watched. Such non-directed perception seems for Joyce to put one in touch with mental forces outside consciousness that manifest themselves as something looking back. When one is not looking at anything in particular, one can almost see the gaze that represents the Other behind the screen.

In "Oxen," the episode in which Bloom's mental contact with Stephen is established with hardly any conversation between them, Bloom stares for a long time at a bottle of Bass ale. As he does so, a heavenly bride appears whose veil I have already remarked:

> It is she, Martha, thou lost one, Millicent, the young, the dear, the radiant. How serene does she now arise, a queen among the Pleiades, in the penultimate antelucan hour . . . coifed with a veil of what do you call it gossamer. It floats, it flows . . . and loose it streams . . . sustained on currents of the cold interstellar wind, winding, coiling, simply swirling, writhing in the skies a mysterious writing till, after a myriad metamorphosis of symbol, it blazes, Alpha, a ruby and triangled sign upon the forehead of Taurus. (414/14.1101–9)

As the focal point of the gaze, the veiled bride Bloom envisions here is the "lost one," Lacan's *"objet a"* as "something from which the subject, in order to constitute itself, has separated itself off" (*Four* 103). Although it is not stated, the word "serene" suggests to me that the bride is looking at Bloom. She may be related to the vision of the Virgin, probably conventional, that Stephen saw in the sky in *Portrait:* "Her eyes seemed to regard him with mild pity" (*P* 105, 116). The "Oxen" veil also derives from a song-related image of a girl with "veil awave" in "Sirens" (271/11.591), and it is parodied by Stephen's mother in her bridal veil in "Circe."

Bloom is mentally approaching the creative power of woman, and this brings him nearer his creator in this episode in which his relationship with Stephen, which has been gestating throughout the book, is the main thing born. The elaborate vision of the veil suggests the possibility of its penetration by Bloom's contact with Stephen. Through the veil's fluttering, the creation of the universe as an act of "mysterious writing" is suggested on the other side. The field finally resolves into the triangle on the ale bottle, and this is presented as Taurus, which Gifford calls the sign of artistic consciousness.

The passage from which I have been quoting (414/14.1078–1109) is a vision in the style of De Quincey of a herd of ghostly animals "trooping" (1091) across a grey wasteland. It turns out to be Bloom's vision, for we are later told that he is staring at the Bass label into which the vision resolves (416/1181). Yet Bloom does not seem to remember this vision, for the narrator later sums up his reverie by saying, "He was simply . . . recollecting two or three private transactions" (1185–89). Stephen, however, does seem to refer to Bloom's vision of "Twilight phantoms" (1083); soon after it, he speaks to Frank Costello: "You have spoken of the past and its phantoms, Stephen said. Why think of them? If I call them into life across the waters of Lethe will not the poor ghosts troop to my call? Who supposes it? I, Bous Stephanoumenos, bullockbefriending bard . . . " (415/14.1112–15).

Stephen expresses Bloom's vision through the images of the bullock-befriending bard making ghosts troop to his call across the waters of Lethe. And the De Quinceyesque style of that vision often sounds like Stephen: "A region where grey twilight ever descends, never falls on wide sagegreen pasturefields, shedding her dusk, scattering a perennial dew of stars" (1080–82). The two paragraphs of Bloom's reverie not only sound like Stephen, but the sophistication of their conceptions suggests him, particularly the veil of writing in the sky. Yet this goes back to Bloom's thoughts about perfume in "Nausicaa," and there are quite a few Bloomian terms here, such as "metempsychosis" (1100), "Martha, thou lost one, Millicent" (1101), and "simply swirling" (1107). Stephen and Bloom, then, seem to be combined in this vision, the most vivid, detailed description of the veil as such in the book. The usual belief is that however much they may echo each other's thoughts elsewhere, only in "Circe" do Bloom's thoughts and Stephen's actually fuse, but here is a substantial example in "Oxen."[7]

The veil in "Oxen," moreover, directly predicts the scene in "Ithaca" in which Stephen and Bloom look at the stars in Bloom's garden, their last scene together, which is dense with suggestions of probing the veil. As "queen among the Pleiades, in the penultimate antelucan hour," the "Oxen" veil is a network among the stars the two men gaze at in the next-to-last hour before dawn. Gifford certifies that the Pleiades were out at 3:00 A.M. on 17 June 1904 (433–34), but he also points out that the sun rose at 3:33 (587), so the "Oxen" veil is set around 2:00 A.M., at the time of "Ithaca." This prediction, which is so difficult to detect that it is hard to believe Joyce could be ironic about it, tends to enhance the significance of the "Ithaca" scene.

To return to the sharing of thought, Lacan, like Gilbert, emphasizes the use of extrasensory perception in *Ulysses*, pointing out that Joyce believed his daughter Lucia to be psychic (*Ornicar?* 8:17, see *JJ* 677–78). In his Rome Discourse, Lacan says, "That the unconscious is the discourse of the other is what appears even more clearly than anywhere else in the studies which Freud devoted to what he called telepathy.... This is the coincidence of the subject's remarks with facts about which he cannot have information . . . " (*Language* 27).

Extrasensory perception demonstrates the power of the Other by taking the mind out of its ordinary self and out of the factual world that corresponds to that ordinary self. The lines Stephen and Bloom share throughout the novel and the predictions in which they are involved, like the mythological and structural references that pop up in people's minds (hundreds of references to wind and rhetoric in "Aeolus," for example), serve to make it clear that the individuals are parts of a larger mental continuum.

Lacan takes a strong stand on the adhesion of the two main figures. He speaks of a "gravitation between the thoughts of Stephen and Bloom that follows its course during the whole novel" and reaches a culmination in the enunciation of "Blephen" and "Stoom" in "Ithaca" (682/17.549–51). For Lacan, this psychic sharing "shows that it is not only from the same signifier that they are made, but truly of the same substance." In this seminar (13 January 1976), Lacan says that the writing of *Ulysses* forms a knot, and gives a diagram of this knot that closely resembles the symbol for the barred subject, S.[8] He remarks here that Stephen also begins with an S, which may suggest that he begins with the same subject. Lacan also says, "Stephen is Joyce insofar as he deciphers [or penetrates] his own enigma" ("Stephen, *'c'est Joyce en tant qu'il déchiffre sa propre énigme'*—*Ornicar?* 7:14). The ambiguity of the two pronouns (one a feminine modifier) may imply that Stephen's enigma (or subject) is also Joyce's, but then Stephen and Bloom are seen here as parts of the same signifier. For Lacan the subject of *Ulysses* is the barred subject of the artist who unites the two protagonists by containing them in opposition.[9]

To return to our gazework, Stephen and Bloom finally actually gaze at each other in "Eumaeus," where they are described with uncertainty about whether they are one or two, "their two or four eyes conversing" (643/16.1091). And the imagery of the gaze in *Ulysses* climaxes in the description of Stephen and Bloom looking at each other on the last full page they spend together in "Ithaca": "Silent, each contemplating the other in both mirrors of the reciprocal flesh of theirhisnothis fellowfaces" (702/17.1183–84). This occurs immediately after Bloom has "attracted Stephen's gaze" to the "screen" in a window of his house that covers a lamp that denotes Molly. Bloom's "affirmations" (1179) of veil worship through this screen seem to leave both figures needing more. They see everything as vanishing: the stars turn unreal, Molly is not reachable, and their own eye contact is uncertain. The sense of loss makes a gap in the veil through which the gaze appears and fades, and this dispersal is the sign of contact with the true Other behind the other. Ragland-Sullivan says, "Authentic analytic consciousness . . . resides in seeing oneself being seen (*se voir se voir*) in the Other (A). In privileged moments such as these, the gaze functions as the reverse side of consciousness and elides itself" (94). All the disappearing features of the nightscape suggest the gaze that elides, the picture that fades, the author/analyst who withdraws to confront his characters/readers with the unknown.

In their final mutual gaze, Stephen and Bloom (with Molly as third person) are both presented as looking at the same thing, namely "the other," which is rendered abstract because they are "contemplating" it. *Contemplate* comes from the Latin for augury, according to Skeat, so it carries a root suggestion that the two men are using each other for temples. "Each contemplating the other in both mirrors" has each seeing his own face in the other's and the other's in his own. The infinite regress of this is followed by words that give the effect of fusion. There is an undertone of fusion in "fellowfaces" because *fellow*, as Skeat says, is based on *félag*, an Icelandic word for a ritual of partnership in which two people put their property in one pile. More striking is "theirhisnothis," in which the fusing of four words in contradictory unity has the effect of breaking down their individual meanings as the mutual mapping of subjects in the gaze evokes a larger Otherness behind the individuals.

This passage completes a sequence in which the possibility is felt of passing beyond the visual field, as *Ulysses* finally does at the end of "Ithaca." But to pass beyond the veil is to go into the realm of dream, a realm in which, according to Lacan, the gaze shows itself (*Four* 75). Lacan emphasizes here that coherence and self-consciousness are impossible in dream. The dream state of vision cannot be apprehended by the organized mind of waking except in distorted, fragmented, indirect form. After all, the waking mind is constituted by the looping of the veil that conceals the gaze.

As personalities, Stephen and Bloom are stuck in the world of separation, of the split between the eye and the gaze, but they can be augmented by a sense of passing beyond these discrete identities to gain a new complex personality. Such a complex has been building through the book toward its fulfillment in "Ithaca," as Lacan points out, and we can see how this new multiple subject operates by looking at the steps that lead up to and follow the mutual mirroring of the two protagonists.

The Intersaid

The Linati schema lists one of the Technics of "Ithaca" as *"Fusione,"* and this seems to refer not only to technique but to content, for Joyce heads the third part or Nostos of the novel, "III *MEZZANOTTE/* (*Fusione di* Bloom *e* Stephen)." This fusion of Stephen and Bloom seems to be signaled in "Ithaca" by the "infusion" and "diffusion" (676/17.357–58) of the cocoa they share. The cocoa is itself a fusion of spirit (which corresponds to Stephen) and matter (Bloom) because it is both liquid and solid. Tea or coffee could not be used because they are solutions, but cocoa is a suspension, and Joyce mentions its "subsolid residual sediment of a mechanical mixture" (690/17.798). Stephen, in his hatred for matter, has been avoiding food all day; and Bloom, as a "stickler for solid food" (635/16.811), has recently tried to get him to eat. The cocoa, a liquid that will deposit Bloom's solid food in Stephen's body is a fine image of imperceptible feelings Bloom deposits in Stephen in the hope that they will sink in later.

The objective world of Bloomsday is increasingly subordinated in the second half of *Ulysses* to a Joycean world of style as the protagonists move toward their contradictory fusion. The cocoa communion is based on shared alienation, but it constitutes their first cause, the mature artist who creates them, and who will result from Bloom's influence on Stephen. Despite his passivity and lack of comprehension, Bloom is an active function of the artist on this level, and Joyce told Budgen that Bloom's role in "Oxen" was that of a "spermatozoon" (*Making* 216). The increasing intervention of the author through stylistic complexities peculiar and personal to Joyce represents a major psychic reality that proceeds through *Ulysses*—the growth of Joyce's mind.[10] Ragland-Sullivan, in her essay "Lacan's Seminars on Joyce" (62,64), emphasizes that in Lacan's view of Joyce, the increasing difficulty of Joyce's language represents Joyce the subject. The subject, however, is never unified in any conventional sense in Lacan: it is made up of a number of agents that "misrecognize" each other (*R–S* 100). In view of this, Stephen and Bloom are capable of constituting the Joycean subject even though they do not succeed in communicating consciously.

The elaborate techniques late in *Ulysses* indicate that the characters sense extensions beyond their ordinary minds. The individual streams of consciousness (which already involve external participation) rarely appear to be unmediated after "Nausicaa." The narrative comes to be dominated by a series of authorial agencies who represent something larger than the individuals.

In "Ithaca," the narrative is never spoken by a single person. It is a fusion of two opposed speakers through the medium of question and answer, neither of which exists apart from the other. The Catechism, on which "Ithaca" is based, presents a youth or novice asking a priestly adept for spiritual knowledge, and therefore its form embodies the relation between son and father. Just as the cosmic but detailed narrative of "Ithaca" exists only through the difference between question and answer, so Stephen, in "Scylla and Charybdis," argues that the universe is founded on the void that constitutes the connection between father and son (207/9.837–42).

One implication of this fundamental analogy is that all knowledge rests on the relation between what is known (the father) and what is not known (the son). This relationship involves the outward-and-inward movement of the dialectic that links subject to object. Stephen and Bloom act out this relationship vividly in the scene in which they stare at each other, an image that reminds me of two cellular nuclei engaged in meiosis. The epistemological significance of this model of father and son springs from the fact that once knowledge settles into being known, it stops having a living relation to the ungraspable reality of flux and becomes opposed to the activity of knowing. The world is built on what we know, but the reality of that world only comes home to us when it violates our principles and makes us realize that it is more than our fantasies about it. Therefore the reality of knowledge is situated in the gap between the incommensurable categories of what is known to us and what is not known.

It is in this gap that Joyce operates as author. This is also the place Lacan refers to when he says that it is always through a gap in the subject's discourse that the unconscious is revealed (*Four* vii). Lacan finds truth at this point of contradiction, and he says that since Descartes' *Cogito, ergo sum* (and especially in Freud), the only source of certainty has been doubt (*Four* 35). Only through being suspended between possibilities can we feel the components of the subject.

The universe of the example of artistic creation that Stephen examines most fully, *Hamlet*, is surely built on the void between father and son, as manifested through a gap. The play's action begins with the apparition of the ghost of the father, and at the end, when Hamlet achieves revenge and father and son are atoned, the ghost leaves the world and that world comes to an end as the drama is completed. Every action in the play contributes to the mystery of uncertainty that connects son to father. Stephen's vision of Shakespeare playing the ghost in Hamlet is Joyce's main model of the artist as Other and superego. This godlike father spirit operates as a function of his son's personality to shape the action and to give his son access to guilt and glory.

The ghost whom Joyce sees as representing the author first appears to Hamlet as a gap in the world, a spot in the field. It enters as the Prince is talking about how men can be corrupted without being guilty, subverted by "some vicious mole of nature" (1.4.24). The identification of the ghost with this spot that reveals something rotten under the surface is soon confirmed when Hamlet addresses the ghost, who is now behind or underneath the scene: "Well said, old mole. Canst work i'th' earth so fast (1.5.170). Stephen expands on the linkage of mole and ghost: "And as the mole on my right breast is where it was when I was born, though all my body has been woven of new stuff time after time, so through the ghost of the unquiet father the image of the unliving son looks forth" (194/9.378–81). This passage presents the mole as the point of continuity between the artist as superego and the figure he creates. The burden of guilt and ideal that the unquiet parent puts on the unliving child is parallel to the drives that the character is attached to by his author.

Freud says that the relation of the superego to the ego is that of father to son (*SE* 21:164). This reinforces the notion that the active perception of reality depends on the difference between an established view and a new one. Thus, for Freud, one's perception expresses not a single agent, but a simultaneous combination of agents, and the same is true of discourse, which expresses the superego and the ego at once. Lacan expands on this idea in "The subversion of the subject," where he speaks of "the right way to reply to the question, 'Who is speaking?', when it is the subject of the unconscious that is at issue" (*Selection* 299). The speaker is a space between persons, a voice in which the forces of an unconscious dialogue fluctuate. This idea receives indirect confirmation from the findings of experimental psychologists that the two lobes of the brain, which work together in normal consciousness, have completely different personalities.[11] Lacan replaces the unified classical subject with the divided Freudian subject: " . . . the place of the 'inter-said' (*inter-dit*), which is the 'intra-said' (*intra-dit*) of a between-two subjects, is the very place in which the transparency of the classical subject is divided and passes through the effects of 'fading' that specify the Freudian subject by its occultation by an ever purer signifier . . . " (*Selection* 299; *Écrits* 800).

In *Ulysses,* where Stephen is generally seen with Bloom's compassion and Bloom is generally seen with Stephen's irony, what is usually speaking at any point is neither Stephen nor Bloom, but a circulation between the two. This circulation is both inter-said, because it lies between two characters, and intra-said because it expresses parts of one mental construct. But the overall mind of the text is as much interdicted as is (for Lacan) the overall mind of any individual: Stephen and Bloom cannot be balanced or synthesized because the subject must remain divided and barred.

The linguistic multivalence of the text constantly expresses this subject on several levels at once, as I have already argued (*Creator* 50–55), with different voices speaking in each word. The simplest example I can think of is a line about Bloom in "Calypso": "Kidneys were in his mind . . ." (55/4.6). The word *in* (rather than *on*) represents Bloom's absorption in kidneys accurately, and he might make the mistake himself; but the narrator also bespeaks Stephen's irony by making fun of Bloom's materialism through the image of a skull full of kidneys. Later the mind of the text has Bloom define the soul as "grey matter" (633/16.752), which fits not only the brain, but the kidney.

What speaks in this polyphony is the mind of the artist. Whether or not Stephen, Bloom, Molly, and the lesser figures add up to the mind of Joyce is insoluble, but there is ample evidence that they are intended to add up to Joyce the creator, the subject he projects as the mind of the text. This figure, like any Lacanian subject, can only be seen as divided and fading; but it is suggested as a goal when the narrative seems to move forward purposefully, and when it is approached, there is a sense of passing through the veil.

NOTES

1. Though the theory of the gaze is not one of the four fundamental concepts, it does take up one of the four quarters of the book, a section called "Of the Gaze as *Objet Petit a,"* 67–119.

2. My translation (compare *Four* 72), of " . . . *c'est là le point essentiel—la dépendance du visible à l'égard de ce qui nous met sous l'oeil du voyant"* (*Quatre* 69). *Voyant* has some of the prophetic overtones of its English equivalent, *seer.*

3. My translation of *"Jamais tu ne me regardes là où je te vois"* (Quatre 95).

4. Lacan points out that the Latin *invidia,* 'envy,' is derived from *videre,* 'to see' (*Four* 115–16).

5. In "Nausicaa," Bloom thinks that "magnetism" is behind "everything," including planetary orbits, gravity, and time. He then defines magnetism as sexual attraction (374/13.987–96). This is part of his tendency to put Molly in the place of God. See my *Joyce between* 157–58.

6. "The *objet a* is something from which the subject, in order to constitute

itself, has separated itself off as organ. This serves as a symbol of the lack, that is to say, of the phallus, not as such, but in so far as it is lacking" (*Four* 103).

7. The two familiar examples of such fusion in "Circe" are the scene with Shakespeare and the dance scene. In the first, Stephen and Bloom look in a mirror to see Shakespeare's face, which combines both of them and speaks for both (567–68/15.3821–53). In the second, as Stephen is whirling frantically toward the end of his dance, a disjointed paragraph freely mingles his impressions with those of Bloom and others (579/15.4140–50, see *Creator* 152).

Daniel Ferrer has examined the scene with Shakespeare to show that it enacts in detail the structure of the Lacanian gaze, but he also shows that the scene dislocates or breaks through this structure (paper for a panel on "Joyce and the Lacanian Gaze" at the Tenth International James Joyce Symposium in Copenhagen on 20 June 1986).

8. *Ornicar?* 7:14–15. Lacan's diagram differs from the symbol in that the two ends of the *s* in the diagram do not quite reach to the slash line that passes through the middle.

9. While revising this book I read the manuscript of Kimberly Devlin's forthcoming and important *Wandering and Return in Finnegans Wake*. Her first chapter shows that Stephen and Bloom are both contained within the dreamer of the *Wake*. She does not identify the dreamer with Joyce, but she does see him as being obsessed with repeating variations on lines from Joyce's work, a rare condition during the time the *Wake* was written.

10. Restuccia says that verbal play late in *Ulysses* makes the text a pure one without any extratextual referent, but her argument shows that this last phase is personal to Joyce. For his effort to conceal or withdraw the divine authority he started with is seen by her as effort motivated by his sexual desire, which enjoys verbal play and being dominated by textuality (167–76).

11. The different personalities of the lobes are described in Ornstein, *Psychology of Consciousness* 18–39. Experiments demonstrating the ability of the two lobes to act independently of each other are recounted in Jaynes, *Origin of Consciousness* 112–17.

5

Through the Veil

Bellocracy

The two most climactic chapters of *Ulysses* feature images of reaching the other side of the veil. They are rending images in "Circe," while the passage is quiet and thoughtful in "Ithaca." But in all cases the attainment of the other side is severely limited or curtailed by the effect of fading that Lacan prescribes: the veil cannot be penetrated for long or vividly because it is constitutive of perception. If the double structure of two separate but reciprocal gazes that relates Stephen to Bloom is penetrated, the effect should be to bring them together, and there are indications of such convergence.

"Circe" is the episode of rending the veil, and this focus is reflected by its technique on the Linati schema, "vision animated to bursting point" (*'Visione animato fino allo scoppio,'* with no word for point). What is conceived of as bursting here is what contains vision, the structure of vision. Both Stephen and Bloom penetrate veils in this episode, but the elements on the other sides of these veils have opposite natures for the two. Stephen breaks a lampshade to reveal gaslight, which implies spirit, while Bloom, in a fantasy, tears off the veil of the Nymph to reveal dark physical putrefaction beneath it.

The sensual colored veil Stephen smashes stands for the physical world he wants to destroy (time and space), while the nun's veil Bloom removes from the Nymph is antimaterial (553/15.3465–69). Because these veils work in opposite directions, one effect of their being removed is to suggest the movement of the protagonists closer together, the unveiling of each to the other. "Circe" was preceded by "Oxen of the Sun," in which the two men conversed for the first time and Bloom began to be attached to Stephen. In "Oxen," Stephen meditated on the "adiaphane" (394/14.385), the "tenebrosity of the interior" (393/380) or the darkness on the other side of the veil, while Bloom had his vision of the veil swirling in space. Both figures were subjected in that scene to preliminary tremblings of the veil.

To understand the meaning of Bloom's removal of the veil in "Circe," it must be seen as the result of a long process of perception in which Bloom sees Bella Cohen. It might seem easy enough, but it takes Bloom 736 lines from the time Bella enters the room to the time Bloom actually sees her, even though he is looking at her all this time: he has to see Bello and the Nymph first. That Bloom does not see Bella before this process is indicated by the way he only addresses fetishes and part-objects at the start of the masochistic fantasy that involves him. He converses with her fan and her boot, and with Bello, but he does not see herself, nor does she speak to him as Bella until twenty pages later when *"The figure of Bella Cohen stands before him"* (554/15.3479). To see why this should be so, I must consider the image of Bella/Bello in relation to Joyce's view of society.

As its name suggests, Bella/Bello embodies the link between beauty and aggression. As the authority that controls Zoe and her clients, it stands for the invisible phallus behind the attraction of appearance; and as the power on the other side of the veil, Bella/Bello represents the forces of society that crush the ego. It is the aggressive organizer or administrator, the type who runs the world. In his notesheets for "Circe," Joyce wrote, "flatty (BC)," showing that he thought of Bella/Bello in Irish slang as a policeman.[1] It smokes a cigar, reads business news, has a son at Oxford, and has friends who are officers and gentlemen. Bella/Bello represents the capitalist Establishment in an episode built on the metaphor of modern civilization as a whorehouse.

It first draws Bloom's attention to its fan, a fluttering screen (open, Bella) which is also a phallus (closed, Bello). The whole interval is established as partly Bloom's projection as soon as the fan speaks, yet the details of this fan-tizzy are suggested by Bella, and the words of her fan express its gestures as Bloom's perception loops through them. The fan refers to the social institutions that contain Bloom when it asks if he is married and subject to "petticoat government" (527/15.2759). It exerts the power of the gaze by telling Bloom that it can see what he is, a line parallel to Father Dolan's "See it in your eye" (561/15.3671). It also assumes authority by a gesture that tells Bloom that they already know each other: *"(folding together, rests against her left eardrop)* Have you forgotten me?"* (527/15.2764). This effort to insert content in Bloom's mind obliterates his rational distinction, and he answers, "Nes. Yo" (only in Gabler 2766). He loses the distinguishing power that separates the external world as the fan draws him into the world of desire.

Though Bloom's fantasies are not conscious, they act out undertones in the relation between himself and Bella/Bello. Joyce brings out the reverberations of these two figures beyond what either could express. The rest of Bloom's day does not suggest that he could make conscious such a hardcore extravaganza, nor could his unconscious be expressed in such polished form. When he passes beyond the veil of reality, the Other is speaking, and its linguistic riches allow Bello to speak more articulately than either party could: "You will be laced with cruel force into vicelike corsets of soft dove coutille with whalebone busk to the diamondtrimmed pelvis . . . (535/2974–77).

The sadomasochism in which Bella/Bello engages Bloom centers on the invasion of the passive mind by an active one that insists that the victim desires his own negation. When Bloom reaches the nadir of negation, being dead and forgotten (544/3230), the Nymph appears. She represents the spirituality that is supposed to follow his sacrifice, but he sees through the falseness of the "ethereal" and snatches her veil, revealing the stench within (553/3470). Only after Bloom removes the veil does he finally see Bella, and now she speaks as herself: "You'll know me next time" (554/3481). This quote from Sacher-Masoch's *Venus in Furs* (identified by Gifford) may be a veiled threat, but Bloom does not respond to it. The primary meaning of "You'll know me next time" is that Bloom has been staring at her all along, without really seeing her, while twenty pages of fantasies passed through some level of his mind.

In rejecting the Nymph, Bloom is overcoming the superego by realizing that the sublime (Bella) is connected to the oppressive (Bello). As the only source of the feeling of freedom, the superego is overcome by invoking a stronger superego; and Bloom is not subject to Bella/Bello's temptation because he cannot appear shameful before the refined young man he is following. Bella/Bello and its attractions are finally obstacles to be passed through to help Stephen. Moreover, because Stephen's "class" appeals to Bloom, the social Other represented by Bella/Bello (an inhabitant of Stephen's world) is a function of Stephen.

One of the major modes of communication in Joyce, possibly the main one, is what people think in the presence (or absence) of each other, rather than what they actually say. Joyce is highly attuned to nuances of influence that pass between people not only without their speaking, but even without their being aware of it. When Stephen and Bloom go through their climactic veil breakings, both are being iconoclastic. This is an unusual attitude for Bloom, and when he rejects traditional values by defying the Nymph, he is probably under the influence of Stephen's rebelliousness, which has led him into the risks of the demimonde. When Bloom asserts himself with Bella, he seems more cutting than he has ever been. His thoughts (though not spoken) may be inspired by Stephen's Gallic sharpness: "Passée. Mutton dressed as lamb. Long in the tooth and superfluous hair. . . . Your eyes are as vapid as the glasseyes of your stuffed fox" (3483–86). Stephen may cooperate with the Other here in inspiring Bloom beyond his usual limits. Would Bloom use "vapid" or "glasseyes"?

Stephen is likewise partly reacting to Bloom when he smashes the chandelier: one reason for his frenzy of defiance is that he sees Bloom as a figure of destiny who threatens to end his youth. Late in "Eumaeus," Stephen sings Sweelinck's variations on *"Youth here has End"* (663/16.1810, Joyce's italics). When Stephen first notices that Bloom has followed him to Nighttown, he says, "A time, times and half a time" (506/2144). This quote from Revelations (12:14, cited in Gifford) suggests that he links Bloom, who talked to him in "Oxen" (a time) and passed him in "Scylla" (half a time), to the end of his world. As Bloom proceeds to give help and advice, Stephen has misgivings about history moving "to one great goal" (563/3718). The kindness of the older man disturbs the younger because it threatens to tie him to human obligation and to cut off his freedom. So the more aware of Bloom's concern Stephen grows, the more frantic he becomes in his revelry:

> BLOOM
> (approaching Stephen) Look. . . . [Joyce's ellipsis]
> STEPHEN
> No, I flew. My foes beneath me. And ever shall be. World without end. (he cries) *Pater!* Free! (571–72/3932–36)

Though other factors intervene, much of this defiance remains present when Stephen strikes the lamp. The two men are under each other's influence when they rend their veils, just as they frequently have psychic contact in "Circe."

I have said that the opposing orientations of the screens breached by Bloom and Stephen imply reciprocity and coming together. Moreover, the objects from which the two men remove screens are transcendent images of what their unveilers worship. This is clearer in Bloom's case: the putrescence that escapes when he takes the Nymph's veil corresponds to the cloacal matter that he is continually devoted to: "I have paid homage on that living altar where the back changes name" (551/15.3405). The decay of excrement makes it an energetic model (only partly parody) of the flux of creative matter that regenerated Stephen in *Portrait* and "Proteus." It is the formless and shifting substance in the bowels of the earth that fertilizes life. Though Bloom is shocked by the Nymph's interior, he completes his vision and gains reality by making contact with the earth.

The Gasjet

In the case of Stephen, we may say that the gasjet represents the sacred because light is traditionally associated with God, and this is true enough, but the situation is more complex. Neither Stephen nor Bloom removes the veil intentionally, and Stephen's intention is to destroy the gaslight, although of course it is significant that he does not. To understand the transcendent significance of the gas, we must trace a specific set of associations that center on one of Joyce's creators. George Russell (AE) asked Joyce to write a series of stories and published three of them under the pen name Stephen Daedalus in the *Irish Homestead* from August to December of 1904, thus becoming the first publisher of Joyce's fiction (*JJ* 163).

The gasjet is a motif in *Portrait,* where Stephen first becomes aware of its "little song" in the background at Clongowes (*P* 12, 14). He finds gasjets again when he goes to seek prostitutes (*P* 100) and a confessor (*P* 141). They seem to be linked to murmuring and to the sacred. In Nighttown, "The yellow gasflames arose before his troubled vision against the vapoury sky, burning as if before an altar" (*P* 100).

The flame of a lamp symbolizes spirit in *Exiles.* In the first act of the play, Richard Rowan tells Robert Hand that he will meet him "at Philippi." This refers to *Julius Caesar,* in which the entrance of Caesar's ghost is indicated by the flickering of Brutus' lamp (4.3.275). In the second act, Richard remains present in spirit after he leaves, and his presence is indicated by three references to a flickering spirit lamp.[2] The gasjet in the musicroom in "Circe" also flickers:

KITTY
(*peers at the gasjet*) What ails it tonight?

LYNCH
(*deeply*) Enter a ghost and hobgoblins. (503/2065–68)

At this point Bloom has just entered with Zoe, but the others do not seem to notice them until two pages later. Bloom is a "ghost by absence" (189/9.174), like Stephen's cuckolded Shakespeare because he has been displaced from his home, but in the brothel also he is absent while present. Thus the lamp is linked to Bloom, and as I suggested Stephen is striking out against Bloom as a benevolent father figure (together with others less benevolent) when he tries to smash it.

A few pages later, after Stephen sees Bloom and refuses to greet him, the piety of a religious gramophone record leads Stephen to think of the Quaker Thomas Lyster, who says, "Seek thou the light" (2246). Lyster is followed by the other participants in the Shakespeare dialogue of "Scylla and Charybdis," climaxing with Russell, who appears as Mananaan Maclir, the Celtic seagod of transformation:

MANANAUN MACLIR
(*with a voice of waves*) Aum! Hek! Wal! Ak! Lub! Mor! Ma! White yoghin of the gods. . . . (with a voice of whistling seawind). . . .

(510/2267–70)

After nine lines of occult mumbo jumbo by Russell, a stage direction says that the light is strangled and *"the gasjet wails whistling"* (2278). As Blamires indicates, Russell turns into the gas, so that his chanting must have been based on the sound of the gas in the background all along (*Bloomsday* 170).

Gifford shows that the nonsense syllables above are quoted from *The Candle of Vision*. In a series of chapters on "The Language of the Gods," AE presents certain letters of the alphabet, phonemes, and syllables as essentially equivalent to the basic elements that constitute the world: "The roots of human speech are the sound correspondences of powers which in their combination and interaction make up the universe." The system is a little like Rimbaud's *"Voyelles,"* or Joyce's schema. For example, *R* represents motion and corresponds to the color red and the form symbol of the line (*Candle* 121). I might add that AE often seems more hypothetical than dogmatic in positing these correspondences. Stephen, however, presents Russell as a god dictating "with a voice of waves" the forms of the world as linguistic signs.

The Candle of Vision describes Mananaan as "one in essence" with his father Lir, the primal creator of everything (156), and says that Lir speaks with many voices at once (153). Both gods are covered with a veil identified with Dana, the mother of the gods (156), who is mentioned by Stephen in "Scylla and Charybdis" (194/9.376). Mananaan is the divine imagination, and his mantle is associated with sound as a creative power (156). In this image, Russell appears as God creating the universe by uttering sounds, a role that matches both the Other and the author.

The linking of AE to Mananaan may have been based on a misunderstanding. Oliver Gogarty (Mulligan), as Gifford reports, believed that AE appeared as Mananaan when his play *Dierdre* was first produced in 1902. In fact, the printed play has no part for Mananaan, and AE apparently played Cathvah, a druid whose voice is heard offstage at the end calling down a vision of the sea to rise and doom the lovers: "Let thy waves flow over them,/ Mananaun:/ Lord of Ocean!" (*Imaginations* 251). Stephen also seems under the impression that Russell played Mananaan, for he identifies Russell with the god here in "Circe" and in "Scylla and Charybdis," when Russell rejects Stephen's theories and Stephen thinks, *"Flow over them with your waves and with your waters, Mananaan . . . "* (189/9.190). For Stephen, AE is a writer who appears as a divinity in his work, a prefiguration of Joyce and a parallel to Stephen's Shakespeare, who can still be heard in his plays as "the sea's voice" (*U* 197/9.479).

The sound of the gasjet, which evokes the nonsense syllables of AE's primal elements, is like the undifferentiated breath that Stephen felt as cosmic in "Proteus" (48/3.403). Stephen's attack on the jet is parallel to his desire to smash God in "Wandering Rocks," even if it meant smashing himself: "Throb always without you and the throb always within.... I between them.... Shatter them, one and both" (242/10.822–25). At the same time that he seeks for his creator, he resents the authority that any author could have over him. But his attempt to demolish his destiny in "Circe" fails to destroy the gasjet and gives Bloom influence in Stephen's affairs. By restoring the lamp (584/15.4284), Bloom takes the side of Stephen's fate, and Stephen's attempt to resist Bloom by wild behavior ends up putting him in Bloom's hands when he gets himself knocked down. Stephen is correct in his intuition that the "commercial traveller" (505/15.2118) is a destiny that cannot be avoided.

While rebellion and patricide are prominent in Stephen's smashing of the lamp, there is also an underlying constructive motive. This is made clearest when he first appears in "Circe," reciting the joyful Antiphon for Paschal time:

> STEPHEN
>
> *(Triumphaliter) Salvi facti sunt.*
>   *(He flourishes his ashplant, shivering the lamp image, shattering light over the world . . .)* (432/15.97–100)

The liturgy he recites triumphantly announces, "They are made whole [or saved]," and he breaks the lamp to release the light it contains. That Stephen is described as mentally breaking a lamp here, 120 pages before he does so on impulse, is strangely prophetic. While Bella's lamp may have annoyed him on an earlier occasion, he rather seems to be breaking a lamp he has not yet seen. This portentous flaunting of the divine perspective underlines the importance of the gasjet scene.

Stephen's constructive aim in "shattering light over the world" is confirmed as he goes on to speak of gesture as "a universal language" that will render "visible . . . the first entelechy" (105–7). This aim follows from his effort to penetrate the forms of language in "Proteus." The idea of saving the world by demolishing the false construction over the source of vision must be at the back of his mind when he finally hits the shade. But the results are disappointing: nothing seems to be saved and the light disappears. What purpose or penetration can be achieved in this dead end?

The most obvious answer is the purpose of skepticism, and this is important, but it is not the whole story. Stephen reveals at the gasjet that the divine framework with which he surrounds even ordinary objects (through such images as Mananaan and light) is built on emptiness. In doing so, he contacts the materiality of Bloom, who has no spiritual inclination, and who gains power over Stephen at that point. Similarly, when Bloom snatches his veil, he sees through his erotic idealism under the influence of Stephen's irony as he effectively enters Stephen's world.

These revelations are not to be seen as solutions. Stephen will remain addicted to metaphysics, and Bloom, to masochism: for them to lose their desires would be terminal. In fact, it seems that they can hardly bear to look at what they unveil. Nevertheless, while each man may find disillusionment, the force that brings them together may have a constructive aim. For each figure, the new insight is part of a rhythmic process that involves possibilities of access to the other side of the veil.

Behind the Veil: A King and No King

The unveiling of the two protagonists to each other is subject to Lacan's restrictions on the gap through which the unconscious is perceived. Lacan says that what appears through the split begins vanishing the moment we see it (*Four* 31), so the Nymph rushes away and the gaslight goes out. The Other behind the field of appearances can be seen only as disorientation, and the unveiling scenes have the value of disassembling the protagonists' frames of reference, preparing them for reconstitution. The access of skepticism that comes on piercing the veil clears the mind to form a new dream. Stephen and Bloom give up their prior assumption to relate to each other. While unveiling can never leave the realm of signs for more than a fleeting moment, the interaction between levels of signs can produce effects that reach beyond consciousness—all of the effects of depth, which surround the meeting of Bloom and Stephen.

An important feature of the veil is its dynamism, which overlaps with multiplicity. What is revealed is bound to be reveiled, but in a new situation. The devel-opment (unveiling) of knowledge is always involved in interaction with the unknown, and the other side often becomes visible. The Nymph, by fleeing, removes her own veil as Bloom clutches it (553/15.3469), making his role far more passive than Stephen's. She illustrates the movement into The unknown that always accompanies the lifting of the veil.

This receding is also represented through sequences or layers of veils, and I have touched on Bloom's tendency to see life as a progress from outskirts to inskirts. In the gasjet scene, a series of some five veils is set up for Stephen, with the implication that it could go on forever, an arrangement that suggests the continuing withdrawal of the source. Stephen's mother is doubly veiled, for her death constitutes its own layer beyond the bridal veil that suggests it. Behind her is the figure of God whom Stephen sees in the lampshade; and behind the lampshade is a mantle, which Zoe adjusts after Mananaan's appearance (510/2281). A mantle is a lacelike hood that is heated to incandescence to provide light around a flame. This one may refer to Mananaan's "mantle" of creative sound. Finally, because of the dramatic technique of "Circe," the gasjet demonstrates that it only exists in language by speaking, like Mananaan, in nonsense syllables, such as "Pooah!" (510/2280) and "Pwfungg!" (583/4247). Language is the ultimate veil, the filter through which everything must be apprehended.

Derrida says that writing is a veil that obscures its subject, not only because it is an imitation that substitutes for what is written about, but because writing constantly refers to a shifting series of linguistic and cultural texts, "A 'floating,' among the texts: the aerial suspension of the veil, the gauze, or even of gas . . . " (*Dissemination* 238). This veil cannot be removed from the written world, and it renders what is written "between here and there, and *hence* between this text and another" (239). The interposition of this curtain makes it impossible to define clearly what is written or how the author is expressed. The words and the meanings behind them keep displacing each other, swirling and folding back on each other along the veil of signs. The author, for Derrida, is only one of the texts that oscillate within his text.

The author Derrida eliminates is the author as a clear statement,[3] but Joyce did not want to appear as a single voice in his work, but as a multiplicity—not as a clear statement, but as a mystery. The obscuring effects of language increase the power of Joyce's authorial presence in his work, a power that depends on uncertainty. Given the reputation for concealed meaning that Joyce built, the more unclear he is, the more the reader tends to be overwhelmed by his mastery.

The multiplication of veiling obscurities is a strong means for creating the effect of divine authority. Kafka's parable "Before the Law" seems at first (when read apart from *The Trial*) to be about a mere legal problem. The theological aspect of the story arises through the endless sequence of gates that is said to conceal the law, and through its ineffability. Each veil in a series implies something beyond it, and the succession of layers evokes an infinite regress pointing to what is beyond conception. If Joyce's characters encounter what cannot be predicted or decided, Joyce must be operating out of the inconceivable realm of the Other in ways that are both transcendent and personal.

McGee sums up the argument against looking beyond the veil: "Lacanian and deconstructive models of reading discover the unconscious in the veil itself, the letter, . . . where outer form is the effect of inner texture and structural rhythm" (11). What he says of the unconscious applies also to the author, and there is value in insisting that these entities can only be effects of the texts. But McGee's sentence already involves something beyond the text by referring to a relationship between outer and inner. If the subject can only be seen as a play between texts, then all that Joyce could know of himself may be fully present on his pages, and his presence is stronger because it multiplies itself.

The projected personality of the author in *Ulysses* has to be granted more vitality than McGee gives it. His analysis of Stephen's Shakespeare discussion in "Scylla and Charybdis" emphasizes that the idea of the author is surrounded by irony, uncertainty, and images of role-playing. This leads McGee to conclude that *Ulysses* is a satire on the idea of the author's authority (38–58). Certainly there is satire, as in the figure of AE as Mananaan, but such a negative view is inadequate. While the author is inaccessible from within his work, his obscurity adds to his authority, and the figure of Shakespeare that Stephen creates has emotional intensity, as does Joyce's projection of himself. This figure is not explicable as a satire of authorship:

> It is the ghost, the king, a king and no king, and the player is Shakespeare who has studied *Hamlet* all the years of his life which were not vanity in order to play the part of the spectre. He speaks the words to Burbage, the young player who stands before him beyond the rack of cerecloth, calling him by a name:
>
> *Hamlet, I am thy father's spirit* (188/9.165–70)

The validity of the role is indicated by the claim that all of Shakespeare's life was a preparation for it. And what Shakespeare says here is given added power by the fact that Bloom thought the same line, *"Hamlet, I am thy father's spirit"* (152/8.67), in the previous episode. Two people might think of the same line from *Hamlet* around the same time, but both Stephen and Bloom misquote the line (1.5.9) by adding the word "Hamlet." This violation of probability demonstrates that the two protagonists make contact with each other through Joyce.

Though Gifford gives a different reading of "the rack of cerecloth," it seems in context to mean a stretch of funeral veil such as is sometimes put before the face of the ghost in productions of *Hamlet*. Joyce conceives of the veil as having a ghostly author behind it. If Shakespeare is divided, "a king and no king," this adds to his completeness as a Lacanian subject.

Joyce's works could not have been written by a combination of linguistic codes and reader responses. However influential these factors may be, it is useful to see the author's mind as a central construction organizing the material. Mahaffey, in *Reauthorizing Joyce,* recognizes that the authority of the word in *Ulysses* is double: " . . . it is both abstract and material, transcendent and immanent, authorized from without by an individual author and from within by the multiple crisscrossing of the sights and sounds of words as they weave and unweave the material network of language" (19). Mahaffey sees the narrative as moving in a rhythm that revolves between author and text.

When the text coheres to form a surface that hides what may be behind it, then the author disappears. At such moments the characters and the readers know what they are thinking, and they and their perceptual fields are clearly defined. But when gaps or splits appear in the coherence of the text, making one sense a level beyond the surface, then some aspect of Joyce is implicated in every variety of the incomprehensibility that is so characteristic of him. As the source of the unconscious, Joyce's activity is felt in the stage before perception, felt as a pre-sense. This stage expresses Joyce's intimate feelings as disorientation and a sense of loss, the sliding of the signifier unhooked.

The minds of the characters continually penetrate the veil of language/ appearance to see new possibilities, and then slip back to consolidate another veil until the next breakthrough. The process of their experience revolves in a *fort/da* movement that loops into and out of contact with the author. The pattern we saw in the chapters of *Portrait* is a model of the rhythm of Joycean thought in general, from the smallest insight to the major stages of life. No part of this pattern is an end, a correct position, or a stable identity, for each phase of the loop leads to the next. But the moment of reaching through the veil is a non-position in which disintegration and incomprehension are felt as the truth of the Other.

Outher Space

In "Ithaca" Bloom and Stephen confront an enormous incomprehensibility in their last scene together as they look at the stars. Because they are hard to see, distant views are like phenomena experienced in semi-conscious states, on the margin of perception that precedes rational articulation. The protagonists of *Ulysses* tend to find messages in the sky from what can only be called a higher being; and Joyce sends such messages, from the cloud over the sun in "Telemachus" (9/1.248) to the shooting star in "Ithaca" (703/17.1211).[4]

For Bloom in "Ithaca," as Joyce supplements his thought, the stars in their remoteness represent the inability of the mind to know its own truth, the barred subject that Lacan sees as the starting point of consciousness: "That it was not a heaventree ... not a heavenman. That it was a Utopia, there being no known method from the known to the unknown ... a mobility of illusory forms immobilised in space, remobilised in air: a past which possibly had ceased to exist as a present before its probable spectators had entered actual present experience" (701/17.1139–1145).

He concludes that the heavens are a utopia ('not place'), an illusion absolutely unknowable, yet he recognizes that they inspire motivation (701/17.1147). If the stars express "a past which possibly had ceased to exist" before its present spectators entered existence, they are something in whose light the gazers may live after the source itself is gone. The pattern corresponds to those of the superego, the Other, and Joyce himself. Joyce's mind continues to operate in his work, constantly coming up with new images and ideas as critics find them. We are doomed to apprehend the barred subject of Joyce as "a mobility of illusory forms"—but then the words that constitute the subject in Lacan present an inscrutable constellation something like the stars.

As the two men see beyond vision into this great distance, the emptiness and detachment from context that they feel makes them aware of their dependence on what is beyond knowledge. They sense what Lacan calls "the central defect around which the dialectic of the advent of the subject to his own being in the relation to the Other turns—by the fact that the subject depends on the signifier and that the signifier is first of all in the field of the Other" (*Four* 204–5). By recognizing that one is a word whose meaning lies beyond comprehension, one gains access to the formation of the subject in the Other.

Because the stars are images of what has vanished, they are suitable emblems of the Other that the two men feel in each other. Lacan speaks of "the Other as previous site of the pure subject of the signifier" (*Selection* 305). This means that when we try to look at the subject, it has vanished, but we can see where it used to be by looking at otherness, what is unknown and unexpected. When we perceive something incomprehensible, our subjectivity is reflected, but when we try to define that subjectivity, we lose it. The tendency of the author to appear as something that is gone also corresponds to Joyce's withdrawal, the way he creates an impression of virtually infinite knowledge, but cannot be pinned down in any particular position when details are examined.

Bloom and Stephen seem to be seeing further here than they have in a long time. One reason they seem to pierce the veil is that vision passes through the sky into space at night. Such penetration, however, is bracketed as limited and illusory: the Milky Way is referred to here as "lattiginous" (698/17.1043), or latticelike, making it another veil, though a more distant and extensive one. Moreover, Bloom seems to retreat from penetration after looking at the stars when he affirms to Stephen the value of the "screen" that represents Molly (702/17.1179). That his breakthrough is illusory and is not sustained consciously, however, need not keep it from being effective. It may prepare for the more palpable experience in this pattern that he will soon have.

Bloom's ultimate unveiling seems to be the most satisfying in the book, but even it is susceptible to deconstruction. At the end of "Ithaca," Bloom reaches the teleological goal of his day when he uncovers Molly's behind and kisses it. Joyce limits this subclimax by emphasizing that Bloom's "osculation" is "obscure" and that his "revelation" is soon followed by a "velation" (734–35/17.2239–45). Like Stephen on the beach, he is kissing emptiness and death as well as inspiration. The sense he feels the most is the least definable one, smell; and his strongest pleasure seems to be "antesatisfaction" (734/2237), an anticipation whose priority defines the object as partly a product of his mind.

As if this were not bad enough for poor Bloom, the analogy between the veil and skin indicates that in Derridean terms, Molly's mesial groove may be seen as a fold in the veil. Derrida says that folds increase the obscurity of the veil by adding layers, shifting the surface, and confusing inside and outside (*Dissemination* 229, 251), so that Bloom's dip into this fold leaves him further than ever from getting through.

Speaking for Bloom, I reply that whatever degree or sense of revelation gives him satisfaction has the effect of creating its own attainment. The obscurity and shifting confusion of his objects, their indefiniteness and movement, constitutes the Other as a dynamic of withdrawal that draws him into expansion. Molly's infidelity, for example, adds to her attraction by making her more uncertain. Realizing that woman is not an essence to be grasped, but a process, Bloom enjoys playing with the veils of Martha and Gerty. To see the veils that they project as letters and stockings, he must imagine some penetration, but because he knows that such penetration is illusory, he can derive satisfaction even from women he almost sees and then loses. Sensing that the key feature of woman is unattainability, he can be gratified by the fading itself: "The sting of disregard glowed to weak pleasure within his breast" (59–60/4.176–77).

While one cannot pass through to clear possession of the other side, one can feel a richness suggested by the stirring the veil sustains. This satisfaction in movement and obscurity is the pleasure Bloom gets from the earth. He does not penetrate on the rational level, but his penetration below the level of reason, while it cannot be articulated clearly, serves and feeds his rational mind. Moreover, the multiplying complexities that obscure what is behind the veil—causing it to double itself, to be neither one thing nor another, and to evade representation—are complications that elaborate the Other behind what can be seen, causing it to have the full richness of the human subject.

While based on illusion, Bloom's pleasure has a basis in the operation of language, that field of illusion. Derek Attridge demonstrates that we can never see through the text because the effect of language corresponding to reality depends on conventions of meaning (*Peculiar Language* 154–55). But if the veil is made up of conventions, then language that breaks convention splits the veil; and while the analingus passage is not one of the most extreme in the book, it distorts its share of syntax and usage, and uses the portmanteau word, which Attridge sees as one of Joyce's most radical devices (195–204): "He kissed the plump mellow yellow smellow melons of her rump, on each plump melonous hemisphere, in their mellow yellow furrow, with obscure prolonged provocative melonsmellonous osculation" (734–35/2241–43). Portmanteaux like "smellow" and "melonsmellonous" violate the givens of diction, as well as the relatively straightforward prose of "Ithaca." They also show the syncopation of a sentence whose loose movement is both hastened and derailed by a dozen strong modifiers.

These breaches of order and wrenchings of frame express the excitement that confuses Bloom's linguistic and ontological boundaries. While the rippling of the veil cannot lead through, it focuses on the field in formation and the sense of what precedes the veil, so it involves the Other. Something on the other side of Bloom's field of language is speaking with Bloom's feeling, for he could never formulate "melonsmellonous." The word combiner on the other side sounds exactly like Joyce, who is heard whenever the veil is probed into motion. Joyce is less active in the conventional, clear, fixed veil than he is in its stirrings, which follow writing techniques that were virtually exclusive to him. Later these techniques were appropriated by modernists and postmodernists, but of course no one has succeeded in sounding fully like Joyce.

The loosening of wordframes in this meloneous funk leads Bloom to a surge of semiotic abundance as well as to further disintegration of language as "Ithaca" concludes. His mind drifts toward the source of formulation, which appears as a feminine function of verbal shifting in the following episode.

NOTES

1. *Ulysses Notesheets* 350. Future references to pages of this text will be preceded by *N.*

2. See my interpretation of *Exiles* in *Joyce between* 108.

3. Derrida's discounting of the author in his early works seems to be strongly counteracted in *The Post Card,* which includes a book-length analysis of *Beyond the Pleasure Principle* called "To Speculate—On 'Freud' " (259–409). Here Derrida builds an elaborate speculation on the most intimate details of Freud's personal life to explain what is really going on in Freud's text. If the only author Derrida eliminates is the unified consciousness in rational control, then I as a psychoanalytic critic have never imagined such an author.

4. Further examples of Joyce's appearance in the sky, and in all aspects of the landscape are presented in my "The Other" 201–6.

6

The Countersign

The Mother of Language

The second half of "Ithaca" leads to "Penelope" because Bloom's acceptance of Molly's adultery moves toward the mental world of the last episode—a world of endless shift in which each individual is "neither first nor last nor only" in an infinite series (731/17.2130). Joyce shows Molly as entrapped in the shifting linguistic construction that is womanhood, which severely limits her awareness of the male-dominated world of power and reason. Nevertheless, she enacts functions of the strength and freedom of women that Joyce supported.[1] First, she shares phallic authority with Leopold, particularly in that she takes the initiative to get satisfaction. And second, she exerts what Joyce saw as an enormous, pervasive power of woman, her ability to create the world through language.

Understanding of why the feminine function should be needed to create words is provided by the ideas of D. W. Winnicott, who studied mothering. Winnicott observes that a mother projects an anxiety-free space in which the child can feel free to expand herself by forgetting the boundary of conflict between herself and the outside world. Winnicott adds that when people are playful or creative, they imagine the protective field of the mother within which the mind can alter the forms of established "realistic" thinking. For Winnicott, such realistic thought, with its clear definitions, is a rigid defensive pose that blocks the mind from seeing anything new or using imagination (*Playing* 118–21).

The traditional role of man has been to deal with hard reality, and his mind could easily grow as armored with rigid thinking as his body, with muscle. One traditional function of woman has been to provide man with an area of sensitivity within which he could open up his mind to alternative views. The major term for this maternal environment in which one thinks creatively is the muse, Kenner's term for the narrator of the last three episodes of *Ulysses* (*Voices* 95–99).

In her essay "Place Names," Kristeva cites further research to extend Winnicott's analysis of the role of the mother in creating language. She shows how through visual and aural images, the mother creates a space of being for the early infant coming into the world. Kristeva associates this undifferentiated space with a term from Plato's *Timaeus* (chapters 16–20) for the formless feminine receptacle of all forms, the *chora,* and she emphasizes that this feminine creative principle precedes the phallus. The baby signals its adjustment to this space with laughter, which appears at the time of the first vocalizations (*Desire* 283–84).

Later, laughter turns to words, and place names are frequent among the earliest words; therefore language is initially attached to a shifting locus derived from the mother (287–88). One implication here is that the foundation or substratum (or solvent) of language is laughter, which is described by Lacan and Derrida as the most essential element of Joyce's writing. Moreover, human awareness of the fields both of perception (the place) and of language is seen here as built on maternal projection. That the field cannot exist without projecting a mother is an indication of how the genders as linguistic systems are dependent on each other, just as masculine and feminine cannot exist except in contrast to each other. Bloom derives his field of perception from Molly, and what he needs from her seems to be not stability, but a dynamism that recalls the formlessness of the *chora* by running beyond any framework.

One of the main reasons for Bloom's acceptance of Molly's infidelity, the one by which he apprehends her mind most fully, appears in the explanation of the jealousy he feels: "Because a nature full and volatile in its free state, was alternately the agent and reagent of attraction. Because attraction between agent(s) and reagent(s) at all instants varied, with inverse proportion of increase and decrease, with incessant circular extension and radial reentrance. Because the controlled contemplation of the fluctuation of attraction produced, if desired, a fluctuation of pleasure" (732/17.2163–68).

In the Rosenbach manuscript of "Ithaca," the eighth word, "its," is "her," while the fourteenth, "agent," is preceded by "source" crossed off.[2] In changing "her" to "its," Joyce may have intended to suggest that the free nature Molly stands for involves both genders. Replacing "source" with "agent" makes Molly's attraction more active. Bloom here recognizes Molly's right to give and take feeling, a dynamism he probably cannot do without.

The "circular extension and radial reentrance" of Molly's feelings specify the outward and inward movement of the loop of desire and perception that Lacan develops. While "reagent" implies chemistry, the idea of two agents "alternately" transforming each other goes beyond chemistry into dialectical complexity. "Circular extension" was modified by "invariable" before Joyce replaced it with the more dynamic "incessant." Bloom sees that Molly has to carry on this dialectical chemistry, and by realizing his need for her vitality, he grants her the power to create his language, giving her the authority of the Other. Man articulates himself through woman in

Joyce. Restuccia sees that Molly speaks for Joyce and controls his pen (143–44), but in emphasizing the perversity of this masochistic use of woman, she overlooks its pervasiveness: how fundamentally man has to use womanly thinking to say anything.

Simone de Beauvoir, in *The Second Sex,* criticizes the representation of woman as the Other because the Other is an object for which man is the subject (xvi–xvii, 132–33). Lacan says that woman must stop being the Other, though by doing so, she will stop being woman (*FS* 94, 160). Two ways for a woman to escape being a mere Other are by assuming a more active, masculine role and by developing the Other as a function of subjectivity. Joyce, in portraying Molly, builds on both of these paths to give her more power; but he also sees that because of the system that contains her, she finally remains dependent on some man for her authority.

Molly is generally in control of her dialogues with Leopold, who tends to play a subservient role with her, and she asserts phallic power by claiming the right to an extra man. If she is acting out Bloom's fantasy here, it is a passive fantasy on his part and she enjoys it. Elaine Unkeless shows effectively that Molly is trapped by conventional roles. But Bloom is trapped too, and if, as Unkeless points out, Molly's tyranny only shows her dependence, then Bloom's subservience shows his. Love tends to make people dependent on each other. Bloom spends the first half of his day working partly to serve her, and the second half avoiding going home because of Blazes. The thought of Blazes, who acts as Molly's phallus here, disturbs Bloom continually, the scepter of her sovereignty over him. If what Bloom needs from Molly is her verbal dynamism, then her femininity is the source of her phallic power. Similarly, Bloom has power over Molly because he gives her freedom as other men would not. So his passivity has a phallic effect in helping him to possess her. The genders have to be seen as constantly interchanging with each other in complex ways.

Critics of Molly argue that she is a male projection, but this need not keep her from being realistic. Her "male" preoccupation with physical sexuality, for example, may be explained by the intense sex she had that afternoon. Lacan's idea that one exists through the Other means that, as Ragland-Sullivan puts it, "individuality is both one's 'true' self and someone else's fiction, thus inherently alien or other" (*R–S* 106). For Lacan, Molly cannot have a true self without being created by someone else's fiction; so she can be both a function of Joyce and an individual. Lacan presents woman as a projection of man (*FS* 156), and in view of the primacy of the mother in forming the self, it is hard not to see man as a projection of woman. The two genders re-create each other constantly by thinking of each other, and Joyce's male protagonists are always moving toward the feminine.

At the end of his narrative life, Bloom completes his movement toward the Other by lapsing into the womb of the unconscious. If one has to surround oneself with mother in order to liberate one's imagination, then when one frees imagination almost completely in dream, one must be mentally reentering the mother's body.[3] His career as a signifier done, Bloom returns to the womb of the imagination; but Joyce's mind must contain this womb to give birth to him. Bloom enters the womb of his creator through the black dot at the end of "Ithaca" that answers the question of where he is. This spot represents the aperture at which Bloom locates his personal god, Molly's genitals. It may be linked to Bloom's superego because it is for him the center not only of transcendent bliss (the ideal), but also of maximum shame and guilt. Through this passageway inward/outward, Bloom dies and is reborn emotionally.

The element most associated with death and rebirth is earth, and Stephen and Bloom both meditate on the earth as tomb and womb throughout the book, especially in "Proteus" and "Hades." Stephen predicts the spot at the end of "Ithaca" in "Scylla and Charybdis" when he speaks of Shakespeare's final goal: "He returns after a life of absence to that spot of earth where he was born, where he has always been, man and boy, a silent witness . . . " (213/9. 1030–1032). "Man and boy" suggests, in conjunction with "always," that the boy remained in Shakespeare after he became a man. Bloom has always been focused on this spot insofar as he has perceived anything at all, for it is his most essential object, his *objet a,* the center of his visual field.

In the last paragraph of "Ithaca," syntax and logic disintegrate as Bloom enters the womb of sleep, where he will float in the unformed primal matter of language. Here in the murmuring sea of the unconscious, he merges with all possibilities, squaring the circle "in the night of the bed of all the auks" (737/17.2329). Bloom joins the name-shifting series of variations on "Sinbad the Sailor," which changes its simple alphabetical nature toward the end to indicate that it could go on forever. This series of adventurers represents every possible impulse that exists potentially in the id or barred subject prior to formulation. What is indicated here is the chain of signifiers, and because it can only reach the text when it is broken by specific words, the chain can only be manifested through the imposition of Joyce as a series of *points de capiton.*

In entering the flowing of signifiers, Bloom enters Molly's field to reconstitute himself as a signifier for the following day. He must partake of the feminine side of life in order to articulate his language, as Lacan indicates when he speaks of "the woman share of speaking beings": " . . . all speaking beings, whoever they be and whether or not they are provided with the attributes of masculinity . . . are allowed to inscribe themselves on this side" (*FS* 150).[4]

Molly inscribes herself on the feminine side of Bloom by her adultery, and the words of hers that echo through Bloom's thoughts are made memorable by the phallic force involved in that adultery. But she also qualifies to be the receptacle of Bloom's self inscription by frequently exceeding all specific definitions. Molly, then, plays both masculine and feminine roles, and the reasonable solution to the problem of gender that Joyce suggests through the Blooms is that each person in a marriage should use both gender codes. This allows him or her to alternate masculine and feminine gestures so that each partner is prevented from monopolizing either gender restrictively. It is dangerous to pretend that gender operates in one direction when it never does.

In her lattitude of perspective, Molly resembles not only the Other, but the subject, the full self at the basis of discourse, being too wide to be captured by any formula. Lacan speaks of the "infinity of the subject" (*Four* 252). In fact, Molly is the subject of Bloom's life in several ways, and this may explain why she is barred. It is ultimately not only her but himself that he desires too deeply for possession.

Molly's Shift

As the embodiment of subjectivity, Molly represents the endless sliding of the signifier by her use of language. Joyce was well aware that the meaning of every word is determined by its position in a sentence. In fact, Lacan's *point de capiton,* the elementary cell that is the simplest form of the origin of the signifier, refers to the structure of interacting forces in a sentence (*Selection* 303). Not a single word thought by Molly, however, has a position in a comprehensible sentence. Molly's discourse gives the effect of expressing the arc of sliding signification of the *point de capiton* without its hook of punctuation; and in this sense, within the limits of language, it suggests pure *jouissance.* Though Molly's phrases and clauses often seem clear, they all ultimately lack the context that would finalize them, and this often adds to their lyrical suggestiveness.

In many cases Molly's words shift their context as they are in progress, changing their orientation from a prior referent to a subsequent one. The words underlined in the passages below are elementary examples of this pattern. Each of these words or phrases starts out connected to the words before it, but ends up being attached to the ones that follow:

> [Mrs. Dante Riordan] greatest miser ever *was* actually afraid to lay out 4d for her methylated spirit telling all her ailments *she had* too much old chat in her (738/18.6–7)

a young boy . . . seduce him I know what boys feel with that down on their cheek *doing that frigging* drawing out the thing by the hour [Bloom] question and answer would you do this that and the other (740/85–89)

[Blazes] cursing him [Lenehan] to the lowest pits *that sponger* he [Lenehan] was making free with me after the Glencree dinner (750/426–27)

the last [stout] they sent from ORourkes was as flat as a pancake he makes his money *easy* Larry they call him (750/451–52)

the poor men [train engineers] that have to be out all the night from their wives and families in those roasting engines *stifling* it was today (754/599–600)

I had everything to myself *then a girl* Hester we used to compare our hair (756/637)

[Apparently Floey Dillon] she wrote to say she was married *to a very rich architect* if I'm to believe all I hear with a villa and eight rooms (758/720–21)

I hate people that have always their poor story to tell *everybody* has their own troubles (758/725–26)

last time Ill ever go there [theater] to be squashed like that for any Trilby and her barebum *every two minutes* tipping me there (767/1042–43)

[Milly] she had me that exasperated of course *contradicting* I was badtempered too (768/1072–73)

These are the simplest kinds of examples of the shiftings that go on constantly on various levels of Molly's discourse of the Other. The relations of these words could be cleared up by punctuation, but the point is that they are not. With the punctuation omitted, there seems to be a moment when each of the underlined phrases changes its mind about its alignment, and they all remain two-faced. Mind-changing and two-faced are terms used to attack the feminine from the point of view of masculine logic, but they could as easily connote vitality. In fact, every word we use does change in transition from its past context to its future one, but we are trained to think of sentences as static structures. By liberating verbal units from containment by sentences, Molly reveals the constant sliding or dynamic interplay of language that corresponds to the actuality of feeling, the source from which language comes and toward which it aims.

The social order that puts Molly in the position of woman oppresses her by separating her from the rational world of power, but it also gives her language a freedom from logical structure, an imaginative mobility that Bloom depends on, partakes of himself, and may convey to Stephen. Further implications of the *jouissance* that appears through Molly's shifting syntax can be developed from a few substantial examples, as when she thinks of nursing: "I had a great breast of milk with Milly enough for two what was the reason of that he said I could have got a pound a week as a wet nurse *all swelled out* the morning that delicate looking student . . . Penrose nearly caught me washing" (754/570–74).

"All swelled out" is distributed at first over the time of Molly's childbearing, but then it is localized on the morning that Penrose almost saw her, so that this image of redundancy ("enough for two") shifts its location in time as well as shifting from possible to actual, leading more than one verbal life. In fact, the images that pass along the many levels of shift in Molly's mind are often not located in time or space. Their main orientation is to the narcissistic flow of her reverie, which represents in its dreaminess the sliding of the signifier.

An elaborate example of Molly's shift takes place soon after she thinks of Lily Langtry, the famous beauty, whose husband made her wear a chastity device. This device leads Molly to several other thoughts as her focus shifts freely. Soon she thinks of a statue of the Virgin with an oversized Christ child: " . . . the infant Jesus in the crib at Inchicore in the Blessed Virgins arms sure no woman could have a child that big taken out of her and I thought first it came out of her side *because how could she go to the chamber when she wanted to* and she a rich lady" (752/497–500).

At first the Virgin seems to be having trouble passing water because of the size of the baby inside her, but the italicized words finally turn out to be about Lily, the "rich lady," who cannot urinate because of her chastity belt. Both belt and baby are imposed on women by the patriarchal order. Sometimes the lines that slide have significant content. In the last two examples, the full breasts and the need to urinate, both shifters linked to babies, represent that "deepdown torrent" (*U* 783/18.1598), the feminine flow of creativity, the streaming of language that cannot stay in a grammatical form, that overflows the boundaries of sentence structure. This *jouissance* beyond the phallic inspires Bloom, who centers his life on cultivating the flow of his wife's feelings even though those feelings hurt him through Boylan.

Molly uses many images of swelling out of containment, such as "you be damned you lying strap" (771/1174). This overflow is often in opposition to Bloom's rational control. In "Cyclops," the narrator remembers that Pisser Burke told him that Molly cried because she "couldn't loosen her farting strings" without Bloom showing her how to do it (315/12.841). In "Penelope" she thinks, "wherever you be let your wind go free" (763/909). She also complains that Bloom once got her a set of fancy breeches that took her "half an hour" to remove so she could urinate, "with it dropping out of me" (745/251–52). Before she actually pees, she thinks, "its pouring out of me like the sea" (769/1123).

Molly is also linked to flow through her singing, which motivates her to make her discourse as continuous as possible. She remembers having trouble singing "Love's Old Sweet Song": "ere oer the world the mists began

I hate that istsbeg" (762/876). The consonant cluster impedes the flow of her voice. Tim Martin mentioned to me in conversation that some singers, such as Joan Sutherland, hardly use consonants.

Perhaps the most powerful effect that Molly's verbal shifts can have is that of beauty or lyricism. Remembering Captain Grove, a companion of her father's on Gibralter, she thinks, "I suppose he died of galloping drink ages ago *the days like years* not a letter from a living soul except the odd few I posted to myself" (757/697–700). The image of Molly posting letters to herself is a model of the loop of desire that reveals her need to create her own feelings through the Other. Like all of the patches of Molly's shift I've been pointing out, this one involves her setting off in a new direction without having separated herself from the old one. The pattern is an analogue of infidelity, and the action it produces might be called a sort of wiggle, that is, the reverberation of two different movements.

There is often a poetic effect in the way Molly's words realign themselves, and it is strong here. "The days like years" is a formula that fits the following account of loneliness, but it exerts it major force by clashing with the hyperbole that precedes it. It would be logical to follow "ages ago" with "the years like days," that is, moving quickly. The reverse formula has the effect of magnifying by close focus an already vast space of time to suggest the archaic, abstract, and infinite while maintaining intimacy. By jumping to something new, Molly creates something touching and beautiful. This poignant beauty corresponds to her feeling, though she does not (and should not) understand how it works. The shift is an example of a gap in discourse through which the subject is glimpsed, and the subject that speaks expresses Joyce as the Other.

Molly's syntactical shifting, combined with her tendencies to contradict herself and to confuse references to persons, places, and times,[5] tends to cause her language to be internal because it blurs external context. This is a step toward the pure language of the *Wake,* which reduces referentiality to a subordinate aura. Of course Molly does convey a good deal of information reasonably clearly: her sliding effects can usually be relegated to a margin or horizon of her discourse. This shifting area of her thinking, however, is the part that Bloom makes it the purpose of his life to promote by sacrificing himself to maintain the flow of her feelings.[6]

The freedom from definition that Bloom supports in Molly provides him with a transcendent source of motivation, a haven of streaming possibilities outside the world of fact. When Molly says, "theyre all mad to get in there where they come out of" (760/806), she recognizes herself as alpha and omega, the origin and goal of all desire and therefore of all discourse and perception. Molly expresses a function of Joyce as the ego ideal, the attractive side of the superego or the Other.

Freud repeatedly maintains that the primary focus of desire is one's own id, and that other objects of desire are like pseudopods of an amoeba, temporary extensions of a fundamental and abiding narcissism.[7] He also says that narcissistic qualities can be highly attractive erotically because the lover makes contact with his own narcissism through that of the beloved (*SE* 14:75, 89). Bloom sustains Molly's narcissism by spoiling her, and this is a way of describing the treasure he invests in her.

For Bloom to allow Molly to contradict herself is to trap her in a dependence, and lovers should maintain respect by controlling the tendency to make such allowances. On the other hand, I suspect that one cannot love someone without allowing that person to contradict himself. Mulligan quotes (17/1.517) from Whitman's "Song of Myself" (section 51):

> Do I contradict myself?
> Very well then I contradict myself,
> (I am large, I contain multitudes.)

One implication of this is that to accept a person's contradictions is to accept the fullness of his humanity, his personal being as opposed to a theory in which it is enclosed. In Molly's case, this includes her masculine aspect as well as the feminine.

Molly designates herself unknowingly as the focus of desire and elicitor of all possibilities when she recalls a joke of Josie Powell's: "when I said I washed up and down as far as possible asking me did you wash possible" (743/204–5). Derrida comments on a line from Mallarmé's prose poem *"Mimique"*: "a hymen (out of which flows Dream)." Derrida says that the hymen, which he equates with the veil, does not disappear after virginity is lost: it remains as a screen on which writing is done (*Dissemination* 211–14). This matches the veil of signs, and so Molly's hymen, her *objet a,* is Bloom's great source of potential images. Projecting her veil, he sees everything through her, and the vision he offers Stephen depends on her.

Penelope's Web

Molly's role as a pre-sense of all that can be seen before it is rationalized, as the unconscious substratum of the field of perception, is suited to her identification with the earth. Joyce's description of "Penelope" in a letter of 8 February 1922 to Harriet Shaw Weaver suggests the unconsciousness of this level: " . . . I tried to depict the earth which is prehuman and presumably posthuman" (*Letters* 1: 180). This aim is typical of Joyce's striving in *Ulysses* for points of view that are more than human.

Some of the most impressive powers that Molly has as the earth that underlies everything are linked to movement. Joyce wrote of "Penelope" to

Budgen on 16 August 1921, "It turns like the huge earth ball slowly surely and evenly round and round and round spinning . . . " (*Letters* 1:170). Whereas men make structures supposed to stand still, the earth never stops moving. This contrast matches the difference between a sentence, which is a fixed structure, and Molly's flow of words. Moreover, in the Correspondences of the Gilbert-Gorman schema, Joyce says not only "Penelope-Earth" but "Web-Movement," so Penelope's web is made out of movement. Joyce seems to see this web as able not only to delay the suitors, but to fascinate. Samuel Butler suggests in *The Authoress of the Odyssey* that the woman who wrote the epic was trying to "whitewash" a Penelope originally associated with scandal. He speculates that "according to the original version, Penelope picked out her web, not so much in order to delay a hateful marriage, as to prolong a very agreeable courtship" (131). This source, familiar to Joyce, links the web to enticement.

The web of Molly's movement is the attraction of her mental mobility. While all of the figures in the book whose thoughts we are given shift the focus of their thinking on every page, Molly shifts to another place every few lines; moreover, her shifts jump over great spans of time, space, and logic, with less control than the mental movements of the others show. As I have suggested, she is often not focused on any particular scene, but sliding between them.

Joyce portrays serious deficiencies resulting from the specialization of part of Molly as the Other. Her visionary power is inseparable from a loss of consciousness imposed on her as a woman. She is half asleep not only in "Penelope" but also in "Calypso," the other time we see her directly. The area of her mind that connects with Bloom and Stephen is below the surface. By framing her in these terms, Joyce insists that in order to occupy the position desire aims at, woman is systematically deprived of the rational part of her her mind, but Bloom is not much better off. She has damaged her brain by living in a sensual drowse for his sake, while he has wounded his crotch by being cuckolded for hers.[8] Joyce knows that they misread each other's interests and that they would be better off if they had not crippled each other emotionally; but he also knows that this is what people often do to each other (perhaps always) when they love, and he doubts that love can be replaced by a rational alternative.

Nor should we overestimate the damage to Molly, or to women. In exchange for the control and logic she gives up, Molly has sharp perceptions about feelings. She is far more intelligent than Boylan, and more clever than Bloom by a wide enough margin so that she knows of his other sexual interests although he does not realize that she knows (738–39/18.34ff.). She understands the movement of desire, the vital principle of all thought, better than the men do, and she leads their minds by her weaving.

Skeat calls the etymological connection between *wife* and *weave* a spuri-
ous "fable," but neither he nor the first OED has any other derivation for
wife, so Joyce may have seen value in the fable. The web Molly weaves is the
veil of appearances that captivates Bloom and aggravates Stephen. The
movement of her narrative jumping weaves it because her freedom from
the fixity of facts is the source of her attraction, and her attraction is what
makes the world appear. Robert M. Adams recognizes that Molly's prose,
"irresistably in motion," weaves the world that the men live in: " . . . Molly
not only is the texture of this world, but the force that creates it by the
spinning of her thoughts" (168).

The weaving of Molly's verbal shifts may be seen as drawing out words
and constructions and running them between meanings to fill in the spaces
in the logical framework of language. The lingering and anticipation with
which she loops her extensions may be essential to giving the world its
solidity, attaching people to it. What makes the world solid may be our
desire to possess it. Moreover, by shifting to a new interest, she draws
attention, so that the same inconstancy that destroys her man also leads
him on. In the inseparability of the genders, he projects this desire to
de-sire himself. Joyce may have had this in mind in a note on Homer's
Penelope: "She weaves a deathshroud for Laertes which is Ul. coronation
robe" (*N* 496). Her weaving at once buries the old (Ulysses' father) and
inaugurates the new, and this double action is the key to the tradition of the
earth goddess-creatrix of death and rebirth.

Molly is highly aware of the role desire plays in creating images. She
remembers Bloom saying, "The sun shines for you" (782/18.1578), and she
hopes to inspire Stephen with vision: "they all write about some woman in
their poetry well I suppose he wont find many like me *where softly sighs of
love the light guitar where poetry is in the air the blue sea and the moon shining so
beautifully* coming back on the nightboat from Tarifa" (775/1333–37).

Here is a far-reaching transition: "find many like me" is in Molly's future,
while "coming back on the nightboat" is on Gibralter a generation ago. The
intervening twenty-three words of flowery description that I have underlined
begin with a line (the first eight words, as Gifford shows) from a song Molly
learned on Gibralter, "In Old Madrid." But Molly may not think of the
oldness of the song at first, and the underlined part is not clearly in the
present or the past: it shifts from one to the other. Such big jumps probably
indicate strong feeling, or sensuality, for it takes strong feeling to draw
together things that are far apart, as in strong poetic figures.

"Poetry is in the air" of this indeterminate space somewhere over a
twenty year span between Dublin and Gibralter, but then poetry is all that is
ever in the air. For we can only see images we have terms for, and these
figures were either created earlier by someone who was inspired, or we are

inspired to create them now. The underlined passage, following "wont find many like me," is devoted to elaborating Molly's sensitivity; and in this way her narcissism projects itself as a veil across the sky.

This veil, however, cannot be projected without positing the response of the Other, which is what inspiration consists of, and Molly's poetry is directed at a vague male figure, most immediately Stephen. Like the men, Molly cannot imagine anything without imagining herself seen back. With regard to her first love, which seems to have been her most passionate, Molly remembers that Lieutenant Mulvey's penis had "a kind of eye in it" (761/18.816).

Molly expresses understanding of how desire creates vision through language when she wishes that her current flame, Boylan, would write a love letter: "if he wrote it I suppose thered be some truth in it true or no it fills up your whole day and life always something to think about every moment and see it all round you like a new world" (758/738–40). The entire visual field is filled with language, and the truth of what appears out of the words that generate a panorama is not physical, but emotional: truth based primarily on the activity that writes it. The man inscribes the images, and what Molly does to inspire this creation is to withdraw. Her sliding lure is parallel to the role of the author who projects authority and then draws back. The letter—which Molly values more than sex at this time, partly because she does not have it—can only be written when Blazes is separated from her. In Derridean terms her perpetual movement is a displacement that subverts the fixed forms of life toward an endless flow of new possibilities. Derrida speaks of writing itself as a displacement, a play of difference that dislocates reality to put it behind a veil (*Dissemination* 181n., 210).

The veil or hymen we see written across the field of sight is a lure that conceals and suggests a reality that can never be reached, so that Derrida defines the present as a mask over a gap (*Dissemination* 215). He calls this gap the cave (*antre*), and says that everything is played out in the cave (222). The *antre* is equated with the space between (entre) representations, and with folds in the veil (or the hymen, which Derrida also sees as folding). I have shown that Molly's veil tends to suspend itself between meanings. Bloom remembers her "Shift stuck between the cheeks behind" (a sentence fragment on 92/6.208), and I have identified her mesial groove with a fold in the veil.

When Molly recalls her first sexual experience with Mulvey, she dwells on the caves in Gibralter: "Saint Michaels cave with the icicles or whatever they call them hanging down and ladders all the mud plotching my boots Im sure thats the way down the monkeys go under the sea to Africa" (760/791–94). Molly associates the cave with the vagina, and the stalactite image here connects with "they once took something down out of a woman that was up there for years covered with limesalts" (760/804–6). Gibralter, the magic, private world Molly goes back to, is a strange female wedge hanging from the bottom of Western Europe. This outcropping of the earth was the goal of Ulysses and the edge of his world. Like the Levant, which Bloom associates with Molly, it is an interface with the otherness of the non-western world. Molly believes that its "caverns measureless to man" include subterranean passages to the dark continent. Kaja Silverman, citing Michèle Montrelay's interpretation of Lacan, says that female sexuality "is censored rather than repressed [as the male is] by the phallus—covered over but not represented or structured by the paternal signifier. For that reason it remains a "dark continent," a real which threatens to submerge not only the female subject but the entire order of signification" (187).

This suggests that the submerged world connected to Gibralter is inside Molly, and at one point she remembers imagining the Rock inside herself when Dr. Collins asked her about difficulty in passing stool (another ironic passage through the veil): "could you pass it easily pass what I thought he was talking about the rock of Gibralter" (770/1163–64). The imagery surrounding the cave suggests that it is not subject to the limitations of time or space on this side of the veil. It is the feminine world of inner space within which Molly's shifting takes non-place.[9]

The cave has terrible associations with the void, the grave, and the transformations of decay, subjects Bloom meditated on in "Hades." The Other always has the frightening aspect of nothingness, and this contributes to the fear and hostility men often feel toward women. Bloom deals with this anxiety by a fetishism that projects Molly's aggressiveness to make what is frightening attractive. It would be better if he could leave the fear behind and release her (as Lacan suggests) from her role of the Other. Joyce, however, means to show the way people actually behave and to leave the ideal possibilities aching in the background. He connects with the depths of his characters through their flaws, their gaps, their dependence on the Other.

Incompleteness

In her closing pages, Molly feels a trembling of the veil that suggests a passage through. An obvious sign of this is that she envisions veils concealing women. One of the possibilities she dreams of is "a nice semitransparent morning gown" (780/1495), and she remembers a velar image from "In Old Madrid": "2 glancing eyes a lattice hid" (782/1597, see Gifford). She also flutters the veil at this time by increasing the rapidity of her cuts from context to context, so that she gushes with images of physical multiplicity during her last fifty lines: "Id love to have the whole place swimming in roses God of heaven theres nothing like nature the wild mountains then the sea and the waves rushing then the beautiful country with the fields of oats and wheat and all kinds of things and all the fine cattle" (781/1557–61).

Molly is sinking into the inner flux of images in her unconscious as she falls asleep. This movement may be seen as an apotheosis, with the flow of Molly's transitions, as the fruit of Bloom's sacrifice, revealing one of the ultimate values of the book as dissemination, the multiplying of images without control.

Molly unleashes here what Lacan says he believes in when he supports mysticism in Seminar 20, "the *jouissance* of the woman insofar as it is something more" ["*en plus*"] (*FS* 147, *Encore* 71). I think that this "something more"—which is also spoken of here as "going beyond" and being "beyond the phallus"—refers to the exhilaration of running from one image to another, of letting feeling flow along the chain of signifiers. While Lacan sees such going beyond as characteristically feminine, he also says some men can do it, and this *jouissance* beyond the phallus is what Lacan refers to as Joyce's symptom. Through Molly's freedom of movement in language, Joyce must be expressing something internalized in himself that he could not express except as a woman.

What distinguishes Molly from the men in *Ulysses?* Joyce's well-known description of "Penelope" starts out with the modifiers "perfectly sane full" (*Letters* 1: 170). I doubt if any man in the book could be called "perfectly sane" in the sense of complete mental health; nor does any seem full to overflowing. They are all burdened by the phallic obsession with power. Lacan holds that women, who do not have to sustain the pretense of the phallus, escape a level of repression and are "closer to the primordial unconscious" (*R–S* 297). Molly is in touch with the free movement of unconscious thinking that Freud calls primary process, which Lacan links to *jouissance* in *Television* (13). Molly is not aware that she speaks for anything primordial, and it may be that it is Joyce's self-consciousness that makes a healthy movement symptomatic. But the creative energy behind all of Joyce's techniques of word choice (based on word changing) appears nowhere else in *Ulysses* with as much purity and thrust as it has here. This free range of metonymic displacement derives its delight from dissolving logical frameworks, so its *jouissance* comes from being beyond the phallic. Even so, it must be added that this movement still has reference to the phallic.

After saying that such feminine *jouissance* supports "one face of the Other, the God face," Lacan adds that "all this comes about thanks to the being of *signifiance*" ("*tout ça se produit grâce à l'être de la signifiance*") (*FS* 147, *Encore* 71). This confirms that "something more" is the overflow into succeeding words, for the productive feminine grace of *signifiance* as 'signifying,' is the endless sliding of the signifier. Rose's definition of *signifiance* as the movement of language away from coherence (*FS* 51) suggests that words are expressive when they break out of their established framework. By putting movement in the place of God, Lacan changes that place to a displacement, and leaves some functions to be accounted for.

The above passage from Molly refers to Nature, a feminine deity Joyce uses to represent the psychic fecundity I have been describing. Joseph Voelker points out that Molly here worships Nature, as Bloom does elsewhere. The power of nature finally glorified is her ability to generate endless forms, but this is only part of what is celebrated here: " . . . rivers and lakes and flowers all sorts of shapes and smells and colours springing up even out of the ditches primroses and violets nature it is as for them saying theres no God I wouldnt give a snap of my two fingers for all their learning why dont they go and create something" (781–82/1562–65).

The creative power Molly worships also has a masculine side. Because speech involves both sliding and fixation, both the arc and the hook of the *point de capiton, jouissance* in language cannot go beyond the phallus without referring to it—at least as something absent. The figure of God, whom Molly refers to as "Lord God" (777/1410), seems to be conventionally masculine for her, and she refers to it as "the first person in the universe" (782/1569), assuming a unified first cause. The superstitions she frequently invokes show a tendency to accept authority she does not understand. In short, she is hooked: mentally and physically, she continues to devote herself to the male principle.

Molly's dependence on phallic authority explains on the psychological level what her bout with Boylan explains on the physical: that she is not fully awake. Only by giving a good part of her will over to male responsibility can she carry on her free flotation. She is not responsible for facts or for making one thing equal another (the phallic function), so she displaces this function onto her faith in a unified first cause, just as woman traditionally seeks access to phallic authority through man (*FS* 145). By emphasizing Molly's functional subjection to the male, her need to consolidate her subjecthood through him, Joyce exposes the inherent unfairness of the gender system. But if he shows her deprived of conscious authority by the system, he also indicates the unconscious power she wields through language; and he sees her weakness as reciprocal to Bloom's.

Bloom is able to see through the myth of God and authority that Molly leans on, but he has his own myth: he is devoted to her, making her the center on which he depends, a phallic illusion he sustains. If the woman has to claim her authority through the male, the man has to give phallic authority to her in order to possess it continually. Their interdependence, while it is articulated by the codes of masculine and feminine, is built on the way the individual has to loop into the Other. Which sides of the code they are on is so far from being inherent that there is a substantial area of Bloom's unconscious that is feminine and it depends on a substantial area of hers that is masculine. This seems to be the most active area of their relation to each other. The enthrallment of his femininity by her masculinity, as represented by Boylan, also enthralls her masculinity to Bloom's femininity because she needs his passivity. Whatever the gender arrangements, it is the depth of their needs for each other that makes love. Because the complexities of these needs cannot be understood, love is bound to entail destructive distortions, but Joyce recognizes that the life it gives is worth the price.

None of the three main figures in the book is capable of representing independent values by himself or herself, and I want to consider how they hinge on each other. Of the various terms for describing the polarity of Stephen and Bloom, one of the most basic pairs is spirit versus matter. Spirit and matter have to be combined to make life, but no one can clearly explain how they connect. Spirit is to matter as possibility is to actuality, and this indicates the distinction between Stephen the idealist and Bloom the pragmatist. In "Nestor," Stephen, who is preoccupied with possibilities that are not actualized, derives from Aristotle a link between the possible and the actual: "It must be a movement then, an actuality of the possible as possible. Aristotle's phrase formed itself within the gabbled verses..." (25/2.67–68).[10] The verses that the phrase blends with are about the rebirth of Lycidas, "*Sunk though he be beneath the watery floor* . . . " (66). This passage predicts that Molly, as the embodiment of movement, will connect the actuality of Bloom with the possibility of Stephen, or that Bloom will move Stephen through Bloom's link to Molly. Of course Stephen does not know his thought is prophetic: the force that moves toward the possibility of unity in the novel is speaking through him.

The connection between the characters, to be sure, is not fully realized. They continue to misunderstand each other, and Joyce leaves open the possibility that the juxtaposition of the three figures is ultimately ironic, so that the indications of their potential to fulfill each other only add to the poignancy as they drift by one another. In a larger sense, Stephen and Bloom are the main components of the subject of Joyce, which continues to combine ironic idealism with a love for the earth. The writing of *Ulysses* brings these opposites together, and the countless hints of their scarcely-possible reconciliation add up to define a spiritual potential that remains invisible behind the actual world. Without this potential, the world could have no *jouissance,* just as Molly's onward flow has to be motivated by desire for the absent phallus. Ragland-Sullivan says that the Imaginary, the element of flux, always aims at fusion (*R–S* 141).

Molly is sinking into sleep at the end, and her identity will dissolve as she joins Bloom in the world they go into and come out of. As John Bishop puts it in *Joyce's Book of the Dark,* " ... night bears darkly prolific powers. Since it is out of this undifferentiated state, every morning... , that all the manifold and splintered facets of the wakeful world emerge" (64). The sleep Molly goes into involves the source of everything, and therefore insofar as there is any purpose, or series of purposes behind the flux, she goes into or toward her author. Neither she nor any of the other characters have ever been fully independent of their author, and the signs of their dependence on this Other are not only the things that come into their minds that they cannot understand, but also the needs they have for one another, which gape across the field they are built into.

Just as none of these figures is capable of independent values, so none is capable of seeing by himself or herself. The material world the men see is a veil that Molly weaves, while the dream screen she is focused on is generated by their letters or signs of love. The masculine provides the form of language and the feminine, the movement. Molly exemplifies and celebrates the maternal ego ideal as an opening up of meaning, but she also worships the masculine principle of unity, for the first cause she invokes at the end is the paternal superego. Both forces are united in the author. The text is a series of knots in which the factors in Joyce represented by the different characters are intertwined in every signifier.

The Answer to the Other

Molly's relation to her author must be seen in order to understand her narrative situation, and this relation can be defined economically by looking at her last brief page and starting with the question of whom she is talking to as the book ends. She seems to be telling in the past tense what she did with her first lover, Mulvey, but in the end she is addressing him to a considerable extent, even while calling him "he." Her closeness to Mulvey, which breaks through her point of view, has a biographical reference: Joyce was haunted by Willie Mulvagh, Nora Barnacle's early lover in Galway (Maddox, *Nora* 20–21).

Although it is primarily Mulvey Molly speaks with, the words "my mountain flower" (783/18.1606) superimpose (with variation) a line of Bloom's from Ben Howth (782/18.1576) on the earlier scene in Gibralter; and Blazes and Stephen also seem to be involved in her feeling here. It may be accurate to say that in Aristotelian terms Mulvey is the formal cause or form of the man she envisions, Blazes is his material cause or physical substance, Stephen is his efficient cause or immediate occasion, and Bloom is the final cause, *telos,* or end. So, as her pronoun shifts indicate, she is addressing a general male principle rather than any particular person. This principle, like Lacan's phallus, is defined by its absence. She is really addressing the Other, to whom she has been speaking all along in her unfocused reverie. The part of Molly that addresses the Other may be called her self, as opposed to the Other that she represents for the men. We might even call it her real self, except that it exists only in relation to the Other.

The most vital image of the Other for Molly is a man: he represents the Other best because he can give her the deepest vision of the gaze and of the loop of desire. Images of gaze and circuit prevail on the last page: "then I asked him with my eyes to ask again yes and then he asked me would I yes to say yes." He reciprocates the asking in her eyes, and on the two remaining lines he feels her "breasts all perfume" and she feels his heart "going like mad," adding another level of reciprocation in which their bosoms both send signals. We do not know if "Mulvey" asks with eyes or voice, but there is a strong feeling of mutual mirroring: she asks him with her eyes to ask her, while he says yes by asking her to ask him, so that she says yes. Moreover, when she says, "asked him with my eyes," she is not only seeing him looking at her, but seeing her eyes from his point of view as he sees her looking at him. The book ends, then, with something powerfully alike to the infinitely regressing cycles of vision and desire that I saw reverberating between Stephen and Bloom in "Eumaeus" and "Ithaca."

The attitude of saying yes constitutes the prime feature of Molly's being. This is one of the implications of Joyce's characterization of her as *"das Fleisch das stets bejaht,"* 'the flesh that always says yes.'[11] Like anyone in touch with his feelings, she lives for the moments in which she can say yes. She says it not only to *jouissance* but to change, risk, and the inevitable unhappiness of love's fading, all represented by the long-gone figure of Mulvey. She gives the man to whom she says it the right to be her phallus, to signify and inscribe, to be her Other and author. In his essay on *Ulysses,* Derrida makes the following statement about the word *yes:* "It always has the form of an answer. It arrives after the other, to respond to the demand or to the question, at least implicit, of the other, that is, of the other in me, of the representation in me of another speech [*parole*]" *("Ulysse"* 233, my translation).

The last line refers to Derrida's concept of *"La parole soufflée,"* 'the stolen word,' according to which whatever we say is spoken through us by an unknown author.[12] Joyce's characters do not know who is speaking through them, but the most useful, comprehensive identity to apply to this polyphonic speaker is the complex identity of Joyce.

The Other, to whom Molly says yes, is the opposing narrative agency that constitutes her discourse. To explain the effect produced by her saying yes to her author, I will turn back to a parallel process that takes place in "Circe" when Bloom is talking to a vision of Mrs. Breen. He presents her with a long narrative explanation of how he happens to be in Nighttown. He is nervous about this locale and about Mrs. Breen's sexy aggressiveness, and is trying to ingratiate himself, and as he is recounting past events, he slips into a parodic woman's voice:

> BLOOM
>
> Because it didn't suit you one quarter as well as the other ducky little tammy toque . . . you honestly looked just too fetching in it. . . . (449/15.555–58)

For the last thirty lines of this dialogue, Mrs. Breen agrees with everything Bloom says and spurs him on to a rising tempo of rapid-fire impressions and opinions. The dialogue ends like this:

> BLOOM
>
> . . . and the poodle in her lap bridled up and you asked me if I ever heard or read or knew or came across. . . . [Joyce's ellipsis]
>
> MRS BREEN
>
> (*eagerly*) Yes, yes, yes, yes, yes, yes, yes. (*She fades from his side. . . .*)
>
> (449/15.569–77)

Mrs. Breen originally appeared as an expression of Bloom's shame, a representation of his feeling of being watched, of the gaze. It seems that when her difference from him disappears, she no longer exists as an object of narration. When she fades, she brings a series of fantasies to a close and restores him to reality, whose gaze is now stronger than hers.

Mrs. Breen's disappearance provides a model of closure for the end of the book. Not only are her yeses parallel to Molly's, but Bloom's "you asked me if I ever heard or read or knew or came across. . . . " includes the phrase "asked me" and parallels the rhythm of Molly's coda. When Molly is overwhelmed by the complete affirmation with which she gives herself to the Other, she unites with her creator. Her tendency to transcend her naturalistic situation here is indicated as her vision flies further than it has to the limits of the visual field. Her thoughts of God and nature see mountains, seas, and countryside swarming with a profusion of natural creatures. Her memory of being with Bloom on Howth Hill, which answers his vision of the same scene (176/8.900–916), presents another vast perspective: "leading him on till he asked me to say yes and I wouldn't answer first only looked out over the sea and the sky" (782/18.1580–82). Then she runs through vivid images of Gibralter and "that awful deepdown torrent O and the sea the sea crimson sometimes like fire and the glorious sunsets" (783/1598–99). These images glare at the edge of overexposure to suggest something beyond the control of eyesight. And the shift beyond the visual field is completed by the mirroring and internalizing tendencies of the final erotic lines.

Molly's passage outside vision goes through the veil, but she does not so much penetrate as receive a flood of impressions. The masculine Other she reaches for confirms her continuity by seeming to give her a love she remembers. And many of the eleven yesses in her last twenty lines are shifters that affirm the validity of the memories before and after them: "where I was a Flower of the mountain *yes* when I put the rose in my hair." But her memories of the past are scrambled and the male figure she assembles is not an actual person. She reaches toward an illusion she needs to sustain her sense of identity.

Both men and women, insofar as they are enclosed in the gender system, depend for existence on their fleeting sense of contact with each other—but the reciprocity of this arrangement is skewed. Though people sometimes achieve balanced contact, gender roles tend to make men penetrate while women receive. By showing how deeply our speechbeing is enmeshed in these language roles, Joyce brings out the need for reform, but he also magnifies the rooted power of the system that any reform must overcome. He implies that it will take more work than we can easily imagine to rewrite the polarities of being, but he embarks on that work.

Molly leaves the scene of eyesight behind to pass into the world of sleep, which may hold hope in that it contains both genders in each person. In sleep, perception is internal, so that the eye looks into its own gaze, and as Lacan says, the gaze shows itself. What one wishes for appears as reality in dream, and the mind assumes the power to create its world. For this reason, when Molly goes to sleep, she joins her author. The world of sleep, which takes place in the field of the Other, is the subject of Joyce's next book, and the *Wake* looks into the mind to reveal the inner origins of the structure of vision.

NOTES

1. Bonnie Kime Scott argues in *Joyce and Feminism* (47, 115) that despite his ironic remarks about women, Joyce was influenced by the ideas of feminists, with whom he was often associated. Strong analysis of the support for women inherent in Joyce's work appears in Bishop, Joyce's *Book of the Dark* 336–85 and in McGee 44–52, 178–80. One of the most direct indications of Joyce's feminist intentions appears in *Exiles,* where Richard, however misguided his method, is struggling to liberate Bertha by giving her the right to adultery.

2. See *James Joyce Ulysses: A Facsimile of the Manuscript P* 684–85 *L* 864–66 *N* 732–33.

3. The idea that the dreamer enters his mother's body is strongly developed in the *Wake,* as Bishop 353–57 shows.

4. Lacan says this while commenting on an elaborate diagram (*FS* 149) with two halves that correspond to the genders. I believe that the diagram indicates that discourse is a balance of masculine and feminine. A commentary on the diagram is given in Melville, "The Place of *Jouissance*" 349–70.

5. Molly's self-contradiction is described extensively by Card, *Anatomy* 38–54.

6. In "Molly's Flow," which reached me as I was revising, Attridge daringly argues that there is no flow because Molly's discourse does not show a breakdown of syntax, but only of punctuation—that the shifting effects are located only in the way she is written, and not in the way she thinks. But "Penelope" consists of nothing but Molly's thought, and Derrida (to whom Attridge subscribes) argues that from its origin, thought is inseparable from writing (*Dissemination* 175, 185). Attridge says that while the reader may be uncertain about Molly's references, Molly is certain (548); and yet it is basic for Derrida that no verbal connection is ever certain. Insofar as Molly has a sense that she knows what her phrases refer to (or for that matter who the "he" is that she speaks of), this may be what allows her to be lost in her shift. That people make mistakes in writing (as Molly decidedly does) shows a level of thought in which grammatical and syntactical connections are unclear, and this probably corresponds to an unvoiced discourse in which words are not accented, so that Molly probably does not pronounce much of her absent punctuation.

One of the things Attridge is right about is that the feminine flow in *Ulysses* is often shared by the male protagonists. In fact, as Attridge suggests, women may not surpass men in such verbal flow. Nevertheless, this area of women's lives has been framed as significant, and I believe that it is useful to recognize the ways in which Molly's mind is conditioned (both entrapped and empowered) by the role of woman.

7. Six references to this analogy are listed in the "Index of Analogies" of the *Standard Edition*, 24: 179

8. That Bloom's cuckoldry applies to all men in Joyce is explained in Hélène Cixous's *The Exile of James Joyce*, which presents exile as Joyce's model for life. Cixous emphasizes that the Joycean male subject always has to find that the woman he loves has loved another before him who cannot be displaced. Cixous equates the prior other with the woman's father and with God (484–503). That Joyce never shows anyone who is at present happy with a sense of possessing love may be one indication that what he presents is not the actual world, but his personal interpretation of it.

9. Erik Erikson describes woman's power of inner space in *Identity: Youth and Crisis* 261–94.

10. Goldman, *Paradox* 141, identifies the Aristotle quote as coming from the first chapter of the third book of the *Physics* (201a).

11. Ellmann points out in a note in *Selected Letters* (285) that Joyce's "flesh that always affirms" is a play on Goethe's Mephistopheles, who identifies himself in the first act of *Faust* as "the spirit that always denies."

12. "*La parole soufflée,*" in *Writing and Difference* 169–95.

PART THREE

"Himself by gazework"

FW 224.25

7

Contending Inwords

Unsetting the Scene

In *Finnegans Wake,* as Bishop indicates (227–32), all perception is internalized by the state of sleep that the book represents.[1] Therefore the circuits of perception and desire appear in pure form acted out on an inner stage. The situation corresponds to Berkeley's assertion that all one ever sees are lights shifting in the eye, and it also dramatizes Lacan's observation that for Freud, the root of the scopic drive is that the subject sees himself *(Four* 194). The components and structure of internal perception are well represented by the fourth chapter of the *Wake* (I.4, 75–103), which I will interpret here. Bishop also demonstrates (317ff.) that the *Wake* shows how we return to infantile material in sleep, as Freud says we do; and I.4 explores the infantile roots of perception and consciousness. For psychoanalysis, these roots not only lie in the past: they are present and active within.

To describe the contents of the sleeping mind of I.4 comprehensively, we may begin by distinguishing two kinds of identification that Ragland-Sullivan, interpreting Freud's terms, describes as forming the psyche in the first years. Primary identification, in early infancy, is a passive, dependent mode of relation to the mother that aims at fusion; while the later secondary identification is an active mode of relation to the father and others that emphasizes language and differentiation *(R–S* 18, 33). The distinction between these two modes is parallel to the one between primary process thinking, the free floating of images in the unconscious, and secondary process thought, the logic of consciousness. In the mind of HCE, the *Wake*'s dreamer, his twin sons, Shem and Shaun, are secondary identification functions, while his wife, ALP, expresses the primary function of fusion. Most of the chapter is taken up with masculine differentiation or conflict in the mind of the dreamer, but his feminine level, which is suggested at the start, returns at the end.

The narrator of most of the chapter seems to be the conservative brother, Shaun: he speaks in the first person plural (which sometimes seems pretentious), he carries out a laborious investigation, and he seems distant from the inner life of the dreamer. His distance at the opening of I.4 seems to be inherited from the end of the previous chapter, in which HCE, having been the subject of many stories, was finally seen from afar as a sleeping monument. In the earliest manuscript, the end of I.3 and the (then) beginning of I.4 are continuous.[2]

Interesting suggestions about sleep occur in I.3. It is presented as a field one is drawn into by one's mother, the first woman in life: "It was the first woman, they said, souped him, that fatal wellesday, Lili Coninghams, by suggesting him they go in a field" (58.29–30). Any woman can (even without knowing it) suggest to a man that he and she enter the field of desire, and in doing so, she will be creating his subject, or "suggesting him." The soup she lands him in is the flowing signification or alphabet soup of sleep, what Joyce calls "say water" (50.34).[3]

In another perspective of I.3, the sleeper is King Arthur, the subject of an old story who is resting, but will rise again. The *Wake*'s world is built on the absence of the sleeper's consciousness, and so he is "Our Farfar and Arthor of our doyne" (52.16–17). This is a typical reference to Joyce the author, who is withheld from the world that is created by his leaving behind the world in which he actually existed. His fatherhood is based on his farness. The waking world cannot be known by the dreamer without disintegrating the dream, yet the *Wake* constantly plays with references to this lost prior world. The framework that encloses dreams is turned inside out by the Arthur reference because we, as functions of HCE, are dreaming him, while he is dreaming us.

At the start of I.4, the field of mental activity is seen from a new perspective as the narrator takes the position of looking at the dreaming HCE from outside. Late in 1925 Joyce read and took notes on Freud's case history of the Wolf Man, in which the dreamer takes the point of view of other figures watching himself (Ferrer, "Freudful" 380). As the narrator speculates on the dreamer's thoughts, that dreamer comes, with the primary-process logic of dreams, to encompass the narrator. The range of perspectives on the dream, from seeing it in the past and the distance, at second or third hand (patterns frequent in the first three chapters) to being swallowed by it, relates to a major paradigm of the *Wake*. If the boundary between dream and wake is radically unlocatable, then sleep appears as a model for waking life.

This rich theme works on many levels. Sometimes the dream is an allegory like Dante's vision of the afterlife as a clarification of the living world, so that the things people say to each other in dream language reveal what would be concealed in ordinary discourse. Sometimes the theme follows Blake's notion that the fall into selfish repression makes our life in the fallen world a state of sleep. But often it follows Freud's idea that the sleeping mind (primary process) is the underlying basis of the waking one.

In the *Four Concepts,* Lacan cites the Chinese story of the sage Choang-tsu, who dreamed he was a butterfly and awoke to think that the butterfly might be dreaming Choang-tsu. Lacan says he was right: "In fact, it was when he was the butterfly that he apprehended one of the roots of his identity—that he was, and is, in his essence, that butterfly who paints himself with his own colours—and it is because of this that, in the last resort, he is Choang-tsu" (*Four* 76).[4]

Lacan suggests that if Choang-tsu were certain that he was "absolutely identical with Choang-tsu," this would be a sign of insanity; but Lacan adds that the butterfly has the more certain identity of the two because he does not wonder if he is Choang-tsu. Self-consciousness is impossible in dream (*Four* 75). In basic ways, the figures we dream are our reality and our outer lives are husks or impositions on that reality. This may explain the pattern late in I.3 whereby Earwicker (HCE) holes himself up and is abused from outside (69–73), for abuse from outside may be a general model for the environment, as it is for a sleeper.

The Study Chapter of the *Wake* (II.2) uses a butterfly to represent the formation of the signifier in terms that resemble the *point de capiton,* combining the sliding of signification with the specifying of enunciation:

> At furscht kracht of thunder.
> When shoo, his flutterby,
> Was netted and named. (262.11–13)

The frightening authority of the father pins down the feminine shift to transfer discourse from the Imaginary realm of flux to the Symbolic realm of language. Much of the *Wake* is concerned with the formation of subjectivity and perception, and the fourth chapter, which concentrates on these themes, opens suspended between primary and secondary processes.

Phrasing in the Fields

The first page of I.4 runs through a series of three possible images that the dreamer may be seeing. Here is the first: " . . . it may be . . . the besieged bedreamt him stil and solely of those lililiths undeveiled which had undone him . . . " (75.3–6). The temptresses behind the veil are as carefree as lilies of the field. This image of lilylips does not last long for the same reason that it calls forth the stuttering of guilt, because it is vaginal.

The next image proposed is also attractive, but not quite as overwhelming: "It may be . . . that he reglimmed? presaw? the fields of heat and yields of wheat where corngold Ysit? shamed and shone" (75.8–11). In this vision the hidden component of the fertility of the woman has become a harvest goddess whose name is an ontological question ("Ysit?"), yet sexuality is still suggested by her "fields of heat." The narrator's uncertainty about whether this image is rooted in the past ("reglimmed") or future ("presaw") is part of a mythologizing tendency. Myth points to a golden age that has been and suggests that it will return. Here as always the golden age is based on the world of childhood we return to in sleep, and though the second vision refers to Byron,[5] it also refers to Thomas Traherne. A famous passage from the *Centuries of Meditations* that runs through Stephen's mind in "Proteus" (3.43) describes how glorious the world looked to the child Traherne before he knew that anything had to die: "The corn was orient and immortal wheat, which never should be reaped, nor was ever sown" (Third Century, number 3). The Byron and Traherne allusions both refer to primeval bliss.

Like the first vision, this one passes quickly. It is the third possibility, which is presented slowly with elaborate parenthetical qualifications, that stays. In fact, the interrupting modifiers show emotions attached to this view. Here are some elements of this last possibility:

> It may be ... that with his deepseeing insight ... he conscious of ene-
> mies ... prayed ... during that three and a hellof hours' agony of silence
> ... with unfeigned charity that his wordwounder (an engles to the teeth who,
> nomened Nash of Girahash, would go anyold where in the weeping world on
> his mottled belly ... for milk, music or married missusses) might ... unfold
> into the first of a distinguished dynasty of his posteriors ... (75.11–24)

His intense focus finally settles on his opponent, and though an inter-lude on HCE's burial will intervene, the conflict with his opponent will return to make the main subject of this chapter. This enemy is depicted here as a satanic serpent, crawling on his belly after woman's milk (see *U* 516/15.2447), and a revolutionary or fallen "engles." As a Shem figure, he resembles the satanic revolutionary Joyce, who commits the central sin of the devil by trying to assume God's position. Roland McHugh indicates that "Nash of Girahash" is based on the Hebrew for cunning (*nasha*), exile (*gur*), and silence (*hasha*).

The enemy is called "wordwounder" primarily because he hits HCE with words, a reference to the namecalling of the previous two chapters. If signifiers are phallic, to throw a name at someone is equivalent to male attack insofar as one aims at a name that will be sharp and penetrating. But each name thrown at HCE develops his identity, for as Bishop points out (131), no term for him is more than a name he is called (none being accurate), and these chapters create HCE by establishing the social threats that define him. He consists of *h*is *c*onciousness of his *e*nemies, being formed by the gaze and by the language of others. Moreover, his possible independence from these names lies in areas in which the words thrown at him cannot keep their clarity, and so he is unconscious of his own potential for opposition. Joyce recognizes his personal responsibility for the opposing force here by giving it his own Shem-like features.

The fact that HCE's mind is shaped by his society explains why he dwells not on beautiful things, but on disturbing ones. Like Bloom in "Circe," he dreams of what threatens him. In fact, he prays here that his enemy should prosper. The text goes on to describe the "distinguished dynasty" of "posteriors" that HCE wishes his wordwounder to have. His "most besetting" idea is that it should form "a truly criminal stratum," thereby (to correct the text) "eliminating [from the oppidump much desultory delinquency] from all classes" by "decasualisation" (76.2–7).[6] In "besetting" the besieged, the idea at once preoccupies him and attacks him, as does the whole final vision he settles on.

It is not enough to say that HCE wishes evil descendants on his enemy, for he prays "with unfeigned charity" (75.19) that the other should be fruitful. His puzzling desire may be explained by a theory in Freud's *Civilization and Its Discontents*—that repression takes such a toll on civilized man that he is bound to have unconscious longings to support antisocial activities. (*SE* 21:111). HCE's sociopathic promotion of a criminal class is excused by the argument that it separates vice from virtue, decasualizing evil. The rationalization that if certain people are bred as criminals, it will be easier to specify others as not being criminals seems bizarre—until one realizes that this is in fact what society does. What is thereby purified is the "oppidump," which may be not only the town (L. *oppidum*) but the Occident, that optimum dump.

The social order that turns the citizen against himself and itself is summed up in a parody of Augustine's orthodox motto, *"securus iudicat orbis terrarum,"* or 'the world [circle of the earth] judges securely.' Joyce renders this as *"sigarius* (sic!) *vindicat urbes terrorum* (sicker!)" (76.7–8). Brendan O Hehir and John Dillon (48) translate, "The assassin [*sicarius*] sets free the cities of terrors [from terrors]," but I think there may be another level. The primary meaning of *vindicare* is 'claim,' while it is the ablative and not the genitive that usually means 'from.' I read it as "Sigarius claims the cities of terror," and see it as depicting the anxious world of civilization ruled by a phallic authority. "Sicker," a parody of *"securus,"* indicates a psychiatric context—and while there may be times when it is possible to think of a cigar as merely a cigar, neither dreaming nor writing tend to be among them. Moreover, the cigar that Bello Cohen smoked in "Circe" linked the image to oppressive patriarchal authority. In the world of this paragraph, society is controlled by a big cigar that is sick, and that is all the more imperialistic for appearing in (sort of) Latin.

After this the paragraph concludes, "and so, to mark a bank taal she arter, the obedience of the citizens elp the ealth of the ole" (76.8–9). The last eleven words give the motto of Dublin in cockney, a dialect Joyce associated with the oppressors of Ireland in the "Cyclops" episode of *Ulysses* (310/12.676–78). "To mark a bank taal she arter" seems to write down an obligation on a bank tally. But it also makes a long story shorter, or a big tale, with the Dutch *taal* ('language') involved.[7] This is the correct use of language, which marks things clearly and cuts off the extra tail of meaning. So the correctness of language, which signifies the obedience of the citizen, is a castration of language's desire, and the confinement of woman to obligation ("she arter").

In his notesheets for "Cyclops," Joyce anticipated *Civilization and its Discontents* by writing, "Altruism saves race, anarchy individual, half & half" (*N* 395). From this perspective, in virtually every situation, a person compromises between serving the state and serving oneself. To serve the state is to express oneself in clear language, for the state operates on the principle that words have clear meanings that allow judgment. The language of the self, on the other hand, moves with the sliding of the signifier away from such determination.

The movement toward and away from definite meaning is a central concern from the start of I.4, which begins its effort to approach what the sleeper is thinking with an analogy: "As the lion in our teargarten remembers the nenuphars of his Nile (shall Ariuz forget Arioun or Boghas the baregams of the Marmarazalles from Marmeniere?) it may be . . . " (75.1–3).

The question of what the lion is thinking of leads to the three possibilities for the sleeper's thoughts that I have touched on, each beginning with "it may be." Though the lion seems to be a mere analogy, the distinction between analogy and reality is not clear in sleep, and the lion image recurs. It comes to refer to the position of the sleeper when it describes what a fight did to its loser: "left him lion" (99.30), and HCE is described in terms of "the tawny of his mane, the swinglowswaying bluepaw" (100.19–20). I like Adaline Glasheen's title for this chapter, "Lion" (xxxiv).

The infrahuman consciousness of animals evoked at the start of "Lion" opens up the field of the unconscious in which all things float undifferentiated. The chain of signifiers is indicated by the metonymous sound shifting of *Ariuz-Arioun, Boghas-baregams,* and *Marmazalles-Marmeniere.* All but the last of these are based on Armenian words. As Nat Halper points out, "Ancient Armenian covered the sources of the Tigris and the Euphrates. This is the traditional location of the Garden of Eden." Armenian is a language of primeval origin. As the lion (*aryuc*) will not forget blood (*aryun*), so man, that bogus bogey, will not forget the objects of sexual desire. These images take us back in the direction of drives that are formed with the earliest articulation and differentiation. The similar words also suggest (without actually embodying it) the idea that newer forms of language do not forget the older forms behind them.

"Those lililiths undeveiled" in the fifth line hark back to the "nenuphars" of the first, which are even more primal than the vagina. A passage on the nenuphar, or Egyptian lotus, from Hilda Blavatsky's *Isis Unveiled* is cited by McHugh in another context: "Wherever the mystic water-lily (lotus) is employed, it signifies the emanation of the objective from the concealed, or subjective—the eternal thought of the ever-invisible Deity passing from the abstract into the concrete or visible form" (*Sigla* 111).

Passage from the subjective to the objective represents birth, and so the lotus from which Brahma created the world in Hindu myth, which Blavatsky sees as the same lily the angel hands Mary at the Annunciation (I 93), is a symbol of the womb. This is the underside or inside of the popular association of the lily with purity. The lion is remembering the source in which he floated: the Nile often stands for the source of civilization or life in the *Wake,* and this is "his Nile." He remembers this flow-ering as he lies trapped in the "teargarten," a German zoo (*Tiergarten*) or English garden of tears, which is both his body and his place in civilization.

The vaginal "lililiths" are conceived of as a secondary, external version of the womb. Lacan says that the imaginary organ that all sex aims at is the lamella, which has the form of the amniotic sac, the timeless, floating enclosure lost in birth (*Four* 198–200). Although it is the focus of vision, the vagina evades vision because it leads to a vanishing point, a gap, the dissolution of the visual faculty in the womb. The labia lead back before language, and Lilith was Adam's mistress before the written history of Genesis. This object cannot be seen, and "undeveiled" is a trick word that seems to reveal, but ends up covering again with a double negative. As Derrida points out, the hymen never disappears.

In the following version of the womb, fertility has been rendered mythological and contained in a structure (the Symbolic) that can only allow something to appear by hiding its inner reality: Ysit "shamed and shone" because she has been divided into two sides, the hidden adiaphane and the ostensible diaphane. These conflicting sides lead to the battle between Shem and Shaun, the main subject of the chapter. With this conflict as subject, HCE assumes his identity as "he conscious of enemies" (75.15).

The four choices through which the paragraph moves are versions of the same subject. As they move from inner to outer, they go from a remembered expansion without form or content to a specific present and future political situation filled with conflict. Freud points out that we can never be sure of what our dreams consisted, but only of what we remember of them (*SE* 4:43). In this passage, the earlier, vaguer possibilities are closer to the open potentiality of dream, but the last one sticks in the mind because it engages opposing forces to articulate consciousness. This consciousness is the shaped dream that rises out of the shapeless unconscious. Throughout mental life, day and night, the shape of conscious vision remains an imposition on the dynamic inner reality of feeling it reveals and conceals.

The opening paragraph, then, traces the assemblage of consciousness as the formation of a vision, making what is visible depend on the interaction of conflicting forces. These forces are articulated most actively as Shem and Shaun, so that consciousness and being are mediated by the masculine conflict at the heart of politics as an externalization of internal process. To create environment (and *H*owth *C*astle needs *E*nvirons), the subject must take on language, and when it does so, it is made subject to language's system of oppositions.

The subject can only exist in words that refer to an unknowable reality in the field of the Other (the totality of language). This is the central defect that desire strives to overcome in every language, including action. It corresponds to what the *Wake* calls "the first riddle of the universe: . . . when is a man not a man?" (170.4–5). When he exists only by expressing something else. When HCE assumes articulation as a speaking being, he is written by another, an intelligence beyond his knowledge. Insofar as his author tries to clarify him—and it cannot help trying to do so as part of the process of forming every word—it denies the inner level of early associations represented by the lotus.

The War in the Word, or *Moi* [tt] and *Je* [ff]

In the second paragraph, the Shaunian narrator tries to leave abstractions behind and return to reality: "Now gode. Let us leave theories there and return to here's here" (76.10–11). The irony is that the "reality" he grabs hold of is built on the development of the first paragraph and is only a dream. In fact, at this point the narrator, in turning from the hypothetical to the declarative, is swallowed by the dream. His assumption that he has a grasp on reality is the prime sign of his delusion. In dream as in Lacan, it is uncertainty that leads to the waking of truth.

Striving for hard realism, the narrator now launches into an elaborate technological description of how HCE was buried in an undersea chamber (76–78). Emphasizing "materially effecting the cause" (76.13) with images of military-industrial engineering, this passage shows in detail how society is designed to bury the unconscious. In the same section, "any number" of public bodies and committees vote HCE and themselves out of existence, illustrating the public denial of the self (76.14–18). Of course he burrows out before long (78.9), and the repressed returns as a series of conflicts, conflicts defined as forming the subject through interpretation. As on the first page, the formation of a conscious self inevitably occasions conflicts between unconscious and conscious, and these conflicts will tend to be acted out by HCE's sons.

Shem and Shaun are always presented as involved in perception, for one of the strongest distinctions between them links Shem to hearing and time, which are understood to be internal, and Shaun to seeing and space. Both sides are constantly found not only in human consciousness, but in the word, for every word is both heard in time and seen in space. It is essential to a word to sustain both levels, whether it be written or spoken. The spoken word imitates the clarity of writing, a clarity that may be linked to consciousness; while the written word imitates the vitality of speech, a vitality that Lacan made virtually equivalent to the unconscious. This is one way in which Shem and Shaun, as sound and sight, compete in every word. Shem tends to represent the unstable, unconscious aspect of self that Lacan refers to as the *moi*, or subject of being, while Shaun tends to be the conscious aspect, or subject of speech.[8] This distinction has a parallel on the visual level of the split between the eye and the gaze.

Bishop presents Shaun the watcher as the figure through whom we see what is visible. Shem, on the other hand, tends to want to sink toward darkness, yet it is out of this darkness that Shem, as the "Autist" (434.35), actually projects what Shaun sees (Bishop 236, 247). In terms used earlier, the guilty Shem is seen by the gaze and sends out vision, while Shaun ("Show'm the Posed," 92.13) is seen by vision and sends out the gaze of social disapproval. Thus the circuit involved in every image is a combination of "shamed and shone." Kimberly Devlin shows that the sense of shame is entirely dependent on a sense of being seen ("See ourselves" 883), and Shem, who is depicted by Shaun, is continually under investigation.

As Bishop indicates, both brothers are essential components of sight (236–40), and they add up to something equivalent to the *point de capiton*. As watching agency, Shaun tends to limit sight, while Shem, as artist, opens up new possibilities of vision. These roles correspond respectively to the authoritative subject of speaking (*je*) and the narcissistic subject of being (*moi*). In a passage that fits Joyce, Ragland-Sullivan uses the distinction to explain Lacan's style: " . . . subjective perception—the *moi*—is elusive, kaliedoscopic, and evanescent, whereas the subject of meaning and speech—the *je*—seeks to "translate" the *moi* while adhering to cultural stipulations. To convey this idea of two modes of meaning fighting to occupy the same space, Lacan frustrates his interlocutors by stylistically holding meaning in suspension . . . " (43).

Shem corresponds to the elusive, subjective *moi,* while Shaun is the *je* that tries to contain the *moi* within cultural stipulations. "Two modes of meaning fighting to occupy the same space" form the subject at the center of this chapter. Images of the split subject and the circuit of vision are used here to show how Shem and Shaun develop out of HCE. They also develop into him, for run-ins between the twins have the effect of adding up to HCE.

Lacan represents the subject of being (*moi*) and the subject of speech (*je*) on one of his main diagrams in such a way as to indicate that they do not relate to each other directly. They can only make contact with each other by passing through otherness, either through the *objet a* or through the Other.[9] The idea of Shem and Shaun connected by otherness appears most prominently in the repeated image of the brothers as two banks with a river between them. Everything flows between their margins in the Study Chapter (II.2), where they appear as notes on either side of each page. Explaining their roles in Latin, this chapter refers to *"ripis rivalibus"* ('banks that share the same stream,' 287.28). The otherness of the river between them is indicated succinctly in I.6. The Mookse (Shaun) finds the Gripes (Shem) on the other side of a stream that focuses his attention on the Other, "the most unconsciously boggylooking stream he ever locked his eyes with" (153.3–4).

If Shaun and Shem are fighting, it is obvious that they are not in contact with each other. They are joined to each other through an irrational complex of emotions they are not in control of. This seems to have been the model for all connections between men in Joyce, as Ellmann says: "Relations between men, he felt, must inevitably have this coloration of uncertainty, jealousy, hostility, and affection; the usual name for this hodge-podge was friendship" (*JJ* 312).

The hostility between men fits in with the idea of secondary identification as discrimination. Men in Joyce make contact with each other through the catalyst of the feminine, as Bloom and Stephen may get together through Molly. In the present chapter, however, the image of the Other that I am concerned with is not a river, but a gap.

The Hole in the Wall

To show how the description of the fight in "Lion" suggests forces struggling to define vision, I will begin with the location of the bout. Kate Strong testifies that it took place where the road "left off, being beaten, where the plaintiff was struck" (80.4). The conflict takes place at the end of the road, on the margin where chaos begins to become civilization. The phrase "being beaten" may indicate that the road was defeated by disorder, but it does seem to suggest by parallelism that the beating of the plaintiff is equivalent to the striking of the road.

On the following page the narrator says that the battle took place "versts from true civilisation, not where his dreams top their traums halt (Beneathere! Benathere!)" (81.15–16). This is where trams do not stop, but it is also below the level of dreams, in the dreamless sleep state where the mind floats without bearings. It is inside Howth Hill (*Beinn Éadair* in Irish), which is equated with the head of the sleeper. But it also refers to an undifferentiated inner realm of primary thinking out of which dreams arise: here the status of anything is to "be neither." And consciousness comes from a place where it does not exist, where it is "not there." In answering the question of where being originates, Lacan describes the place of the Other in terms that remind me of the Kabbalah: " 'I' am in the place from which a voice is heard clamouring 'the universe is a defect in the purity of Non-Being' " (*Selection* 317, *É* 819).

Lacan says that the movement of desire encircles the *objet a* in order to attain "the dimension of the capital Other" (*Four* 194). This is one reason why Issy, as the object of desire, usually appears in Shaun's corner when Shem and Shaun argue; but it also helps to explain another feature of some run-ins of the twins, the hole in the wall. Historically, the Hole in the Wall was a pub near Phoenix Park, but this should not keep its name from having other meanings.[10] The circuit of desire in Lacan passes through the rim, a circular opening that penetrates the interface between self and other, or inside and outside (*Four* 178, 194). We look at the boundary between inside and outside when we look at our eyelids, so that in sleep the rim is projected before us on the field of vision.

The conflict at the center of "Lion" is located again by the main witness in the trial that reviews and reenacts that conflict. This witness is called W. P. (witness for the prosecution or "Wet Pinter"), and his identity shifts. As he is telling how one Hyacinth O'Donnell (87.13) attacked two kings, and he starts to report what Hyacinth was asked at the scene of the crime, this interrogation takes his place. For the balance of his testimony, W. P. turns into a questioning of Hyacinth. As at the beginning of the chapter the speaker was taken over by the answer to a question he asked, so here he is taken over by a questioning he reports.

The back-and-forth action of the questioning repeats the action of the fight. Tindall (88) points out that O'Donnell, as a "mixer [fighter] and wordpainter" (87.13), combines both Shaun and Shem, and therefore he is HCE. At the thought of the old crime, the prosecution witness (Shaun) turns into his father, and so he is "patrified to see, hear, taste and smell, as his time of night" (87.11–12) how the attack took place. Entering a sort of dark night of the soul, he is overwhelmed by the action on many levels and it makes up his world of sleep. The way he returns to the father by going back to the fight suggests that the father is made up of conflict, as a number of titles for God in the book suggest: "Foughtarundser" (78.16, based on the German *Vaterunser,* or 'our father'), for example, or "In the name of the former and of the latter and of their holocaust. Allmen" (419.9–10). The origin of being is the conflict between new and old ideas represented by "Lion."

In the question-and-answer sequence involving Hyacinth, he is asked if the attack was about a conflict between brothers. His reply folds into the give-and-take so that it is actually given by his questioner: "About that and the other. If he was not alluding to the whole in the wall? That he was when he was not eluding from the whole of the woman" (90.20–22). It may be because the gap and the movement through it constitute personality that the hole is the whole. And it is both the opening in a woman and the passage to another level "such as turly pearced our really's" (90.30, a reference to Persse O'Reilly, one of HCE's names). Discourse is a back-and-forth movement in this passage, alluding to specific meaning, but eluding it. These forces are represented by the split in the narration between question and answer. In fact, the passage indicates that if a man does not allude to the hole, he is eluding woman. Lacan says that perception of the female genitals is confrontation with a lack that constitutes the subject as a symbolic representation (*FS* 113). This hole corresponds to the black dot at the end of "Ithaca."

The origin of the wall itself appears in the first chapter, where Finnegan, the archaic form of HCE, is a hod carrier who spends his time making walls. "(There was a wall of course in erection)" (6.9). The wall expresses phallic pride here, and it is bound to lead to a fall. The masculine structure of logic and language has to be breached because it is written over reality. As the latest form of the veil of appearances, the wall is more rigid, but also more penetrable and artificial. From the perspective of the *Wake,* the material world is a facade that does not sustain interest. As HCE's ancestor who formed the existing world, Finn tends to stand for the author, so it is logical that his wall is linked to writing.

In "Freud and the Scene of Writing," Derrida argues that all perception is based on a model of writing in which every new image has to conflict with and try to fit into an established trace. (*Writing* 196–231). An earlier reference to the hole in the wall presents this scene of back-and-forth strokes as the scene of writing: "Now by memory inspired, turn wheel again to the whole of the wall. Where Gyant Blyant fronts Peannlueamoore. There was once upon a wall and a hooghoog wall a was and such a wallhole did exist" (69.5–8).

This passage suggests that the whole wall is a hole, a hole approached by a circuit ("wheel"). At this hole we find the mirroring of a giant pencil. McHugh indicates that *blyant* is Danish for 'pencil' and *peann-luaidhe mór* is

Gaelic for 'big pencil.' Joyce regarded Scandinavians and Celts as the two main groups that merged in the Irish. The opposing mirror-pencils represent writing as composed of conflicting forces. If we wonder where the pencil comes from, it seems relevant that the last sentence echoes the opening of *Portrait:* "Once upon a time and a very good time it was . . . " The pencil comes from the artist.

The hole reaches outside the world to the source of creation. Here the subject of being (*moi*) and the subject of speech (*je*) make contact with each other through the Other. Another name for the location of the conflict is "Guinney's Gap" (90.13), a reference to the Ginnungagap or Great Void of the Eddas. Campbell and Robinson describe it as "the interval of timeless formlessness between world aeons" (46). It is here, according to Scandinavian myth, that the world was made from the dead body of a hermaphroditic giant, Ymir. In this creation, "the sparking of life" came "from the cataclysmic fusion of the twin polarities of fire and frost" (Magnusson 44, 47). In Joyce's "ginnandgo gap" (14.16), there can be no light without conflict: "Let there be fight?" (90.12).

Internal Competition

What happens in the fight is very hard to determine. The description of it begins with the statement that "the attackler . . . engaged the Adversary" (81.18–19), which immediately obscures who is responsible by making both men antagonists. In the first version of this argument (*FW* 35–36), HCE (who is probably the "Adversary" in I.4) assumed he was attacked when the Cad greeted him in distorted Gaelic, thereby demonstrating that the attacked can be the attacker. Moreover, the antagonists change identities frequently with the appearance of phrases like these:

> . . . the same man (or a different and younger him of the same ham) asked . . . (82.10–11)

> the wartrophy eluded at some lives earlier (83.14)

These changes imply about the figures before us both that they are phantasms of the sleeping mind and that they return through history. When the trial takes place, there is no indication that any of the parties in the court have any particular connection to those in the original incident. One of Joyce's points seems to be that in your effort to find the truth about people, you tend to be working with a different truth today than you were working with yesterday.

If the battle represents the inner struggle out of which the subject is formed in Lacanian terms, it should center on castration as physical equivalent to the lack in the gap. In fact, the turning point in the conflict seems to occur when "a woden affair in the shape of a webley (we at once recognize our old friend Ned of so many illortemporate letters) fell from the intruser who ... (did the imnage of Girl Cloud Pensive flout above them ... ?) whereupon became friendly ... " (82.16–20).

The "intruser" seems to be the Cad, and a son attacking the father tends to find himself disarmed. In *Portrait,* for example, as Stephen is daydreaming about strangling an old man, Stephen suddenly turns benign: " ... with him I must struggle ... till he or I lie dead, gripping him by the sinewy throat till ... [Joyce's ellipsis] Till what? Till he yield to me? No. I mean him no harm" (*P* 252).

In "Lion" the wooden gun (Webley) that falls is designated as phallic by the phrase "our old friend Ned." On the following page, it may be "a coctable" (83.15). This phallus is bad tempered as "illortemporate," but it is also the Logos, the authority behind the Gospel readings that begin *"In illo tempore"* ('at that time,' identified in McHugh). The son's attempt to kill the father is an attempt to become God, or Woden. The gun is also a signifier "of so many ... letters."

The anxiety of being separated from this phallic signifier presses the fighters into an uneasy and short-lived friendship. As this happens, the "Girl Cloud" of Issy flouts above them, so they are reconciled through the Other. But even before they make up, their conflict involves them in a larger entity, the structure of their interaction: "The pair ... struggled appairently for some considerable time, (the cradle rocking equally to one and oppositely from the other on its law of capture and recapture), under the All In rules ... (81.33–82.2).

This refers to Bruno's idea of equal opposites, which is emphasized at the end of the trial. As Joyce put it in a letter, " ... every power in nature must evolve an opposite in order to realize itself ... " (*Letters* 1:226). The fight passage suggests balance, but that is undercut by the imbalance between "to one" and "from the other," suggesting that such arrangements need not be fair. The idea that self is realized by fighting is suggested by images of the pair making a parent and of the rocking cradle. They create each other through the rigorous definitions of hostility, as a later description of the anger of the brothers suggests: " ... And each was wrought with his other" (252.14). And by creating each other, they create functions of the mind of the sleeping giant and his book.

Good indications of how these functions work appear in the sixth or "Questions" chapter (I.6), and in the ninth question of this chapter, which is widely regarded as describing the *Wake.* This passage explains what could be seen in "an earsighted view of old hopeinhaven" (143.10). Joyce regarded hearing as an interior sense, so this line suggests an inside view of hope in its haven—which is also a view of a beautiful city (Copenhagen). Here one sees "all the ingredient and egregiunt whights and ways" (143.11), men and paths coming and going, as one would see in a city or in a mind linked to many circuits. The ways in which the mind "recourses" (143.12) through its history are presented as follows: " . . . the reverberration of knotcracking awes, the reconjugation of nodebinding ayes, the redissolusingness of mindmouldered ease and thereby hang the Hoel of it . . . "(143.12–15).

This "earsighted view" suggests an alternation of ears and eyes, corresponding to Shem and Shaun. Bishop points out that sound tends to be more unstable and unconscious than sight because sounds cannot be located or fixed (287–88). The ears, linked to Shem, tend to break words down into unstable sounds, so that they crack the knots that bind words together, suggesting reverses and errors by their reverberations. The eyes, linked to Shaun, see words clearly, rejoining their knots and binding them. But then the ears dissolve them again. Thus, words are taken apart and put together again in a continuous cycle with a hole hanging near it.

This process anticipates current neuropsychological research, which sees language as formed by different areas of the brain working simultaneously, some of them involving sight, and others, hearing.[11] To give an arbitrary suggestion of such complexity, the reading of one word might involve three different areas of the brain that work on visual material and two that work on auditory, as well as other channels, such as memory. Such a redundant procedure is bound to involve competition, and a current theory of neural Darwinism holds that images that reach consciousness are selected from a large number of competitors.[12] All of this is in line with Freud's idea of overdetermination and with Lacan's complicated knot constructs.

Shem and Shaun, as personalities that operate at the gap where language originates, can be linked to the two lobes of the brain. Experiments have shown that these lobes have opposed personalities, but they interact to form consciousness (Geschwind 224–26). Shem may be linked to the right lobe of the brain and feeling, while Shaun relates to the left lobe and logic. "Lion," the first chapter in which the twins are clearly differentiated, is a study of the divisions in HCE, and these are reflected through a series of images of language that expresses more than one speaker at once.

While puns and portmanteau words are the major means in the *Wake* of giving language multiple levels, a number of other patterns are added to those here. Translation, for example, expresses two mentalities at once, and Ezra Pound's Chinese translation is used to depict HCE with a tongue speaking one language and a jaw speaking another: "A maundarin tongue in a pounderin jowl? Father ourder about the mathers of prenanciation"

(89.24–26). The answer carries on the ideas of "mau" and "pou" in the question. The meandering mother tongue is linked to the kabbalist MacGregor Mathers and to the occult world that precedes definite forms. The father, as forthright as big-jawed Ezra, puts language in order. Speech has to combine a solid structure that closes where it opened with another part that is flexible to a degree that tends to be obscene when it becomes visible.

The "tongue in . . . jowl" passage, which is based on "tongue in cheek," an idiom for irony, is a solid example of the Wakean theme that all discourse involves both a masculine side and a feminine one: " . . . every telling has a taling and that's the he and the she of it" (213.12). The masculine side of narrative here is more directly relatable to the mathematical etymology of the word *tell* as 'recount.' But the feminine side, "taling," not only carries the less-than-true connotations of *tale,* but suggests a tail, something extra that hangs on the end of a story irrationally.

The passage goes on to play with references to Ogham, one of the languages Joyce learned about from R. A. S. Macalister's *The Secret Languages of Ireland.* This Druid code was written in marks alternating above and below a horizontal line, so Ogham is a model of language formed on two sides of a central division. After this, the question and answer (also on either side of a division) are "Hokey jasons, then, in a pigeegeeses? On a pontiff's order as ture as there's an ital on atac" (89.34–35). Epexegesis is adding a word or words to a statement to clarify or modify it. This is what Derrida calls a *supplément,* and it has the effect of contradicting the original statement. That is, if I say, "A tall blond man," and then, "A tall blond man with a pig," the pig causes a change in the man; and Festy King, the main defendant of the trial, is alleged to have been with a pig, presumably a pigeegeeses (and a hyacinth, 86.14). Even such a slight change as putting something in *ital*ics can make it go against its original meaning, or change its reference; so that the tail is on the attack as sure as it is on a cat. The line also implies a head on a tack, which becomes untrue when it turns into a tail. Every perception is a conflict between the new, supplementary impression that arrives and the established trace into which it must fit. By going beyond, every supplement forms a loop through which new and old interact. No matter how thoroughly the new image either is subsumed by the old one or overwhelms it, they both continue to change each other.

Since the Pope gives the word of God, the tail on a "pontiff's" bull goes lolly or hangs loose (lolls) on the end of the Deity, "As a gololy bit to a joss?" (89.35–36). Joyce uses *joss,* the pidgin word for a household deity, five times in the *Wake,* usually with divine overtones (177.6, 472.15, 611.14, 27), punning on his name. A joss is also an incense stick, and as such, it can have a little burnt part drooping at the top; but as it burns, this grey tail may grow bigger than the body. Similarly, Joyce's work began as an extension or appendage of his life, but as his career progressed, the part of him consumed in his work came to dominate the rest of his life. The truth of the work is an interplay between the written supplement and its creator, both changing each other as they proceed. In fact, the passage I am examining (89.24–26, 89.29–90.1) is itself an epexegesis, having been added to the fourth chapter a decade after an early version of I.4 appeared in *Transition* (1927) (*JJA* 46:185, 49:412–13). It changes the chapter by adding emphasis to the idea of the new transforming the old.

The unfaithful nature of truth, the fact that it changes constantly, is demonstrated by the next phrase, "Leally and tululy," which asserts loyalty to two different women, Leah and Tallulah.[13] This line is a not-very-sophisticated version of Japanese-English dialect. In relation to China, Japan was originally a cultural and geographic tail, curling off the mainland at Korea. But eventually, Japan became more advanced, so that the tail wagged the cat.

"But, why this hankowchaff and whence this second tone, son-yet-sun?" (89.36–90.1)? The Hankow chap, Sun-Yat-Sen, may be equated as a rebel with Shem, who later appears as a handkerchief picked up from the riverbank (158.34). The central Chinese city of Hankow, which was taken by Japan in 1938, the year this passage was added, had installed Sun-Yat-Sen's revolutionary government in 1911. The Republic of China was a historical epexegesis that tried to transform the country, the new voice ("second tone') of a follower ("son") that became a leader ("sun").

The Vanishing Verdict

The significance of the idea of epexegesis can be understood in a Lacanian context. The identifications that a child takes on seem to supplement his well-being, but he is really taken over by these extensions, so that finally the source of his being lies in the Other and his identity is external to him. As a result, even the highest achievement of the human spirit, such as sacrificing oneself for mankind, is only an "apexojesus" that does not really belong to its achiever; and the same alienation applies to the most intimate parts of one's body, which are what the context of "apexojesus" indicates, for it is a point on the diagram of ALP in the Study chapter (296.10). In this sense Joyce's work no more belongs to him than his personal life—except insofar as he makes this dispersal his own discovery and creation.

Conflict with others, which is the central subject of "Lion," is presented here as lacking a logical basis because it is really internal. Its main purpose is to deny that one is ruled by the Other, and the points of pride people quarrel over tend to be defenses of this impossible goal. On an internal level, the trial that tries to understand the initial conflict corresponds to the cognition that follows perception. But the trial ends up repeating the conflict because the subject can only be expressed in oppositions. There can be no verdict of resolution.

Norris argues that the attempt to separate oneself from the Other is a great source of hostility in the *Wake* (*Decentered* 77), and this principle explains many features of the trial. When, as I have shown, W. P., the accuser, turns in effect into Hyacinth O'Donnell, the accused, this is a sign that the two are really the same, both parts of one dreamer. And when the trial climaxes with the "loudburst" of Pegger ('thrower') Festy, who swears by everything he can think of that he never threw a stone, the dreamer is finally denying that he attacked himself. Perhaps the most painful feeling behind any of our afflictions is the sense that somehow we caused them ourselves, and this feeling results from our attachment to the Other.

Pegger, "the senior king of all" (90.36–91.1), seems to be the same man as Festy King. As this "testifighter" (92.4) concludes, his protestations break out of proper language or Castilian and he makes everyone follow him into a vulgar Spanish pot of rank stew: (" . . . in his excitement the laddo had broken exthro Castilian into which the whole audience perseguired and pursuited him *olla podrida*) outbroke much yellachters . . . " (91.36–92.3).

The *olla podrida* is their embarrassment over his protestations, which are in themselves vehement enough to show he is wrong: he cannot stop pegging. They laugh partly because they are disturbed. And Festy, like Robin at the end of Hawthorne's "My Kinsman, Major Molineux," is "reluctingly" (92.4) obliged to join the laughter despite his opposition. The criticism of the crowd represents the gaze and the Other, and this is not the only level on which Festy is joining his opposite.

As the trial ends, the voices of the defendent Festy and the witness for the prosecution are indistinguishable from each other. Here Joyce plays on Bruno's motto, *"In Tristitia Hilaris Hilaritate Tristis"* ('In sadness mirth; in mirth, sadness,' cited by McHugh): "The hilariohoot of Pegger's Windup cumjustled as neatly with the tristitone of the Wet Pinter's as were they *isce et ille* ['this and that'] equals of opposites, evolved by a onesame power of nature or of spirit, *iste* ['that'], as the sole condition and means of its himundher manifestation and polarized for reunion by the symphysis of their antipathies" (92.6–11).

McHugh shows that most of this is based on the summary of Bruno's theory by Coleridge cited in my Introduction. Pegger's Windup may be that of a baseball pitcher, but it connects to a motif of getting the wind up, which primarily means being frightened.[14] The complementary mingling of their "laughtears" (15.9) is a sign that P. W. and W. P. cannot exist without each other, that an action by one is a reaction by the other. Manifestation takes place between the two, and what is manifested is a power that involves the whole family: it expresses both brothers interacting and includes both genders, "himundher."

The larger "power of nature or of spirit" that they manifest must be related to the dreamer of whom they are parts. In mentioning this power the narrator, leaning on Bruno, is assuming the ability to see beyond life, and it hardly seems ironic. The other end of the narrative has become visible, but then it tends to appear in dream. If I dream of a conversation or conflict, I have to be speaking, and therefore thinking, all parts. But I cannot be conscious of thinking for two minds at once, even though every thought I have is addressed by someone to someone else within. Family, society, and education render me addicted to the idea of unified personality, and terrified to inhabit my contradictions—but then I dream.

One of the most common features of dream is revelation (unveiling). This means, for example, that I can hear someone else say something that surprises me in dream and then awake to confirm that it came from "another"—that is, it was something I did not know before. What happens here is that the Other shows itself. The moment at which Festy and the Witness fuse is a "symphysis" ('growing together') in which the parts of the dreamer sense the totality in which they are joined. This growth is not a synthesis, for it is dynamic and does not last. Of the various images of fusion in Joyce, the one this resembles most is the scene in the "Sirens" episode in which Bloom and Simon Dedalus are joined in the sound of a song (*U* 274–76/11.695–754).

Lacan says that "in the so-called waking state [*dans l'etat dit de veille*], there is an elision of the gaze" (*Four* 75; *Quatre* 72). In dream, however, the unstable essence of the gaze shows itself (*Four* 76). When Choang-tsu dreams he is a butterfly, it means that he sees the focus of perception fluttering in its reality as gaze (*Four* 76). Lacan also says here that Freud's Wolf Man was frightened by a butterfly because "the beating [or 'pulsation,' *battement*] of little wings is not so very far from the beating of causation." These are images of the fluttering of the veil that convey to the waking mind the inexpressible idea of the gaze showing itself.

If my mind shifts from being my own to being someone else's, the blinding jump involved in that transition brings the mind that passes through it into contact with a higher level of mind that is able to contain both. Similarly, sudden jumps from one level of reality or language to another evoke the power that exerts these transitions. The constant transformation of perspective in the *Wake*—often from one word to the next and within each word—is like the butterfly in exerting a fascination that lures one beyond the veil: "What are so many figures, so many shapes, so many colours, if not this gratuitous *showing* [*ce* donner à voir *gratuit*], in which is marked for us the primal nature of the essence of the gaze" (*Four* 76; *Quatre* 72).

If one approaches seeing the Other in dream, such a vision cannot be sustained, at least not to waking (*veille*) knowledge. In what we know of dream, "It shows—but here, too, some form of 'sliding away' of the subject is apparent" (*Four* 75). Once a glimpse of the power behind manifestation has been given, the two brothers separate, but they have been decisively transformed by their contact with the Other. In fact, they have taken on their identities, for Shem and Shaun are first named here (94.11–12), and after their "cumjustle" (a word with sexual overtones), they begin playing their typical roles, which were not nearly so clear before. Shaun, the "willingly pressed" (W. P., 92.14), is adored by the girls, while Shem (Festy) disgraces himself and withdraws into art (93).

The verdict of the court seems to confirm the mingling of Shem and Shaun that took place at the climax I have described. The four old "justicers" (92.35) represent justice as the way it "just is," and have no power to originate. If the shift from the fight to the trial went from perception to cognition, the part of the chapter after the trial seems to concentrate on memory. The old men can "do no worse than promulgate their standing verdict of Nolans Brumans" (92.36–93.1). I take this to mean, 'Not willing in a fog,' for *nolens* is legal Latin for 'unwilling' and *la brume* is French for 'fog, haze, uncertainty.' It also refers to the logic of Bruno of Nola, whereby any distinction is inseparable from its opposite.

The striving of each of the twins to differentiate himself from the other and assign responsibility seems to be defeated by this judgment of confusion; but the actual differentiation of the twins arises from their dependence on each other. They can no more be separated than time, which is linked to Shem, and space, which is linked to Shaun. (Neither time nor space can be defined without referring to its opposing mode.) When they recognize that they are inseparable, each articulates himself by interaction with the other, and so they are "polarized" by their "symphysis" (92.10). This follows Hegel's dialectic, with its emphasis on the idea that something can only form itself through its opposite so that "the Thing has its essential being in another Thing" (*PS* 76).

The contact of the twins with the Other that climaxes with the overlapping interception of the trial has powerful formative effects because it connects them to the source of their creation. Not only do Shem and Shaun appear, but Shem tends to become Joyce, and the letter that stands for the book takes on a more definite form than it has yet had, both here and in the following "Letter" chapter (I.5).

While there are many autobiographical references throughout the *Wake*, the paragraph that begins with the passing of the verdict has so many that Festy seems to turn into Joyce as he turns into Shem, a combination indicated by the final word of the paragraph, "Shames!" (93.20). Most of these biographical references are cited by Susan Swartzlander (473–75). Joyce's attack on established language is represented by Festy's "having murdered all the English he knew" (93.2). McHugh indicates that *tomme lommer* is Danish for 'empty pockets,' so Joyce mocks his own improvidence (93.3). Festy is a "firewaterloover" (.7), issues "gash from a burner" (.11), and is a "Parish [Paris] Poser" (.14) with "all the wrong donatrices," a reference to the curious group of patronesses who supported Joyce.

Festy as Shem is also seen "showing off the blink pitch to his britgits to prove himself (an't plase yous!) a rael genteel" (93.4–5). This suggests that when Joyce wore an eye patch, he felt as if he were posing as a British gentleman. Moreover, this relates to the later phrase "the blinkpoint of so eminent a spatialist" (149.18). Festy, like any writer, has a point of view, though in keeping with the theory of the gaze, his point of view is a blink: where he looks from cannot be seen. Or what looks through him cannot be seen, and yet there are many clues to its identity.

The Winking Blinkpoint

The letter generated by the trial is the *Wake* itself and the discourse of human history generated by the conflict between the subject of speaking and the subject of being. With the end of the trial, " . . . everybody heard their plaint and all listened to their plause. The letter!" (93.22–23). The letter or signifier is constituted by the plaint of Shem and the applause of the plausible Shaun in everyone; and for the balance of this page, everyone contributes his little bit of song to the letter.

The letter binds all members of the family together: "It made ma merry and sissy so shy and rubbed some shine off Shem and put some shame into Shaun" (94.10–12). It seems to embody a process whereby each gives qualities to her or his opposite; but at the center of it is a gap or blink point, the artist's point of view.

> What was it?
> A . . . . !
> ? . . . . 0 ! (94.20–22)

The narrator starts to say what it is, and then there is a blank that calls out the response of "O!" which may itself stand for the unknown. This unspeakable center is the sin, split in the veil, or displacement of frame that generates what can be seen of the difference between words or family members. Within this difference they interact. "And that was how framm [frame] Sin fromm Son, acity arose . . . " (94.18). Yet this gap of sin also carries the sign of alpha and omega, the beginning and the end, which is linked to "jas jos."[15] This sin goes back to the sin that Stephen used to separate parts of his being and create himself in *Portrait.* Those earlier sins are behind the use of sin and the reference to it here and throughout the *Wake.* Sin is the area in which Joyce the *sinthome* works.

The place of the Other is approached at the point of the unknown, the emptiness in the "O." Norris says of the point of view in the *Wake,* "The vantage point of the work is not an area of consciousness, but rather is a place where the unconscious—the essentially 'unknowable' self—tries to communicate with the dreamer's conscious self" (99). As this point of the Other is approached, the mental agents of the *Wake* run into conflicts that define and develop them. These conflicts act as *points de capiton* to form the subject of Joyce as a series of verbal connections.

A great enlargement of vision results from the conflict of this chapter. This vision stands in contrast to the four old men, whose attempts to go over the case on the next few pages can only distort things in senile rambling. Yet they contribute to the vision by evoking the depth of time and the obscurity of the mind. The realization that follows from the trial is a negative reaction to this obfuscation. A narrator breaks into their drivel with "Well?" (96.25). This narrator resembles Shaun in that he claims authority, but something that knows more than he does speaks through him, a negative authority that seems real and Joycean. Nothing could be more personal to Joyce than this negation, and there is no greater assertion of his creative power:

> Well, even should not the framing up of such figments in the evidential order bring the true truth to light as fortuitously as a dim seer's setting of a starchart might (heaven helping it!) uncover the nakedness of an unknown body in the fields of blue or as forehearingly as the sibspeeches of all mankind have foliated (earth seizing them!) from the root of some funner's stotter all the soundest sense to be found immense our special mentalists now holds (*securus iudicat orbis terrarum*) that by such playing possum our hagious curious encestor bestly saved his brush with his postcrity, you, charming coparcenors, us, heirs of his tailsie. (96.26–35)

In this sentence, as skeptical as anything in the *Wake,* the evidence from the trial and subsequent tellings is a scattering of figments framed arbitrarily. In fact, the original manuscript of 1923 was even more skeptical, giving "fictions" for "figments" and "any truth" for "truc truth" (*JJA* 46:51). The evidence is less likely to reveal the truth than someone with poor eyesight making a chart of the sky is likely to discover a new heavenly body—or someone who has never seen a woman's body (with "blue" as 'obscene'), to draw it nude (or make a blueprint of it).

The remarkable turn after "blue" indicates that it is just as unlikely that the languages of humanity could discover reality by arising haphazardly from ignorance through desire. All language begins by being focused on the *objet a,* in this case, the genitals of a farmer's daughter, which correspond to the gap of embarrassment that can make a man filled with desire ("funner") stutter.[16] All languages are brothers (sibs) because they have unfolded in folly from this root, being seized by the mater-ial attractions of earth. They were no more forehearing of what they would describe than the dim seer foresaw. And yet everything known, all the soundest sense, has foliated through them, for we do not know anything that is not expressed in language. I assume that "all the soundest sense" starts out as the object of "foliated," though it ends up beginning a new clause.

Joyce refers in the *Wake* to Pope's distinction in "An Essay on Criticism" between sound and sense (121.15, 522.29). Therefore "the soundest sense" (which was originally "soundest opinion" in the manuscript) is a confusion of two different things, suggesting that the sense of language can never be sound (valid) because it is always subject to feeling. The opposition between sound and sense corresponds to the one between the poet Shem and the rational Shaun.

There is no unified sound sense, then, and the fact that its judgment is supported by *"securus iudicat orbis terrarum"* only confirms that it is conventional. The passage insists on the Lacanian principle that there is no necessary connection between language and what it represents. Thus all of the origins that language tries to convey—the facts of history and the identity or identities of its author(s)—are unreachable. The effect of this sundering of language from truth is like that of the defeat of the tower of Babel, and it is by the analogy with Babel that we can understand how Joyce is playing a godlike role here.

Derrida says that Joyce, in arranging difficulties of interpretation, left his followers "an institution that, like God with the tower of Babel, he has done everything to render impossible and improbable in its source, to deconstruct it in advance."[17] Like the God of Babel, Joyce has left his followers drifting among fragments of a truth that can never be put together, that was never coherent, the truth of language. For Joyce to do this, however, is to claim virtually absolute authority, to speak for the Other. On an intellectual level, God's dissemination of his language at Babel is the maximum assertion of his power in history. The more unknowable He is, the more He inhabits the powers of the Other in everyone: the powers to create language and to multiply interpretation. By preserving the gap of his ineffability, he maintains an ability to bring people and words together to generate fruitful conflict. What is withheld remains as source.

The clause that turns out to start with "all the soundest sense" argues that just as our knowledge of the universe comes from language that proceeds blindly from a gap, so this knowledge has been made possible not by what our ancestors presented, but by what they concealed, by the other end of their testimony. When he "saved his brush with his posterity" (.34–35), Festy not only saved his tail and his rear end, but maintained his contact with future generations; and he did so by "playing possum." One reading of this is that the consciousness that was withdrawn from the world was given to a creativity that sprang from contact with an inner flux. Perhaps he is called "hagious curious encestor" because the qualities of this inner world were holy, strange, and taboo (incestuous). The initials of this 'title show that as Festy retreats into the past and the distance, he becomes HCE as well as having qualities of Shem. He seems to be the creative aspect of the father.

The word "such" before "playing possum" indicates that the playing corresponds to the three creative activities in the first half of the sentence: framing figments, setting starcharts, and foliating language. These may be inner games of poetry, astronomy, and grammar, but the point here is that they all proceed blindly, all are imagined. All pretend 'to be able' (Latin *possum*). From this perspective, cultural activity is useful or prepares for the future when it is original. To repeat the past is to kill it: one can only carry mental life on by making it new. This is why Joyce designed his work to be constantly reinterpreted. And it seems that one makes it new, or escapes established signification, by denying the existing world and turning inward. The image of this inward turn that now appears is that of a fox hiding in the woods from the hunting parties of men.

Lost in the Words

The rest of I.4 is concerned with the familiar pattern of inquiry about HCE (Festy-Shem) as a figure in hiding. In his foxy phase, he reeducates his intestines so that he can feed on his own substance as a ruminant. Earlier, after HCE had burrowed out of his grave, he hid "feeding on his own misplaced fat" (79.13), but now that he is more Shem-like, his auto-diet-act becomes more sophisticated. He hides, "miraculously ravenfed and buoyed up, in rumer, reticule, onasum and abomasum, upon . . . the creamclotted sherriness of cinnamon syllabub, Mikkelraved, Nikkelsaved" (97.14–17). McHugh says that the rumen, retinaculum, omasum, and abomasum are parts of a cow's stomach, and syllabub is a drink made from cream and wine. Joyce's versions of these terms, however, suggest that HCE is living on rumor (or stories), ridicule, masturbation (onanism), and abomination—a Joycean diet that will not be cookbooked.

HCE is redigesting the contents of his mind, and to ruminate can mean to ponder. The substance he is digesting is sinful syllables formed by the opposition between Mick and Nick (Shaun and Shem). But these are the products of the whole process of the chapter, a process in which two changing male figures struggled against each other to form a series of signifiers. For HCE to digest the results of their struggle is to consolidate the subject made by all these word crossings or *points de capiton.*

By the introspective activity referred to as "playing possum," and insofar as he avoids the huntsmen who would yoke him to society, HCE has made us all "heirs of his tailsie" (96.35). While "tailzie" is a Scottish legal term for the limitation of inheritance, the primary effect of the last syllable, an epexegesis, is to make the tail diminutive and improper. HCE relates to us not through his public front, but through his private back. As hairs, we are offshoots or excretions of his tail, but as heirs, we inherit his supplement. What he has conveyed to us is not his substance, but the little thing that hung out behind him like his writing or the odd signs he gave off unofficially—unconsciously, for one cannot see one's tail. These undertones give his soul to us better than official discourse.

The forest in which HCE hides is a forest of words, for "The war is in words and the wood is the world" (98.34–35), a sentence that plays with the way words are influenced by sound similarities ("war . . . words . . . wood . . . world"). HCE conceals himself in the subconscious sliding built into the forms of language, an undergrowth of overtones. In naming their letters after trees, the Celts recognized Rimbaud's idea that each sound has its own character. In the world of word wood, each role of personhood depends on words and their sounds: "Maply me, willowy we, hickory he and yew yourselves" (98.35–36).

The structure of motifs in this passage reappears in one of the best novels based on the *Wake*, Russell Hoban's *Riddley Walker* (1980). The central event of *Riddley Walker*, a nuclear holocaust or "abnihilisation of the etym" (*FW* 353.22), takes place in the "hart of the wud." Hoban's novel indicates that this phrase includes not only a stag in a forest, but the heart of the world, of volition ('would'), of insanity (*wood* as 'mad') and of the shapeshifting word. Hoban's vision illuminates the *Wake*, especially the setting of this chapter in the heart of the signifier.

Festy/HCE in hiding is not visible because he represents a part of humanity that is submerged. In *Ulysses*, the image of the hunted fox was linked to Shakespeare (193/9.337) and Parnell (492, 572/15.1762, 3952), and Swift was seen running from the mob "to the wood of madness" (39/3.110). The implication was that the creators of human consciousness have tended to generate the power of vision insofar as they were persecuted. Festy as fox is associated with "silence" (98.2), "exile" (98.5), and "cunning" (99.23). In fact, he seals himself up hermetically to become "Jams jarred"

(98.19). The private identity that must be concealed from the public is the source of vital communication that works through what is not known.

For the rest of the chapter (in brief), people speculate on the hidden figure's identity as he circulates through history; and on the last seven pages, these speculations break down into two groups divided by rubrics into male and female views. The male impressions of the missing HCE, under the heading of "Assembly men murmured. Reynard is slow!" (97.28), tend to accuse him of weakness, suggest that he is dead, and reduce him to an abstraction. This demonstrates an invidious masculine logic of discrimination.

After this the female views of HCE, starting with the line, "Dispersal women wondered. Was she fast?" (101.1), tend to focus on a shapeshifting woman who is seen as responsible for HCE's fate. Having mentioned several possibilities, the women declare that all of them are true, and that the listener should relax, for the conflict has ended in feminine victory: "Now listed to one aneither and liss them down and smoothen out your leaves of rose. The war is o'er. Wimwim wimwim!" (101.6–7). It gives vim to his whims when the women win. They soothe and revive HCE, and the chapter ends with ALP nursing HCE, and all of us: " . . . and we list, as she bibs us, by the waters of babalong" (103.9–10). Anna is seen here as dictating our discourse. This fits with HCE's response to her in a song near the end about marriage: *"Goo, the groot gudgeon, gulped it all"* (102.32, Joyce's italics). He is turned into a baby when she puts a bib on him and bids him listen. *Bib* is also the Latin root for drink, and the activity of drinking seems split between them as she nurses him with language. She provides the streaming of speech designated by the word "babalong" whenever we let words flow through us.

Great though ALP's authority over the stream of consciousness may be, it is limited by her devotion to HCE. Her streaming is directed toward him: " . . . she who will not rast from her running to seek him till, with the help of the okeamic, some such time that she shall have been after hiding the crumbends of his enormousness in the *a*reyou *l*ookingfor *P*earlfar sea, (ur, uri, uria!) . . . (102.3–7, my italics).

She aims to hide HCE's body in herself in intercourse, and this will return him to the situation of being buried under the sea that he entered on the second page of the chapter. There was sexual angling involved in the earlier burial, as references to Izaak Walton indicated. It took place near a stream with willows that were also hosiery: " . . . a troutbeck, vainyvain of her osiery and a chatty sally with any Wilt or Walt who would ongle her as Izaak did to the tickle of his rod and watch her waters of her sillying waters of . . . " (76.26–30).

The underwater grave was "an inversion of a phallopharos" (76.34), which is one way of describing a vagina (see *FS* 128). If HCE's burial had sexual overtones, ALP's sexuality has overtones of death because when he is hidden in her, she will finally rest from her running.

The passage about ALP's goal looks forward to its reversal at the end of the *Wake*, when it is the male as ocean that she will sink into. This is indicated by the phrase "with the help of the okeamic," which, I fear, refers to the body of water the Liffey is headed for, the Irish Sea. Evidently the person who needs love sinks into the ocean of the beloved, no matter which gender is involved, and this illustrates Lacan's idea that sexual roles are independent of biological gender.

Another important figure of the interchangeability of sexual roles is the kiss. In the *Four Fundamental Concepts* Lacan uses as the main model for his theory of sexual relations a structure called the rim which corresponds to oral and anal sexuality. The feelings that loop through the rim, passing from inside to outside, need not be differentiated by gender. This is the looping of signification that constitutes the subject, and Lacan seems to regard this level of sexuality as more fundamental than the genital (*Four* 178–94).

ALP often remembers HCE in conventional phallic terms: "That was the prick of the spindle to me that gave me the keys to dreamland" (615.27–28). While his phallus gives her power to dream, it also takes away her consciousness, putting her in the passive position of Sleeping Beauty. But ALP can give the key herself, for she is associated with Arrah-na-Pogue, the heroine of Dion Boucicault's play of the same name. Arrah frees a man from prison by passing a message through a kiss.[18] Issy, the younger, more aggressive version of ALP, says, "you can eat my words for it as sure as there's a key in my kiss" (279, lines 7–8 of note). A woman can easily be teaching a man, and therefore taking the active role in kissing, whether or not her tongue goes forward.

In II.4 the four old men remember kissing ALP in terms of passing into an Egyptian afterlife "in Arrah-na-pogue, in the otherworld of the passing of the key of Two-tongue Common" (385.3–5). The oral fusion of kissing here becomes a model of the linguistic circulation that forms the subject. The sharing of language conveys the world of the Other.

Like the mother in the poem Stephen writes in "Proteus," ALP dies kissing her deity, for "Lps. The keys to. Given!" indicates a kiss on the last line of the book. This Oedipal image of God gains power if we remember Stephen's preoccupation with kissing his mother in the first chapter of *Portrait*. But on the level on which Joyce takes the place of God, ALP is kissing the Other of her author as the narrative sinks back, at the end, into the oceanic mind it came from. One of the beauties of ALP's final gesture lies in her repeating the act around which her life has centered, the giving of her self. She says that although HCE told her earlier that he'd give her the keys of her heart, " . . . now it's me who's got to give" (626.32). The keys she gives seem to hold the power to create the *Wake*, for the word "Given!" is followed by the sentence that opens the book:

> Given! A way a lone a last a loved a long the
>
> .   .   .   .
>
> riverrun, past Eve and Adam's, from swerve of shore to bend of bay, brings us by a commodius vicus of recirculation back to Howth Castle and Environs. (628.15-3.3)

This arrangement dramatizes the tendency of every sentence to loop into the Other through the *point de capiton*. Filled with the feeling the book has accumulated, it passes through the outher and returns charged with the book's potential. The pattern parallels the prostitute in *Portrait* whose kiss at the end of Chapter 2 gave Stephen the ability to see his life as a cyclical narrative near the beginning of Chapter 3. In the earlier example, as in the later one, society is so organized that the phallic power of the woman is no help against her oppression: she is allowed to give such power, but not to hold it.

The Feminine Coda

The parallels between the fourth chapter of the *Wake* and the last one are extensive, if not unique. Joyce originally planned to have ALP's letter appear at the end of I.4, but he ended up putting it at the end of the last chapter, which makes up Book IV.[19] Both chapters start with external views of the sleeper asleep, which are followed in both by descriptions of him buried (595), after which he is described as having disappeared and then awakened with overtones of resurrection. HCE's underwater crypt in Lough Neagh (76.22–23) seems to parallel the hut Kevin makes for himself in the middle of lake Glendalough (605–7). These constructions are described in meticulous detail, and Kevin, like his father, submerges into a state of self-communion.

In each chapter the burial of the father is followed by conflict between his sons. In both chapters the two brothers engage in public debates that resemble trials and center on perception, the latter example being the dispute between the Archdruid Balkelly and St. Patrick (611–12). The first debate even prefigures the second by having (as we have seen) a Chinese questioning a Japanese (89.36, compare 612.12–17), in a passage added in 1938. Though both debates end mysteriously, Shem seems to lose both. After this, there is a period of decline, following which ALP appears to revive the victim. She announces her position, speaks of her husband, and moves toward the sea.

There are of course many differences between the chapters. The earlier one moves into the world of dream to unfold its characters, while the later one leaves it behind. But the similarities mean that on an important level, both chapters tell essentially the same story, a story of masculine conflict leading to paternal decline and feminine vision that echoes through all of Joyce's work.

The way in which the conflict leads to the letter in both chapters shows the relation between two systems in the subject. The indefinite subject of being must be attacked by the definite subject of speech and they must interact before perception is possible, and so before the discourse of the Other can be heard. The situation is similar to the pattern in *Portrait* whereby Stephen had to be attacked before he could be motivated to generate a new vision of his mother (and of himself). Stephen was always attacked by a masculine function of himself in order to achieve contact with a feminine function that would allow him to reshape his inner and outer worlds. In this perspective, the death or "dispersal" that ALP heralds when she appears may only be the dissolving of an ossified form of the self.

All of Joyce's major works move toward a final uncertainty that focuses on a woman's mind. At the final moment, she is always thinking of a beloved who is lost, but there is always a hope connected to the idea that she still gives love. This is true of Gretta Conroy in "The Dead," Bertha in "Exiles," Molly in *Ulysses*, and ALP in the *Wake*. *Portrait* seems to be the exception, but I have shown that all of its chapters lead to final encounters with the feminine. In fact, if one looks at the last ten lines of *Portrait*, one finds the terse style of a diary powerfully evoking the feeling of a woman being separated from what may be the main love object of her present life: "Mother is putting my new secondhand clothes in order. She prays now, she says, that I may learn in my own life and away from home and friends what the heart is and what it feels. Amen. So be it." While not as climactic as the revelations of women that end the other books, this passage is essential to the final vision of Stephen at which *Portrait* aims. Not only is her anguish the measure of his commitment, but she defines his purpose, as he recognizes by saying, "So be it." He leaves the soul of his mother only to return to it within himself, and her prayer may operate unconsciously as the scenario for his meeting with Bloom in *Ulysses*.

While the pattern is not as prominent in earlier works as in *Ulysses* and the *Wake*, all of Joyce's books organize life as a process of perception that progresses toward realizing the mind of a woman. Moreover, starting with the vision of the dead that Gabriel Conroy has after realizing his wife's feelings, the image of the depth of the woman's soul is presented as the source of perception as well as its goal.

Lacan says that man commonly seeks the Other through woman (*FS* 151), and Rose says that when the subject addresses demand for love to another person, that person becomes the locus of certainty or Other (*FS* 32). This suggests why Lacan says that the God face of the Other is supported by feminine *jouissance* (*FS* 147). Nevertheless, Lacan insists that it is dangerous to confuse woman with God, that it denies the humanity of woman and separates both genders from the vitality of uncertainty (*FS* 160). As Rose puts it, "To believe in The Woman is simply a way of closing off the division or uncertainty which also underpins conviction as such" (*FS* 51).

Joyce, however, focuses on woman *as* uncertainty, and so the goal of his work is the locus of displacement that Lacan identifies with the source of truth. Joyce does not forget the otherness of the Other: he approaches it through a structure that keeps it in motion. Lacan's mystic belief in "the *jouissance* of the woman" as "something more" (*FS* 147) refers to the ongoing shift or "babalong" of feminine discourse that Joyce's mature work celebrates.

Joyce avoids deifying woman by focusing on her desire, which always ultimately appears as a sense of loss. Gabriel is thinking of his wife's lost lover and of the failure of his own love for her at the end of "The Dead." As *Exiles* ends, Bertha expresses her longing for the husband she used to love, and Kenner (*Dublin's Joyce* 90–93) has shown substantial verbal parallels between the play's end and the end of the *Wake*. We have seen May Dedalus's sense of loss at the end of *Portrait;* while at the close of *Ulysses,* Molly's thoughts combine Mulvey with Bloom as a youth. ALP, as she finishes the *Wake,* contrasts her "puny" (627.25) husband with what she used to think he was and longs for her father. In every case the loss the woman thinks of expresses the depth of her subjectivity, drawing back veils as no other feeling could in accord with Lacan's principle that the subject is built on a sense of loss. Perhaps it is because identity springs from separation that only by seeing the woman's loss can the artist see his own soul.

In ALP Joyce recognizes a level of woman that rejects her man and turns back to infantile need for an absolute father. By going back before social articulation, Joyce reaches a deeper level of woman's mind than Molly represented, and a deeper level of his own. The full realization that the drive toward the object of desire depends on the fantasy of an absolute parent leads beyond the idea that love aims at something possible, and so it reaches toward recognition of the root of consciousness as a need that can never be fulfilled. The only way to recognize this need is to project its impossible goal, which in this case goes beyond the object of love to approach the object of being.

The obscurity of the *Wake* facilitates, rather than prevents, the penetration of the veil, so that the appearance of an obstacle represented by the wall of language is an illusion, a dream wall. When we confront the obscure surface of the text with open minds, we feel something stirring behind it that a clear text would hide. By speaking not with words as they are conventionally understood, but with suggestions (parts of words) that constantly disintegrate, the text speaks from outside social codes, from the other side of rational discourse, where the subject enacts its strangeness in the obscurity of the object.

NOTES

1. Attridge, in his recent article "*Finnegans Wake:* The Dream of Interpretation," argues that the *Wake* need not be read as a dream, or that the dream metaphor is only one way of interpreting it. I feel obliged to reply since I make use of the dream model. The evidence Attridge uses to deny that the *Wake* is primarily a dream is not conclusive. He says that the reason Joyce emphasized that the *Wake* was about sleep from as early as 1926 on was that he wanted to provide an easy way in for *Wake* readers. In this area Attridge assumes that he can be certain of Joyce's deconstructive intention and that it was other than what Joyce stated. Attridge is correct in arguing for new ways of looking at the *Wake* and against certainties, but this does not mean that we should reject what is most likely. The idea of dream is generally present in the *Wake,* though I agree with Attridge insofar as he argues that dream is only one level that combines with many others.

2. As Hayman points out, the 1923 first draft of I.4 was an "appendix" of I.3. See the volume of the *Joyce Archive* on the *Wake, Book I, Chapters 4–5: A Facsimile of Drafts, Typescripts, & Proofs.* As this is vol. 46 of the *Archive,* the standard form for the citation is *JJA* 46:vii, 3, 89.

3. Bishop 262 cites this phrase.

4. As a Taoist, Choang-tsu saw yin and yang interacting to make up everything in the universe. While yin and yang are often simplified as male and female, they really include all opposites, such as light and dark—including two pairs that the anecdote involves, dreaming/waking and self/other. Thus Taoism resembles Bruno's coincidence of contraries, and so it coincides with Joyce's vision as well as Lacan's.

In case this seems far from the Modern novel, let me point out that the interaction between male and female forces pervades the world of Woolf's *To the Lighthouse* (1927). Here the relation between the feminine Mrs. Ramsay and her masculine husband forms the center from which all of the other characters derive their vitality and their perception. That Woolf wrote a novel so dominated by yin and yang at a time when she was strongly involved with Vita Sackville-West gives me an opportunity to note that my emphasis on masculine and feminine does not exclude gays. Lacan uses homosexuals to prove that gender systems have no relation to biological gender, that anyone can use both systems (*FS* 76). My impression is that gays make extensive use of the imagery of the male-female polarity and even sometimes exaggerate it.

5. Roland McHugh, *Annotations* 75, points out that *FW* 75.9–10 parodies the

well-known lines from Byron's *Don Juan,* "The Isles of Greece, the Isles of Greece!/ Where burning Sappho loved and sung!" The song about Greece appears between stanzas 86 and 87 of Canto III. Because the pages of McHugh's *Annotations* are arranged to correspond to pages with the same numbers in the text, future notes for this book will not be needed, and references to McHugh will be to this book unless otherwise indicated.

6. The words in brackets appear in a 1927 typescript of this passage, and seem to have been left out of the final text by accident. See *JJA* 46:89–90.

7. McHugh cites *taal.* There are many Dutch words in this area of the text. Bishop 360 points out that references to Dutch refer to what is below the surface as "nether lands."

8. The distinction between the *moi* and the *je* is developed in *R–S* 23, 42, 51–52.

9. This is the Schema L, which appears on *R–S* 2 and in *Écrits* 53.

10. People spoke of a hole in the North Wall near this pub where voters put in an empty hand and came out with money. For an account of the pub and a list of references to it, see Mink 446.

11. One of the main works on the interaction of seeing and hearing areas of the brain in speech is Norman Geschwind, "Disconnexion Syndromes in Animal and Man (1965)" in his *Selected Papers* 106–236. Geschwind's technical work is explained effectively and related to reading by Israel Rosenfield, "A Hero of the Brain."

12. Gerald M. Edelman, *Neural Darwinism: The Theory of Neuronal Group Selection* 4–22. The implications of this theory are well explained in Rosenfield, "Neural Darwinism: A New Approach to Memory and Perception."

13. The name Tallulah was probably available to Joyce, for Tallulah Bankhead became an international star with *Faithless,* 1932.

14. See Hart 225 for references to the motif, and see *Brewer's Dictionary* under *wind* for the meaning of the phrase.

15. Riquelme 10–13, 24 speaks of the motif of alpha and omega in the *Wake* and says it stands for the artist as "jas jos" (*FW* 184.2).

16. Campbell and Robinson gloss this line as saying, "All the rumor and action of *Finnegans Wake* develops from the stuttering of HCE in the park encounter" (92n).

17. This description of Joyce studies appears in *"Ulysse Gramophone"* 235. An English version appears in *Ninth* 37.

18. The standard description of Joyce's use of *Arrah-na-Pogue* is Atherton, *The Books at the Wake* 157–61.

19. The first draft of the letter and typescripts of part of it, dated 1923–24, appear in *JJA* 46:281–89.

Reweave: The Gift of Tongue

Perception in Joyce searches toward its cause in desire, moving toward apperception, which means both seeing fully and seeing oneself. As the text grows aware that the objects it frames are products of convention, it moves toward finding reality in the structure of its own process. The three images of the field of desire that I focus on represent progressive elaborations of a Joycean subject constituted by the process of perception.

In *Portrait*, satisfaction comes from entering the flux of a world filled with possibilities for the development of the artist as self-creator. Here the forms the artist studies have reality as sources of creation and identity. But in *Ulysses*, because the Father has struck down the mother, the world appears as a veil of signs, evoking the feeling that reality is beyond, to be sensed only in hints that flicker through language. Stephen and Bloom continually try to determine the relation of their sensations to reality by experiment, and the imagery is so arranged that they are generally seen as striving to penetrate the veil. This striving is always disappointed on the conscious level, but on levels below consciousness, it has beneficial effects that are represented by a prominent image in all of the novels, the kiss.

The *Wake* takes place in a world of sleep where the gaze behind the veil can show itself. While there are references to the "veiled world" (*FW* 139.1), the veil in its role as the inescapable illusion of the physical world is far less prominent and effective in the *Wake* than in *Ulysses*. The specific images that present themselves in the *Wake* are arbitrary forms generated sporadically in vain efforts to conceal the disturbing opposition of the Other. The wall of language is an artificial construction full of holes, and it convinces no one. HCE builds it continually to assert his phallic authority, which depends on public standards: " . . . where theirs is Will there's his Wall" (175.19–20). This masculine effort to fix reality in a definite form is stiff without being solid, a network of signifiers that, like the phallus, will not last long in any particular form. HCE is often shown fallen down at the foot of the wall because building this barrier separates him from the source of vitality.

What the wall tries to hide is perceived everywhere in the *Wake*, for the world of things is replaced by the wordshifting behind it. Almost all we can see is the other side of language, for the otherness behind each word is constantly made apparent by the shifting of words away from what they seem to say. The goal of vision is reached when language points as far as it can to all the possibilities behind it, as in the final "the," which leads to the whole book. When language spreads in this way, the field of signifiers enacts the full swarming that constitutes the inner world, so that one perceieves the origin of one's perceptions. At this point, the Other reveals the subject, as Joyce's realization of the life of the opposite gender is his realization of his own life.

Such maximum points of vision, however, are not clear because they are in motion. ALP's last line, for example, embodies ongoing movement: "A way a lone a last a loved a long the." The entire fragment is made up of sound shifts that function metonymically, and its rhythm drives it forward. Isolated from its goal, it represents pure motion, the slide without the hook. This is exemplified strongly in the word "the," which bounds lightly toward a noun it never reaches. Like ALP's whole soliloquy (619.20–628.16), this line streams with *jouissance,* the verbal shift that Lacan calls Joyce's symptom because he recognizes the ability to change words as the heart of Joyce's powers.

Movement, which is equivalent to feeling, is the only way to penetrate the veil (or wall) because when the obstacle is shifted, it loses its solidity and contact is made with the other side. At least the space on that side answers the movement on this one. On the other hand, because the veil can only be penetrated by motion, and reconstitutes itself whenever one stops to get one's bearings, whatever is behind it can never be seen clearly. If the other side cannot be consolidated, however, neither can language ever be seen as a pure veil without evoking a beyond. Lacan shows that such a thing would not be visible. So every movement and every displacement of language speaks for something beyond the veil. This may indicate why Joyce, Lacan, and Derrida give movement a privileged status beyond criticism, an almost sacred role.

In *Portrait,* where each chapter forms a coherent image of Stephen, the major movement is the shift between moments of stasis at which perception fixes on epiphanies at the end of each narrative unit. In *Ulysses,* however, the veil is perpetually swirling as the moment of perception slides into verbal connections beyond it because language is transformed by extra levels of stylistic experimentation. In the *Wake,* the coherence of language and vision, as represented by the wall, cannot sustain any credibility, cannot appear without negating itself. When I reach a point where I can make sense of a sentence in the *Wake,* I wonder what I am missing.

The question of whether the veil is passable or not depends for its answer on the view one takes of it, like the question between waves and particles as the basis of matter in physics, for the veil operates in both ways. Arnold Goldman's *The Joyce Paradox* remains valuable in pointing out that Joyce's works move in simultaneously opposing directions that can only be selected by differing ideologies. According to Bakhtin's *Problems of Dostoevsky's Poetics* (90–100), any ideology in a polyphonic novel is only one voice in a structure that gets its vitality from the opposition between voices.

If the idea of impenetrability and that of passage are both active in Joyce's novels, how do they relate to each other? They may be seen as alternating in a rhythm that follows the model of each chapter of *Portrait* to constitute a fundamental structural unit of the novels. At the beginning of each unit is an effort to make perception and language clear, to consolidate a masculine position. As the unit proceeds, however, the attempt at a unified male position disintegrates through its own contradictions, and the unit ends with an expansion into the feminine.

Early in each chapter of *Portrait,* Joyce is distant from Stephen as Stephen earnestly engages in being a student, a whoremonger, or a sodalist. But by the end of the chapter, Stephen achieves a transcendence that brings him close to Joyce. His intimacy with his author is expressed in the feminine aspect of language that represents Stephen's Other: irony is subordinated to enthusiasm at the end. The distant attitude that Joyce has toward Stephen early in each unit corresponds to the naturalist view of the figure trapped by his social system. In this view the veil cannot be penetrated, but each chapter ends with a sense of passing through.

Similarly, in *Ulysses,* Joyce is distant from Stephen and Bloom at the start as they are distant from each other. In "Telemachus," for example, the narrator says of Stephen, "Pain, that was not yet the pain of love, fretted his heart" (5/1.102). Joyce moves in on Stephen through the "Telemachiad," which increases its interiority with each of its three chapters. Then he spends the rest of the novel approaching the subject formed by the opposition between both protagonists. As Joyce grows closer to them, he imposes his own stylistic devices to take them out of their ordinary reality and move them closer to the unconscious flow in which they will finally be joined. The ends of Joyce's works usually focus on an image that strongly tends to be construed as a passage through the veil: the powerful, pervasive image of the kiss.

The communicative force of the kiss, one of Joyce's most valued images, may be questioned by deconstruction, and it is so questioned by Joyce. The last kiss in the narrative proper of *Ulysses,* at the end of "Ithaca," is Bloom's reverse kiss on Molly's rear end. We are not inclined to see essential communication in a reverse kiss (though it may be strongly felt) and Molly soon says that she has no expressiveness in that quarter (777/18.1403).[1] If changing the locus of the kiss seems to negate its communication, then the semantic truth involved in this gesture may only be a convention of language. Every element of Joyce's work is similarly dependent on convention, but it is unfair to that work to assume that Joyce intended to communicate nothing but skeptical criticism.

Joyce would not represent life as fully as he did only to dissect it, and the displacement of language from meaning that he emphasizes may be the very substance of life. Lacan sees "Being (the subject)" and "Meaning (the Other)" as largely mutually exclusive, and portrays them as two circles that overlap in about a fifth of their area (*Four* 211). The overlapping area is darkened and labeled "non-meaning," implying that being and meaning, or subject and Other, can only meet in non-meaning, which Lacan describes as a phase of uncertainty or alienation in the circuit between self and Other, and describes also as the realization of the unconscious. If the subject can only make contact with the Other in obscurity, then obscurity is what the kiss conveys; and this confusion can be conveyed as well (or better) in the most debased version as in the most exalted one. Such confusion is the dynamic feeling of life, the element in which we live most of the time when we are not consciously controlling our thoughts. Through the kiss we feel it in others and so in ourselves.

Passage through the veil of signs is equivalent to communication, the arrival of a real message. Shari Benstock points out that for Lacan, a message always reaches its destination, while for Derrida, a message never truly gets there.[2] That is, Lacan insists that all language has a structure that communicates, while Derrida insists that the complexities of that structure make it go astray. In fact, both the idea that discourse always reaches its goal and the idea that it never does so are too absolute. What happens in most discourse is that the impulse to communicate combines with the tendency to disseminate or wander, and the two factors alternate or interplay. This process is represented in Joyce's use of the veil image.

The opposing views of Lacan and Derrida may be related to their professions. Derrida's philosophical interest in demonstrating his logical power may make him resist recognizing beneficial effects that can be rationally disintegrated. On the other hand, Lacan as an analyst was obliged to believe in the possibility of communication, without which there could be no hope of cure. Lacan puts it this way in Book II of his Seminars:

> The analysis must aim at the passage of true speech, joining the subject to an other subject, on the other side of the wall of language. That is the final relation of the subject to a genuine Other, to the Other who gives the answer one doesn't expect, which defines the terminal point of analysis. (246)

The sign of the genuine Other is the answer one does not expect, the very unexpectedness of the answer. This means that the penetration of the veil is always caught in a shift, that the other side is seen only in movement.

In "The direction of the treatment," Lacan sees the analyst as presenting himself as the subject who knows and then withdrawing his authority, which acts something like a bullfighter's cape (*Selection* 271). When the analysand finds that he cannot reach the truth of the analyst, he is forced to find his own truth; but unless the analyst projected the veil of authority, the patient would not be drawn forward to progress. This is a powerful mode of activity for the image of the author as deity that Joyce projects, everywhere to be sensed and nowhere to be pinned down, in his work. As a novelist, Joyce combines the doctor and the philosopher in that he wants to communicate in order to cure, but the truth he aims to teach centers on what cannot be communicated and how incommunicable it is. By withdrawing the veil, by disintegrating the lure of coherence, the Lacanian analyst and the Joycean artist exert an authority more effective and creative than any clearly defined authority could be.

To show how the drawing back or dissolution of the veil in the later work follows a continuous policy of Joyce's, and to examine some issues involved, I want to return to a prefiguration of this pattern in his first novel. The organ of Joyce's authority is manifested as the *objet a,* which appears as a hole in the veil, virtually a black hole, surrounded by strong feeling and obscurity, and intensely charged with language. The function of the author appears through woman because the *objet a* conceals the Other. A fundamental version of the *objet a* appears when Stephen finds his manhood by kissing the prostitute: " . . . conscious of nothing in the world but the dark pressure of her softly parting lips. They pressed upon his brain as upon his lips as though they were the vehicle of a vague speech; and between them he felt an unknown and timid pressure, darker than the swoon of sin, softer than sound or odour" (*P* 101).

The mysterious pressure at the rim, surrounded by the code confusions of synesthesia in the last eleven words, is her tongue. This linguistic organ, which includes all of the senses in its taste and pressure, conveys to Stephen new powers of language as well as a new conception of himself, as we see in the equation scene that follows on Stephen's vice. He sees the equation as "a widening tail, eyed and starred like a peacock's" on which the numbers that appear and disappear are "eyes opening and closing" and the eyes are "stars being born and being quenched" (*P* 103). Nowhere before the kiss scene has his imagination attained the level of figural complexity seen in this conceit.[3] So the gift of tongue is a priceless one that comes from the source of art, one fundamental to Stephen's assumption of his destiny.

The image of the kiss has motivated Stephen's development from very early in the book. The first questions he asks himself that are quoted directly center on "What did that mean, to kiss?" (*P* 15). He noticed ambiguities in words earlier, but this is a big step forward in cognition because he introduces the abstract category of meaning here and wonders about motivation: "Why did people do that with their two faces?" This problem institutes a series of unanswered questions throughout the book that serve as powerful tools for his development, focusing his concentration and building his awareness of himself as an inquirer. Such questions arise when he is suspended between a masculine threat and a feminine attraction, as the kissing question arises because Wells taunts him for kissing his mother. Stephen cannot think actively without referring to the polarities of the kiss.

The dependence of Stephen's thought on the feminine, the situation indicated by the kiss, raises questions on the political level about the social reality involved in this gift. To answer desire, the kiss must seem to be given freely, but tongue is an expensive gift (even a quarter of a pound). And while the idea of the gift has aristocratic associations with largess, there is an economic reality behind the question of who has to pay. In the scene in which Stephen initiates his consciousness with a kiss, it is a prostitute who gives. In *Ulysses* Stephen defines a prostitute as one who "buys dear and sells cheap" (633/16.738). All of the women involved in the continual gift of tongue are both actual women and creations of Stephen's imagination: they must have a reality that can surprise, but they are also used as screens on which Stephen projects his exploration of himself. Through woman he expresses his feminine side not only to construct his masculinity, but to express himself "wholly."

From the perspective in which the Other is an effect of material and social causes, the man who draws his linguistic sustenance from woman is parallel to the artist who draws on society's support to create a private beauty while others go needy. Like God kissing Stephen's mother, both the seducer and the artist may be seen as parasites draining those who are less fortunate. Joyce was aware of this view, but he knew also that he could not give up the dependence of man on woman or that of the artist on cultural privilege: his works are devoted to heterosexuality and extravagantly difficult to read. It is not likely that men should completely give up their dependence on women, or that artists should not ask support beyond their utility. What the man and the artist can do is to recognize the arbitrary nature of their advantages and use this recognition to liberate their subjects into consciousness, so that dependency can be alternated rather than being one-sided.

Joyce justifies his authority by his mission of forging the uncreated consciousness of the human race; and with this aim, he makes his authority stronger by questioning the unfairness of his own position. He emphasizes the inseparability of male discourse from the feminine power of language and presents authorized language as hopelessly lost among verbal alternatives.

By rendering these aspects of the Lacanian unconscious, Joyce draws back the veil to articulate the hierarchical injustice involved in the kiss that connects man to woman and author to text. Whether he was a man or a woman, Joyce would have to use phallic functions of will and discrimination to focus on feminine reality; and he would also have to discover through feminine language the truth at the foundation of his subject.

In *Portrait*, Stephen aims to liberate the soul of Irish womanhood, "the imaginations of their daughters" (*P* 238), which he repeatedly envisions as "a batlike soul" locked away from consciousness of itself by social restraints (*P* 183, 221). He frequently fears that he has misjudged E——. C——., that his mind breeds "vermin" and that she is beyond the images he projects on her (222, 233, 252). His last impression of her is a lurching suspicion that he was all wrong about her: "I liked her and it seems a new feeling to me. Then, in that case, all the rest, all that I thought I thought and all that I felt I felt, all the rest before now, in fact . . . O, give it up, old chap! Sleep it off!" (252, Joyce's ellipsis). His contact with the Other here is indicated by strong dialogism, the feeling of arguing with himself.

Admittedly, Stephen could not gain this insight into E——. C——. unless he had broken with her and was in the process of leaving her, and there were earlier passages of his that sympathized with her after attacking her. Nevertheless, his sharp recognition, seventeen lines from the end, of how he distorts her constitutes one of the significant goals of the book: he recognizes patterns of delusion that have infested his mind from early in the novel. This is one way in which seeing himself honestly is inseparable from empathizing with a woman.

One of his most penetrating insights into woman occurs during the writing of the villanelle of the temptress. In this poem he asks four times, *"Are you not weary of ardent ways?"* (*P* 223), indicating that woman must be tired of playing the role of the Other. The villanelle is a poem with feminist intentions in that it strives to recognize a reality in woman that sees through her right to claim devotion, a reality that Joyce presents at the end of the *Wake*.

Stephen's intention to build a knowledge of the mental life of woman is carried on in *Ulysses*, which presents a searching analysis of the evils of prostitution and the complexities of marriage. It leads to the revelations of Molly's deformed beauty in which entrapment and flow are bound together by the organization of gender. By articulating Molly's inner speech and the underside of the city's motivation, Joyce draws the locus of desire onto the rational side of the veil. He thereby shifts the focus of uncertainty to a deeper level, moving from the surface appeal of woman steadily deeper into the complexities in which she is enmeshed. This entangling movement is also a discovery of the author and his male protagonists, but it can only be made through the vision of woman as *objet a*.

Joyce's exposure of the role of woman was part of his searching critique of all areas of modern society. This critique was dependent on his interaction with himself for its depth, its ability to go below the surface. He recognized that his penetration of society proceeded from his communion with himself in blasphemous religious terms in the 1904 broadside "The Holy Office": "Myself unto myself will give/ This name, Katharsis-Purgative" (*JJ* 166). Taking from his own reflection the power to purge his culture, he sees himself through seeing the realities of his world and sees those realities through seeing himself. The circuit that connects self to Other carries the full range of social language, but this cultural and historical material is conditioned by the personal channels that make it accessible.

Just as Joyce's revelation of social realities depends on his ability to get outside himself, so does his power to write. This last is the most fundamental result of his devotion to women. The movement into the field of woman as a movement into dream is the entry into the space of writing. At the beginning of Book III of the *Wake,* for example, Joyce presents the contact between the writer and his work as a kiss through which the pen sees: "Pensée! The most beautiful of woman of the veilch veilchen veilde. She would kidds to my voult of my palace, with obscidian luppas, her aal in her dhovc's suckling. Apagemonite!" (*FW* 403.14–17).

The sense of expansion that ALP gives is represented through the wide wild world as veiled with many violets (German *viele Veilchen*). The world as veiled is also the field of perception and the page (vellum). In an action that kids, or expresses the spirit of humor in *jouissance,* she touches the vault of his palate with her kiss (obscene lips), and this inspires the monumental creation of the vault of his palace, if only in thought (*la pensée*). "She would kidds" also represents the drive to reproduction. The softness of her touch contains wisdom, the owl in her suckling dove, which is also all, or totality. At the same time, she uses the phallic power that Stephen called "woman's invisible weapon" (*U* 196/9.461), for the "key" in her kiss (*FW* 279.n.8) is a pointed tool, an awl. Her ability to give freedom entails power. McHugh points out that the Agapemones were a sect that emphasized "love feasts," and the kindness that ALP feeds the narrator seems to throng his imagination with warning or prophecy (Latin *monita*) at the rate of a page a minute.

The influence of this violet muse on the narrator is described six lines later as turning his vision inward: " . . . as nighthood's unseen violet rendered all animated greatbritish and Irish objects nonviewable to human watchers save 'twere perchance anon some glistery gleam darkling adown surface of affluvial flowandflow . . . " (403.32–404.1).

The odor of the violet, parallel to the movement into sleep, makes discrete objects disappear into a flow of so and so.[4] What is seen here is prior to the construction of the human watcher, and the preposition that connects the seer to what is seen is "anon," which indicates that it is not yet there, but still to come, and suggests that identity is lost in anonymity. The goal of perception and desire in Joyce's fiction, as I have shown, has always been the merging of the individual into a flux. The maternal force of this flux—seen here as an affluent ALP, "affluvial"—generates and multiplies new forms to make up the entire narrative or total taletelling of life: "The untireties of livesliving being the one substance of streams-becoming. Totalled in toldteld and teldtold in tittletell tattle" (*FW* 597. 7–9).

The untiring continual discovery of the feminine as the reality of linguistic otherness supports and gives life to Joyce's text by keeping it in motion. The kiss is a fine image of this motion in tongues because it combines liquid with a sliding that can hardly be stopped. Derrida sees a similar pattern when he presents discourse as a mixing of "two tongues at once" in *The Post Card,* kissing both his (apparent) wife and language (183–84). The movement into otherness involves both feminine and masculine functions. Not only does the opening of space allow the displacement of words, but the intentional pushing back of the veil that Stephen initiates carries through all of Joyce's experimental techniques, bringing what is unknown into language in order to focus on what remains beyond. The newness of language is the shifting of the diaphane of authority by the movement of feeling, and the process of this shift takes place through a give-and-take of perceptual looping.

The kisses that end and punctuate Joyce's main works are realizations of extensive identities that are enhanced by their concluding positions. The identities affirmed by these kisses are not those of discrete individuals, but of circuits of interchange. They enact the loop that Lacan locates at the rim in the field of the Other. It has been circling through all of Joyce's narrative, but now, at the moment toward which the rest has moved, it is articulated as reaching itself as a point of departure in the Other.

The movement toward the Other in the final kisses is prefigured by Stephen's confronting of this function at the end of each *Portrait* chapter, but it is fully developed in the otherly motions of Molly in her erotic reverie and ALP in her passage toward death. ALP could never intentionally wield the exalted dignity of her final passage, just as no realistic figure (except a Joycean), could consciously approach the language of the *Wake*. Yet the true expression of the intimate otherness of death makes ALP's soliloquy one of the ultimate presentations of the subject that the Jesuits taught Joyce to meditate on. As the male Other addressed by Joyce's major women moves further from consciousness, it moves toward the source of language and the vast burden of Joyce's responsibility both to flow and to terminate. This level of his subject could not be apprehended by Joyce except through a woman's point of view not only because it is his womanhood, but because it is his manhood.

As the subtlest enactment of the circuit between self and Other, the kiss that is always being approached in Joyce's novels (but never physically reached after Chapter 2 of *Portrait*) is the most vital model for the looping not only of perception and speechbeing, but of narration. When the text sees or hears an image it has not known before, when it reaches a new thought or enters a significant action (one whose end is not known), it engages the field of the Other. This field operates through a tissue of signifiers charged with an unknowable otherness behind them, and to activate the field, Joyce has to project the effect of a receding authority that will motivate his characters and his readers.

Lacan's concepts and structures serve to reveal how life is literally lived in revolutions, and how the scenes and selves we weave to consolidate these revolvings continue to pulse with their movements and forces. The opposing ideologies in Joyce's work are caught in this rhythm. The few patterns I have examined here are only a part of Lacan's system, and of Joyce's. But the phenomenology or phonemenology that I trace here is active with variations in all fictions, including life. In representing the looping of signification and in projecting the multiplicity and movement of authorial activity, Joyce reveals the framing of interior monologue, and the dynamic of opposition in which narration is involved. Here are further areas where critics can expand their technology by observing his technique.

NOTES

1. Insofar as Molly implies that she has no feeling in this area, she contradicts herself on 784/18.586–587.

2. Benstock, "Nightletters" 233n. The passages from Lacan and Derrida that Benstock refers to are in John P. Muller and William Richardson, eds., *The Purloined Poe: Lacan, Derrida and Psychoanalytic Reading* 53, 201.

3. The only exception may be the scene in which Stephen falls asleep in the infirmary (*P* 26–27). Here waves of fire turn to waves of water that speak, but it is debatable whether Stephen could express this consciously.

4. American violets have little odor, but the European sweet violet is fragrant.

Works Cited

Adams, Robert M. *James Joyce: Common Sense and Beyond*. New York: Random, 1966.

AE. See Russell, George.

Aquinas, St. Thomas. "Commentary." *Aristotle's De Anima in the Version of William of Moerbeke and the Commentary of St. Thomas Aquinas*. Trans. Kenelm Foster and Silvester Humphries. New Haven: Yale University Press, 1951.

Atherton, James S. *The Books at the Wake: A Study of Literary Allusions in James Joyce's Finnegans Wake*. New York: Viking, 1959.

Attridge, Derek. "*Finnegans Wake:* The Dream of Interpretation." *James Joyce Quarterly* 27.1 (1989): 11–29.

——. "Molly's Flow: The Writing of 'Penelope' and the Question of Women's Language." *Modern Fiction Studies* 35 (1989): 543–65.

——. *Peculiar Language: Literature as Difference from the Renaissance to James Joyce*. Ithaca: Cornell University Press 1988.

Aubert, Jacques. *Introduction a l'esthétique de James Joyce*. Paris: Didier, 1973.

——, ed. *Joyce avec Lacan*. Paris: Navarin Editeur, 1987.

Bakhtin, Mikhail M. *The Dialogical Imagination: Four Essays*. Trans. Caryl Emerson and Michael Holquist. Ed. Michael Holquist. Austin: University of Texas Press, 1981.

——. *Problems of Dostoevsky's Poetics*. Ed. and trans. Caryl Emerson. Minneapolis: University of Minnesota Press, 1984.

Benstock, Bernard, ed. *James Joyce: The Augmented Ninth: Proceedings of the Ninth International James Joyce Symposium, Frankfurt, 1984*. Syracuse: Syracuse University Press 1988.

Benstock, Shari. "Nightletters: Woman's Writing in the *Wake.*" *Critical Essays on James Joyce*. Ed. Bernard Benstock. Boston: G. K. Hall, 1985.

——, and Bernard Benstock. "The Benstock Principle." *The Seventh of Joyce*. Ed. Bernard Benstock. Bloomington: Indiana University Press, 1982.

Berkeley, George. *Principles, Dialogues, and Philosophical Correspondences*. Ed. Colin Murray Turbayne. Indianapolis: Bobbs-Merrill, 1965.

——. *Works on Vision*. Ed. Colin Murray Turbayne. Indianapolis: Bobbs-Merrill, 1963.

Bishop, John. *Joyce's Book of the Dark: Finnegans Wake*. Madison: University of Wisconsin Press, 1986

Blake, William. *The Poetry and Prose of William Blake*. Ed. David V. Erdman. Garden City, New York: Doubleday, 1965, 1970.

Blamires, Harry. *The New Bloomsday Book: A Guide through Ulysses.* London: Routledge, 1988.

Blavatsky, Hilda P. *Isis Unveiled: The Master-Key to the Mysteries of Ancient and Modern Science and Theology.* 2 vols. 1877. Los Angeles: The Theosophy Co., 1977.

Boheemen, Christine van. *The Novel as Family Romance: Language, Gender, and Authority from Fielding to Joyce.* Ithaca: Cornell University Press, 1987.

Boswell, James. *Life of Johnson.* London, Oxford, 1953.

Brewer, Ebenezer Cobham. *Brewer's Dictionary of Phrase and Fable.* Revised. New York: Harper and Bros., 1953.

Brivic, Sheldon. *Joyce between Freud and Jung.* Port Washington, New York: Kennikat, 1980.

——. *Joyce the Creator.* Madison: University of Wisconsin Press, 1985.

——. "The Other of *Ulysses.*" *Joyce's* Ulysses: *The Larger Perspective.* Ed. Robert D. Newman and Weldon Thornton. Newark: University of Delaware Press, 1987.

Brown, Susan Sutliff. "The Geometry of James Joyce's *Ulysses:* From Pythagoras to Poincaré . . . " Diss. University of Southern Florida. 1987.

Bruno, Giordano. *The Expulsion of the Triumphant Beast.* Trans. Arthur D. Imerti. New Brunswick: Rutgers University Press 1964.

Budgen, Frank. *James Joyce and the Making of Ulysses.* 1934. 2nd ed. Bloomington: Indiana University Press 1960.

Butler, Samuel. *The Authoress of the Odyssey.* 1897, 1922. Chicago: University of Chicago Press, 1967.

Buttigieg, Joseph A. *A Portrait of the Artist in Different Perspective.* Athens: Ohio University Press, 1987.

Campbell, Joseph, and Henry Morton Robinson. *A Skeleton Key to Finnegans Wake.* New York: Viking, 1944.

Card, James Van Dyck. *An Anatomy of "Penelope."* Madison, N.J.: Fairleigh Dickinson University Press, 1984.

Carpenter, William. *Death and Marriage: Structural Metaphors for the Work of Art in Joyce and Mallarmé.* New York: Garland, 1988.

Cixous, Hélene. *The Exile of James Joyce.* Trans. Sally A. J. Purcell. New York: David Lewis, 1972.

Clément, Catherine. *The Lives and Legends of Jacques Lacan.* Trans. Arthur Goldhammer. New York: Columbia University Press, 1983.

Cohn, Dorrit. *Transparent Minds: Narrative Modes for Presenting Consciousness in Fiction.* Princeton: Princeton University Press, 1978.

Coleridge, Samuel Taylor. *The Friend I.* Ed. Barbara E. Rooke. Vol. 4 of *The Collected Works of Samuel Taylor Coleridge.* London: Routledge & Kegan Paul, 1969.

Curran, Constantine P. *James Joyce Remembered.* London: Oxford University Press, 1968.

Davis, Robert Con, ed. *Lacan and Narration: The Psychoanalytic Difference in Narrative Theory.* Baltimore: Johns Hopkins University Press 1984.

De Beauvoir, Simone. *The Second Sex.* Trans. H. M. Parshley. New York: Bantam, 1961.

Derrida, Jacques. *Dissemination.* Trans. Barbara Johnson. Chicago: University of Chicago Press, 1981.

——. *Of Grammatology*. Trans. Gayatri Chakravorty Spivak. Baltimore: Johns Hopkins University Press, 1976.

——. *The Post Card: From Socrates to Freud and Beyond*. Trans. Alan Bass. Chicago: University of Chicago Press, 1987.

——. "Two Words for Joyce." *Post-structuralist Joyce: Essays from the French*. Eds. Derek Attridge and Daniel Ferrer. Cambridge: Cambridge University Press, 1984. 145–59.

——. "*Ulysse Gramophone: L'oui dire de Joyce*." *Genese de Babel: Joyce et la création*. Ed. Claude Jacquet. Paris: *Editions du CNRS*, 1985. 227–64.

——. *Writing and Difference*. Trans. Alan Bass. Chicago: University of Chicago Press, 1978.

Devlin, Kimberly J. " 'See ourselves as others see us': Joyce's Look at the Eye of the Other." *PMLA* 104 (1989): 882–93.

——. Wandering and Return in Finnegans Wake. Princeton: Princeton University Press, forthcoming in 1991.

Eco, Umberto. *A Theory of Semiotics*. Bloomington: Indiana University Press 1979.

Edelman, Gerald. *Neural Darwinism: The Theory of Neuronal Group Selection*. New York: Basic, 1987.

Ellmann, Richard. *The Consciousness of Joyce*. New York: Oxford University Press, 1977.

——. *James Joyce*. 1959. 2nd ed. New York: Oxford University Press, 1982

——. *Ulysses on the Liffey*. New York: Oxford University Press, 1972.

Erikson, Erik H. *Identity: Youth and Crisis*. New York: W. W. Norton, 1968.

Felman, Shoshana. *Jacques Lacan and the Adventure of Insight: Psychoanalysis in Contemporary Culture*. Cambridge: Harvard University Press, 1987.

——, ed. *Literature and Psychoanalysis: The Question of Reading: Otherwise*. Baltimore: Johns Hopkins University Press, 1982.

Fenichel, Otto. The Psychoanalytic Theory of Neurosis. New York: W. W. Norton, 1945.

Ferrer, Daniel. "The Freudful Couchmare of Λd: Joyce's Notes on Freud and the Composition of Chapter 16 of Finnegans Wake." *James Joyce Quarterly* 22.4 (1985): 367–82.

Fraser, Alexander Campbell. *Berkeley*. Edinburgh: Blackwood, 1909.

Frye, Northrop. *Fearful Symmetry: A Study of William Blake*. Princeton: Princeton University Press, 1947.

Freud, Sigmund. *The Standard Edition of the Complete Psychological Works of Sigmund Freud*. Ed. and trans. James Strachey et al. 24 vols. London: Hogarth, 1953–74.

Genette, Gérard. *Narrative Discourse: An Essay on Method*. Trans. Jane E. Lewin. Ithaca: Cornell University Press 1980.

Geschwind, Norman. *Selected Papers on Language and the Brain*. Dordrecht, Holland: D. Reidel Publishing Co., 1974.

Gifford, Don. *Joyce Annotated: Notes for Dubliners and A Portrait of the Artist . . .* 2nd ed. Berkeley: University of California Press, 1982.

——, with Robert J. Seidman. *Ulysses Annotated: Notes for James Joyce's Ulysses*. Berkeley: University of California Press, 1988.

Gilbert, Stuart. *James Joyce's Ulysses.* 1930. 2nd ed. New York: Vintage, 1955.

Gillespie, Michael Patrick, with Erik Bradford Stocker. *James Joyce's Trieste Library: A Catalogue of Materials* . . . Austin: Harry Ransom Humanities Research Center, 1986.

Girard, René. *Deceit, Desire, and the Novel: Self and Other in Literary Structure.* Trans. Yvonne Freccero. Baltimore: Johns Hopkins, 1966.

Glasheen, Adeline. *A Third Census of* Finnegans Wake: *An Index of the Characters and Their Roles.* Berkeley: University of California Press, 1977.

Goldman, Arnold. *The Joyce Paradox: Form and Freedom in his Fiction.* Evanston: Northwestern University Press, 1966.

Gordon, John. *James Joyce's Metamorphoses.* Dublin: Gill and Macmillan, 1981.

Gose, Elliott B. *The Transformation Process in Joyce's* Ulysses Toronto: University of Toronto Press, 1980.

Gottfried, Roy K. *The Art of Joyce's Syntax in* Ulysses. Athens: University of Georgia Press, 1980.

Gregory, Richard L. *Eye and Brain: The Psychology of Seeing.* World University Library. 3rd ed. New York: McGraw-Hill, 1978.

Halper, Nat. "Armenian." *A Wake Newslitter* 16 (1979): 19–24.

Hart, Clive. *Structure and Motif in Finnegans Wake.* London: Faber and Faber, 1962.

Hayman, David. *Joyce et Mallarmé.* 2 vols. Paris: *Lettres Modernes,* 1956.

——. Ulysses: *The Mechanics of Meaning.* 2nd ed. Madison: University of Wisconsin Press, 1982.

Hegel, Georg W. F. *Phenomenology of Spirit.* Trans. Arnold V. Miller. New York: Oxford University Press, 1977.

Herring, Phillip F. *Joyce's Uncertainty Principle.* Princeton: Princeton University Press, 1987.

Hoban, Russell. *Riddley Walker.* New York: Washington Square Press, 1982.

Iser, Wolfgang. *The Implied Reader: Patterns of Communication in Prose Fiction from Bunyan to Beckett.* Baltimore: Johns Hopkins University Press, 1974.

Jaynes, Julian. *The Origin of Consciousness in the Breakdown of the Bicameral Mind.* Boston: Houghton Mifflin, 1976.

Joyce, James. *The Critical Writings of James Joyce.* Ed. Ellsworth Mason and Richard Ellmann. New York: Viking, 1959.

——. *Dubliners.* Ed. Robert Scholes. New York: Viking, 1967.

——. *Exiles.* New York: Viking, 1961.

——. *Finnegans Wake.* New York: Viking, 1939, 1958.

——. *The James Joyce Archive.* Ed. Michael Groden, et al. 63 vols. New York: Garland, 1978.

——. *Joyce's Ulysses Notesheets in the British Museum.* Ed. Phillip F. Herring. Charlottesville: University Press of Virginia, 1972.

——. *Letters of James Joyce.* Vol. I. Ed. Stuart Gilbert, New York: Viking, 1957; reissued with corrections 1966.

——. *A Portrait of the Artist as a Young Man: Text, Criticism, and Notes.* Ed. Chester G. Anderson. Viking Critical Library. New York: Viking, 1968.

——. *Selected Letters of James Joyce.* Ed. Richard Ellmann. New York: Viking, 1975.

——. *Stephen Hero.* Ed. John J. Slocum and Herbert Cahoon. 2nd ed. New York: New Directions, 1944, 1963.

——. *Ulysses.* New York: Random, 1961.

——. *Ulysses: The Corrected Text.* Ed. Hans Walter Gabler. New York: Random House, 1986.

——. *Ulysses: A Facsimile of the Manuscript.* Ed. Clive Driver. New York: Farrar, Straus and Giroux, 1975.

Jung, Carl Gustav. *The Collected Works of C. G. Jung.* Ed. Sir Herbert Read et al. Trans. R. F. C. Hull. 20 vols. Princeton: Princeton University Press, 1953-73.

Kawin, Bruce F. *The Mind of the Novel: Reflexive Fiction and the Ineffable.* Princeton: Princeton University Press, 1982.

Kenner, Hugh. *Dublin's Joyce.* 1956. Reprint. Boston: Beacon, 1962.

——. *Joyce's Voices.* Berkeley: University of California Press, 1978.

——. *Ulysses.* Rev. ed. Baltimore: Johns Hopkins University Press, 1987.

Kershner, Richard Brandon. *Joyce, Bakhtin, and Popular Literature: Chronicles of Disorder.* Chapel Hill: University of North Carolina Press, 1989.

Kristeva, Julia. *Desire in Language: A Semiotic Approach to Literature and Art.* Trans. Thomas Gora, Alice Jardine, and Leon S. Roudiez. Ed. Leon S. Roudiez. New York: Columbia University Press 1980.

——. "Women's Time." *Signs* 7.1 (1981): 13–35.

Lacan, Jacques. *Ecrits.* Paris: *Editions du Seuil,* 1966.

——. *Ecrits: A Selection.* Trans. Alan Sheridan. New York: W. W. Norton, 1977.

——. *The Ego in Freud's Theory and in the Technique of Psychoanalysis.* The Seminar of Jacques Lacan: Book II. Trans. Sylvana Tomaselli. Ed. Jacques-Alain Miller. New York: W. W. Norton, 1988.

——. *Encore. Le Séminaire de* Jacques Lacan: *Livre* XX. Ed. Jacques Alain Miller. Paris: *Editions du Seuil,* 1975.

——. *The Four Fundamental Concepts of Psycho-Analysis.* The Seminar of Jacques Lacan: Book XI. Trans. Alan Sheridan. Ed. Jacques-Alain Miller. New York: W. W. Norton, 1981.

——. *The Language of the Self: The Function of Language in Psychoanalysis.* Ed. and trans. Anthony Wilden. New York: Delta, 1968.

——. *Les quatre concepts fondamentaux de la psychanalyse. Le Séminaire de* Jacques Lacan: *Livre* XI. Paris: *Editions du Seuil,* 1973.

——. *"Le sinthome." Ornicar?* 6 (n.d.):3–20; 7 (n.d.): 3–18; 8 (1976): 5–20; 9 (n.d.): 32–40; 10 (n.d.): 5–12; 11 (n.d.): 2–9.

——. *Television* and *Dossier on the Institutional Debate.* Trans. Denis Hollier, Rosalind Krauss, and Annette Michelson (*Television*), and Jeffrey Mehlman (*Dossier*). *October* 40 (1987): 1–133.

——, and the *école freudienne. Feminine Sexuality.* Ed. Juliet Mitchell and Jacqueline Rose. New York: W. W. Norton, 1982.

Lemaire, Anika. *Jacques Lacan.* Trans. David Macey. London: Routledge and Kegan Paul, 1977.

Macalister, R. A. Stewart. *The Secret Languages of Ireland.* Cambridge: Cambridge University Press, 1937.

MacCabe, Colin. *James Joyce and the Revolution of the Word.* London: Macmillan, 1978.

Maccoby, Hyam. *The Mythmaker: Paul and the Invention of Christianity.* New York: Harper and Row, 1986.

Maddox, Brenda. *Nora: The Real Life of Molly Bloom.* Boston: Houghton, 1988.

Magnusson, Magnus. *Hammer of the North: Myths and Heroes of the Viking Age.* New York: Putnam's, 1976.

Mahaffey, Vicki. *Reauthorizing Joyce.* Cambridge: Cambridge University Press 1988.

Maher, Michael. *Psychology.* Manuals of Catholic Philosophy: Stonyhurst Series. New York: Benziger Brothers n.d. [Probably about 1893.]

Mallarmé, Stéphane. *Selected Prose Poems, Essays, and Letters.* Ed. and trans. Bradford Cook. Baltimore: Johns Hopkins University Press, 1956.

McGee, Patrick. *Paperspace: Style as Ideology in Joyce's* Ulysses. Lincoln: University of Nebraska Press, 1988.

McGrath, F. C. *The Sensible Spirit: Walter Pater and the Modernist Paradigm.* Tampa: University of South Florida Press, 1986.

McHugh, Roland. *Annotations to* Finnegans Wake. Baltimore: Johns Hopkins University Press, 1980.

——. *The Sigla of* Finnegans Wake. Austin: University of Texas Press, 1976.

McIntyre, J. Lewis. *Giordano Bruno.* London: Macmillan, 1903.

Melville, Stephen. "Psychoanalysis and the Place of *Jouissance.*" *Critical Inquiry* 13 (1987): 349–70.

Mink, Louis O. *A* Finnegans Wake *Gazeteer.* Bloomington: Indiana University Press, 1978.

Muller, John P., and William J. Richardson, eds. *The Purloined Poe: Lacan, Derrida, and Psychoanalytic Reading.* Baltimore: Johns Hopkins, 1987.

Noon, William T., S.J. *Joyce and Aquinas.* New Haven: Yale University Press 1957.

Norris, Margot. *The Decentered Universe of* **Finnegans Wake**: *A Structuralist Analysis.* Baltimore: Johns Hopkins University Press, 1976.

——. "Narration under a Blindfold: Reading Joyce's 'Clay'." *PMLA* 102 (1987): 206–15.

O Hehir, Brendan, and John Dillon. *A Classical Lexicon for* Finnegans Wake. Berkeley: University of California Press, 1977

Ornstein, Robert E. *The Psychology of Consciousness.* 2nd ed. New York: Harcourt, 1977.

O'Shea, Michael J. *James Joyce and Heraldry.* Albany: State University of New York Press, 1986.

Peake, Charles H. *James Joyce: The Citizen and the Artist.* Stanford: Stanford University Press, 1977.

Plato. *Phaedrus.* Trans. R Hackforth. *The Collected Dialogues of Plato.* Ed. Edith Hamilton and Huntington Cairns. Princeton: Bollingen, 1961. 476–525.

——. *Timaeus.* Trans. H. D. P. Lee. Baltimore: Penguin, 1965.

Racine, Jean. *Phèdre.* Paris: Librairie Larousse, 1971.

Ragland-Sullivan, Ellie. *Jacques Lacan and the Philosophy of Psychoanalysis.* Urbana: University of Illinois Press, 1986.

——. "Lacan's Seminars on James Joyce: Writing as Symptom and 'Singular Solution.' "

Compromise Formations: Current Directions in Psychoanalytic Criticism. Ed. Vera J. Camden. Kent, Ohio: Kent State University Press, 1989.

——. "More French Connections." *James Joyce Quarterly* 26.1 (1988): 115–24.

Restuccia, Frances L. *Joyce and the Law of the Father.* New Haven: Yale University Press 1989.

Rimbaud, Arthur. *Rimbaud: Selected Verse.* Ed. and Trans. Oliver Bernard. Baltimore: Penguin, 1962.

Riquelme, John Paul. *Teller and Tale in Joyce's Fiction: Oscillating Perspectives.* Baltimore: Johns Hopkins University Press, 1983.

Rosenfield, Israel. "A Hero of the Brain." *New York Review of Books* 21 Nov. 1985: 49–55.

——. "Neural Darwinism: A New Approach to Memory and Perception." *New York Review of Books.* 9 October 1986: 21–27.

Russell, George W. (AE). *The Candle of Vision.* New Hyde Park, NY: University Books, 1965.

——. *Imaginations and Reveries.* New York: Macmillan [1915].

Saintsbury, George. *A History of English Prose Rhythm.* 1912, 1922. Reprint. Bloomington: Indiana University Press, 1965.

Sandulescu, Constantin-George. *The Language of the Devil: Texture and Archetype in Finnegans Wake.* Gerrards Cross, Buckinghamshire: Colin Smythe, 1987.

Sartre, Jean-Paul. *Being and Nothingness: An Essay on Phenomenological Ontology.* Trans. Hazel E. Barnes. New York: Philosophical Library, 1956.

Schlossman, Beryl. *Joyce's Catholic Comedy of Language.* Madison: University of Wisconsin Press, 1985.

Scholes, Robert, and Marlena G. Corcoran. "The Aesthetic Theory and the Critical Writings." *A Companion to Joyce Studies.* Ed. Zack Bowen and James Carens. Westport, CT: Greenwood Press, 1984.

Scholes, Robert, and Richard M. Kain, eds. *The Workshop of Daedalus: James Joyce and the Raw Materials for* A Portrait . . . Evanston: Northwestern University Press, 1965.

Schwarz, Daniel R. *Reading Joyce's* Ulysses. New York: St. Martin's Press, 1987.

Scott, Bonnie Kime. *Joyce and Feminism.* Bloomington: Indiana University Press 1984.

Senn, Fritz. *Joyce's Dislocutions: Essays on Reading as Translation.* Ed. John Paul Riquelme. Baltimore: Johns Hopkins University Press 1984.

Silverman, Kaja. *The Subject of Semiotics.* New York: Oxford University Press, 1983.

Skeat, Walter W. *A Concise Etymological Dictionary of the English Language.* New York: Harper and Brothers, 1882.

Swartzlander, Susan. "Multiple Meaning and Misunderstanding: The Mistrial of Festy King." *James Joyce Quarterly* 23.4 (1986): 465–76.

Tindall, William York. *A Reader's Guide to Finnegans Wake.* New York: Farrar, 1969.

Traherne, Thomas. *Centuries.* New York: Harper and Brothers, 1960.

Unkeless, Elaine. "The Conventional Molly Bloom." Women in Joyce. Eds. Suzette Henke and Elaine Unkeless. Urbana: University of Illinois Press, 1982. 150–68.

Vitoux, Pierre. "Aristotle, Berkeley, and Newman in 'Proteus' and *Finnegans Wake.*" *James Joyce Quarterly* 18.2 (1981): 161–75.

Voelker, Joseph C. " 'Nature it is': The Influence of Giordano Bruno on James Joyce's Molly Bloom." *James Joyce Quarterly* 14.1 (1976): 39–48.

Weir, Lorraine. *Writing Joyce: A Semiotics of the Joyce System.* Bloomington: Indiana University Press, 1989.

West, James King. *Introduction to the Old Testament: "Hear, O Israel."* New York: Macmillan, 1971.

Whitman, Walt. *Leaves of Grass.* New York: Mentor, 1954.

Whittaker, Stephen. "Joyce and Skeat." *James Joyce Quarterly* 24.2 (1987): 177–92.

Winnicott, Donald W. *Playing and Reality.* Harmondsworth: Penguin, 1974.

Wisdom, John Oulton. *The Unconscious Origin of Berkeley's Philosophy.* London: Hogarth, 1953.

Woolf, Virginia. *To the Lighthouse.* New York: Harcourt, Brace & World, 1955.

Yeats, William Butler. *Mythologies.* New York: Macmillan, 1959.

Index

A Note on the Author

Sheldon Brivic is a member of the English faculty at Temple University. He is the author of *Joyce between Freud and Jung* and *Joyce the Creator*. His articles have appeared in *James Joyce Quarterly, Massachusetts Review, Novel, ELH,* and elsewhere.